Contents

Foreword	1
Prologue	2
1. We Meet for the First Time	7
2. Second Date - Hurricane!	11
3. Tent Camping & Expressing Myself	16
4. I Love You	19
5. A Whirlwind Courtship with Long Talks	22
6. Surprise! Sasha's 40th and My Surprise	26
7. Planning A Marriage in a Different State	29
8. Getting Married, October 1997	35
9. Honeymoon and Shark Attack!	39
10. Real Estate: Of Money and Upgrades	41
11. Of Interest Rates and Accumulation	45
12. Before Jumping Ship, Look Both Ways	48
13. Being Childless in a Child-Centered World	51
14. The Scare and The Happiness	54
15. Heartbreak and the Start of Anxiety	57
16. Of Fun and Free Fall	59
17. Summer of Fun in 2001	63

18.	Where Were You When The Sky Cried?	67
19.	Sales Through Technology	70
20.	Refusal of the Call	74
21.	The Journey Begins	78
22.	How To Buy Big Ticket Items	82
23.	Preparing to Buy Our Vacation Home	84
24.	Lessons Learned	87
25.	Idyllic Life Fraying	90
26.	Sabbatical 2006	93
27.	Choosing Frugal and Selling All	97
28.	Selling the House and Everything In It	100
29.	Living in a National Park	103
30.	Too Hot! Feeling Burned	106
31.	Into the Woods	109
32.	Old Hand Camping Host	111
33.	The Great Recession	115
34.	Cabin Living	118
35.	Truck Camper Rally	122
36.	Festivals and Full Timing	125
37.	A Summer of Weird Weather	128
38.	Weddings and Birthdays	133
39.	Gods Conspiring Against Us	137
40.	New Start in Frugal Creativity	140
41.	Sasha's Retirement	144
42.	Sasha Volunteers	149

43.	Hot Happenings	152
44.	Season of the Bugs	155
45.	We Move to New Adventures	157
46.	The Grand Adventure Towards Norm	159
47.	Start of New Adventures	163
48.	Upgrading the Toyhauler	166
49.	Whirlwind with National Parks	169
50.	New Decade of RVing	172
51.	Future Buying with Boondocking	174
52.	Cheap Months for Living and Learning	177
53.	Health Insurance and Dumpster Diving	179
54.	Four-Wheeling in a One-Ton Truck	182
55.	Sasha and Lockhart Basin, Who Will Win?	185
56.	Blow Out!	188
57.	A Unique Thanksgiving	190
58.	Perfect Rig & Truck	194
59.	Drive to Canyonlands and Grand Canyon	198
60.	More Programs, Less Hiking	201
61.	Mouse Problems and Close Encounters	203
62.	Another Health Scare	206
63.	Do You Want To Change Jobs?	209
64.	Back to Lake Mead and Lost Power	212
65.	Social Expansion of Legs and Brains	215
66.	Changes and Added Stress	217
67.	Heritage and Family Visits	220

68.	Tax Tribulations	223
69.	Astronomy Dreams and Nightmares	225
70.	Sky Adventures Before Family Visits	228
71.	Family Visits and Misunderstandings	230
72.	Of Hiking, Hotness and Sadness	234
73.	The End of My NPS Career	238
74.	Snapped with Feelings of Guilt	240
75.	Therapy and Travel	243
76.	Arguments With Family	246
77.	New Year With High Hopes	250
78.	The Long Walk Out of The Desert	252
79.	Traveling Across New Lands	256
80.	Becoming a Forest Ranger	258
81.	Internet Land and PTSD	261
82.	We Work to Play	264
83.	Government Shut Down	268
84.	Into The Desert to Renew	271
85.	Living In the Desert	274
86.	Our Adventure Vehicle	277
87.	Who Is YNC?	280
88.	Dipping Our Toes in Real Estate	283
89.	Winter Work First Time Ever	286
90.	Book Seller with Grants	290
91.	Following the Sun	294
92.	Florida Living	299

93. Trying to Find My Groove	303
94. We Start to Drink	310
95. Relationships	314
96. Beginning of the End	317
97. Decisions Made	320
98. Desert Decisions	324
99. Finding Fun Communities	327
100. We Come Full Circle	330
101. Plans Become Actions As I Turn 50	332
102. Celebration of Life	335
Epilogue: Where Are LauraNSasha Now?	337
About the Author	339

To the men in my life: Dad, Uncle Joe, Dad J, and of course, to Sasha.
To Dad: thank you for encouraging me to write this book.
To Uncle Joe: thank you for your help about finances and frugality.
To Dad J, thank you for believing I could do whatever adventure I wanted.
And to Sasha, my soul mate and life adventurer.

Prologue

Being an adventurous person was not in the plan. I always had my head in a book almost as soon as I could read. The adventures went on inside those pages but not with me. Most of my childhood was typical. I am from the suburban town of Westfield, New Jersey (NJ).

My parents: Mom and Dad, Mom's sister Tina and brother-in-law Joe (Aunt Tina and Uncle Joe), and Mom's parents (Grandma and Grandpa F) bought a summer home together in Avon-by-the-Sea, NJ. We went there every summer. That might be unusual.

The traveling spirit came early. From when I was four years old until college, we would go "down to the shore." My sister, Karen, is two years younger than me. My first cousin, Denise, is four months younger. And Stephen, Denise's brother, is seven years older than me.

Growing up, the Jersey shore was the best. Avon-by-the-Sea was the perfect place for families. Belmar was for college kids, and Ocean Grove was for seniors.

I went to college knowing my field of study: Environmental Science. University of Rhode Island (URI) did not have that field, but geology was close. So I got a science degree and found enjoyable jobs.

The college was near the beach too, and I considered studying oceanography. But that would need a Master's degree, and I was sick of school.

When I graduated in May 1990, the US Geological Society laid off half its geologists. What that meant was the geology graduates were going to have to do something else. While I contemplated my future, I got an offer from a professor at URI to work in the field in Montana. The Milwaukee Public Museum would hire me. I worked as a field geologist for a program called Dig for Dinosaurs. My work included driving people to onsite within Makoshika State Park, Glendive, Montana. I studied the type of ancient environment each bone or fossil found.

It was an easy job and one I loved. It allowed me to travel west. I saw some beautiful places, some of which I would only visit almost 30 years later.

Sasha was born for adventure. He and his parents lived in Serbia, Yugoslavia, for his first four years. Then, on vacation, they traveled west to Detroit, Michigan, to escape communist rule. His Mom's family moved to Detroit after World War II. His grandfather moved there after being in a prisoner of war camp. The American soldiers freed him and got him set up in Detroit. His parents moved again after his brother Bo and sister Yvonne was born. Finally, they settled in Bethesda, MD. His Dad was a urologist, and the dinner conversations were quite interesting.

The year 1968 was a lucky year for us both. I was born in October. Sasha became a naturalized citizen in the spring at 11 years old. He visited his Dad's parents living in Valjevo, Yugoslavia (Serbia) that summer and had a grand time. He was traveling alone, with family throughout the stay, but no parents. So when the Soviets invaded Czechoslovakia on August 21, 1968, his parents freaked out. And his parents ensured he was on the next plane ride out.

Sasha always tells of this harrowing taxi ride to the airport. The taxi driver drove fast, and no beast had time to move out of the way. He arrived at the airport and hustled onto the plane in record-breaking time.

Sasha's family routine became skiing, traveling, and making friends in their new country. They had huge parties every December for Saint Nickolas, called Slava. The celebration happened on December 19. It was the perfect time for the family's friends to celebrate.

Sasha studied at the University of Maryland for a year. Then, he headed west to Colorado State University in Fort Collins, Colorado. While getting a degree in Speech Communications, he was more interested in filming others. I do not think he started using the degree until after Colorado. Instead, he was a ski bum, staying in the state to ski in the winter and work in restaurants throughout the year.

It was not until he fought with a tree that he returned to the District of Columbia (DC).

He and his friend, Todd, were skiing in the remote backside of a mountain. It was the last run of the day when Sasha lost control and slammed into a ponderosa pine tree. His femur bone broke, and he was in terrible pain. Todd skied down the mountain as fast as he dared and got help. He saved Sasha's life.

With a broken bone and six months of recovery, Sasha returned to DC in 1984. He found work as an audiovisual (AV) specialist and started working "real" jobs.

In the early 1990s, Sasha started working for AVWashington (Avitecture). He designed systems for the federal government's ABC of organizations, such as the CIA, FBI, and their ilk. When I met him, he was Senior AV Designer with a cool red Jeep and a healthy tan from going to the beach each weekend.

My work was in the environmental geology business, looking for oil in all the wrong places. I cleaned the soil and groundwater of contaminants in New Jersey and surrounding states.

Going to Oregon to try for a master's degree in hydrology, I never achieved more than a B minus. Yet, I excelled at cross-country skiing, mountain biking, and making beer.

Coming home to New Jersey, back to my parents, I was twenty thousand dollars in student loan debt. With another job cleaning oil spills in groundwater, I was outside. It was one of the dirtiest jobs I had ever worked, but it allowed me to pay off my debt.

My sister Karen, moved from Westfield to Bethesda to teach in the county school system. I would go south to visit her. She invited me for one summer weekend in July of 1995. I brought my mountain bike, hiking shoes, and a bathing suit. She thought riding the biking trails on the C&O Canal would be fun sometime that weekend.

Little did I know how much riding I would do.

Chapter 1

We Meet for the First Time

I left work in New Jersey as I had packed my car that morning with everything I needed for a fun weekend. I headed south with commuters from New Jersey and New York going to the beach. Getting to Bethesda took four hours, where I met Karen and her roommates. We had a late dinner and talked briefly before bed on Friday night.

The following day, we went over to a friend of Karen's, Mark W., who was having a little pool party. It was July in the hot summer with high humidity, and pools were the thing. We might have swam. Karen introduced me to Mark's friends. Most of them were older than Karen and me, and her boyfriend James was also there. Everyone seemed nice and friendly. I found them to be interesting people with various jobs and interests. My traveling adventures of being out west and in Europe kept them entertained. My job as a female geologist who was lithe and athletic seemed to intrigue them.

Once we got home from the afternoon pool party, Karen, James, and I went to dinner. They suggested two options for the evening: either we go to a bar, or there was a pool party in Arlington, Virginia (VA) that we could attend. Of course, we needed to bring something to the party.

As I said before, I had $20,000 in debt and was trying to be frugal. If I go to a bar, the drinks are expensive, and I could do that in New Jersey. Or I could experience something different, a rooftop pool party in Virginia. Which one would you choose?

James drove to Virginia, where I bought a four-pack of hard lemonade, and James got a six-pack of beer. The pool party was on the rooftop and decked out for serious partying, although I doubt anyone was swimming.

I came into the party carrying the four-pack of hard lemonade, and the first thing I heard was this booming, joyful laughter. Realizing some of Karen and James' friends were in a small cluster around the laughing man, I beelined it over there. I wanted to know who it was who had that laugh.

Sasha says that when we were introduced, he took notice right away.

He thought, "Who is this girl who walked over to a bunch of guys carrying hard lemonade?" So he decided then and there to get to know me better.

The party was a whirl after our meeting. His booming laughter rang over and over as we talked. He told me of his adventures, and I told him of mine. At some point, his friends became bored with the party and wanted to go to a jazz club down the street. So Karen, James, and I went to the club with them. The music was loud, but we did not care.

Sasha and I kept talking to each other. He was the easiest person to talk to that I had ever met. He had a wealth of knowledge about everything.

Karen and James decided to leave the jazz club a few hours later and return to Bethesda. I did not want to go, no, not yet!

Karen said, "Ask Sasha if he could drive you to James' house. He is a dependable guy."

And when I asked, he said, "Sure, of course!" While he lived in Alexandria, VA, most of his friends lived in Bethesda, MD, across the Potomac River.

Karen and James left, and Sasha, his friends, and I stayed at the club until it closed at 2 am.

As we returned to the rooftop party to get Sasha's car, we saw the fire department breaking up the party. Sasha said, "You know it is a great party when the hook and ladder break it up!"

But the night was just getting started. His friends insisted that they were hungry and needed nourishment. I knew exactly how that felt when my friends and I went clubbing. We would hit a diner before heading home. While Northern Virginia does not have diners, they have IHOPs, and we went there.

As breakfast is my favorite meal, I bought eggs and bacon with a side of pancakes. Sasha and I kept talking. I cannot remember what we discussed, but everyone soon realized we liked each other.

He asked me for a date for tomorrow and said he would call me in the morning to firm up where we would go.

Ultimately, he drove his friends home, as the breakfast had not soaked enough alcohol for them to go over the river.

Once we got on the road, I realized Sasha had this fantastic music collection; I had not heard a commercial once. While I considered myself a radio gal, switching stations as I went through states, he had a mixed tape of his favorite music. By the time he dropped me off, we had listened to some great tunes. Similar taste in music was a definite plus for him.

The following day, I woke up, and Karen asked, "What happened last night? You got in late!"

I told her about Sasha, the jazz club, the fire truck, and IHOP. I said that I might have gotten in around 3 am. She asked me skeptically, "Do you still want to go for a bike ride?" and I said, "Sure, why not?"

Karen and I took that ride for an hour or two. When I returned, Sasha called and said he would pick me up, and we could bike along the C&O Canal. Thankfully, that area is very flat and easy to ride, and it is a popular place to go. From there, we went along the Billy Goat Trail, a hiking trail over large boulders. I was having a great time, but it was humid and warm. I know I was sweating profusely.

I remember drinking Gatorade and water. I remember the rocks. Lots of rocks.

I do not remember what we talked about while we were hiking. I remembered he smoked. He was not a chain smoker, but he had a cigarette every time we took a break. Still, it was an enjoyable, fun hike for the both of us, and we biked back to his Jeep.

As we returned to my sister's house, I gave him my email address (softrock@hotmail) and phone number, and he gave me his email too. Finally, I said goodbye to my sister and headed out. I had a four-hour drive back to my parent's house and had to work the next day.

As he kissed me goodbye, I thought, when will I see him again? Even though he saw me at my "sweatiest," I had the most excellent date and needed to see him again soon.

Chapter 2

Second Date - Hurricane!

Life seemed to go back to normal for me after that weekend. I went back to work and back to seeing my friends. I told my parents and friends about this great guy I met in Virginia.

All of my friends from high school had started pairing up. I felt left out. Finding someone when you least expect it was fantastic and fun. He was completely different from anyone I had ever met.

We started with emails back and forth. His email had his picture, and I told my Mom, "umm, he did not have a mustache when I met him!"

When I asked him about it, he said that he and his friends had mustaches and decided collectively to shave them off for the summer. Good, I thought, as I liked him without the mustache. He looked much younger without one. As he was twelve years older than me, looking that much older would scare my parents more.

We were trying to figure out how to connect again. Sasha suggested going white water rafting down the Gauley River in West Virginia. For me, that was an eight-hour ride each way. While I was up for making road trips, it seemed a little much. Mom kept saying, "What about the sleeping arrangements?"

"MOM!" I said, "I have a tent from Oregon days." I did not think she was amused.

Instead, Karen and James decided to rent a beach house in Corolla, North Carolina (NC). It would happen in August, giving everyone time to make arrangements for extra days off from work.

I asked Sasha, "Would you like to go?"

He said, "Yes!"

He did not ask about the sleeping arrangements. This date would be four days. I had never done anything like this. I am unsure if he encouraged me to take risks or if I decided to break out of my "good girl" mentality, but it felt like bliss to take a chance.

I would drive down to his place in Alexandria, and from there, we would take his Jeep to North Carolina. He was prepared for the beach and even brought his white-water kayak. We had beach chairs, coolers, and water, and I got this beer I had made in a Styrofoam cooler. He obtained his music, snacks, and everything you could think of for a fun time. I was pleasantly surprised by his preparedness.

He had enough music tapes for the ride down and back without having to hear the same song twice. I was amazed by that. I only ever had two tapes in my collection, a Queen's album called Highlander and a RUSH mixed tape.

Imagine my surprise when Bohemian Rhapsody came on, and we both started singing. And then the actual moment came – we both started head-bopping simultaneously! WOW! I loved that moment. I KNEW I liked him.

Before the trip, I told Sasha that he would be surrounded by my sister and her friends to ensure no shenanigans would happen. It was only our second date. So instead, he slept on the pull-out couch for the first two nights.

On the first full day, we went to the beach. In North Carolina, you can drive on the beach. Unheard of in New Jersey, where every square inch of the beach has a person on it. But North Carolina beaches also do not always have lifeguards nor sections designated where to surf or swim.

Sasha planted an umbrella firmly in the sand where we had shade. The ocean was beautiful and was at low tide. Perfect for swimming, surfing, and talking. I remember only us swimming and playing in the waves at the beach.

The next day we took a bike ride. There are boardwalks perfect for riding bikes. Sasha knew the best places to go, and I happily followed his lead.

At one point, we got off our bicycles and walked to a pier. It was beautiful being surrounded by the water reeds, the hum of the insects, and the chirping of some small birds nearby. We were talking about something when he turned and looked at me.

I looked into those blue eyes, the color of the sky above, and he kissed me. It was the most beautiful kiss and embrace.

He later would tell everyone that he decided to kiss me then and there or else fall into the bay. I am glad he made the right decision.

As I said, Sasha slept on a pullout couch while I shared a twin bedroom with Karen's friend Christine. That night after such a beautiful day and kiss, we asked her to switch with Sasha.

He and I pushed the twin beds together. While we enjoyed each other's company, I was not ready to head down that path entirely. You see, I was still a virgin. Yes, I had made it through high school, college, and graduate school, but I had never found someone I fully trusted enough to give my heart, soul, and body. I was closer to Sasha than I had ever been with anyone, but I could not do it yet.

However, I liked him even more, the next morning. We had an excellent breakfast, and on this day, we would go out to the bay with his kayak. He would show me how to use it, and I knew I would love it.

When I was younger, I was a surfer gal. I liked to have the ocean around me, feel the wave movement, and understand the surf. Even though I was tall, my center of gravity and balance were fluid and low. So when it was my turn to take the kayak, I took it as quickly as the board.

When I returned the kayak to him, he took it out. Again, his powerful strokes helped him glide through the water. It was poetry in motion, almost like a ballet on water.

But then I heard a honk. I looked around, and there were Karen and James. They came out to warn us that a hurricane was coming and the visitors had to leave the island! Oh NO! We had to return to the house, as our stuff was there. I waved my hands to get Sasha's attention, and he dug into the water.

He said, "What's up?"

I said, "We had to go back for our things as a hurricane was coming up the coast and would hit North Carolina!"

We gathered everything from kayaking and headed back to the beach house. Karen had left it unlocked and told me to lock it up afterward. As we were headed back to the beach house, we noticed a LONG line of cars going in the opposite direction. They probably thought us nuts!

We packed our stuff quickly and got our bikes, chairs, and kayak onto the Jeep. We decided that while Karen and James might go inland for a day and return, we went to Virginia.

Off we went into the traffic where everyone else was trying to get off the island. And Sasha's Jeep was a stick shift—something I did not know how to drive.

My Dad had tried to teach me how to drive a stick shift in high school. We had an Omni back then, which was Dad's commuter car. It got excellent mileage.

While I could get it to move at a slow speed, when I tried to shift gears, the car would jump forward and then stall. I got a jump, a stall, and an angrier Dad each time I tried. I think he was bumping his head trying to help me. Finally, the lessons stopped when the muffler fell off. And that was the end of the lessons in stick shifting for me.

But this ride with Sasha was taking a toll. It took four hours to get off the island. We still had to go through Virginia. It was between Richmond and the beltway that Sasha asked me to drive.

We changed seats, he popped the clutch, and I was driving a stick shift on Interstate I-95.

I managed to drive for a few hours while Sasha slept. In time though, the DC and Northern Virginia traffic started to creep in. I could slow down a little and still be in the same gear, but I was getting worried. What if I had to switch gears?

I finally woke Sasha up for him to take over. I pushed in the clutch as he switched gears down until we made it stop at a pull-off.

Later that day, we got to Sasha's house. We got our gear out of the Jeep and fell into a deep snooze. We were worn out from the journey.

Trouble was around the corner when we woke up. His toilet was being repaired. His only toilet. It was completely unusable. His plumber must have figured we would not return so early and took off.

Since we could not use the toilet and because Sasha's sister Yvonne lived so close, we went to her house to use the bathroom. She invited us to stay the night.

The following day Yvonne and her husband John invited Sasha's parents and us to enjoy a crab BBQ. So on our second date and I met his parents.

A welcoming, happy couple who took me in and realized we were meant for each other. Sasha's Dad, Milorad, told me early on that he could see we were soul mates, even if we did not realize it ourselves.

Who else would I have been with who liked the outdoors as much as I, who enjoys the beach, swimming, reading, talking, and does the head bopping in time to the music? And who introduced me to his parents so quickly and easily, as though it was no big deal? Sasha did.

And after a fabulous crab dinner with my new friends and boyfriend(!), I headed back up to New Jersey. We would figure out when we could meet again.

Chapter 3

Tent Camping & Expressing Myself

Once I got home, I found another time to be together. His family was as fun as he was and so welcoming. At the time, Grandma C, Dad's mom, lived with my parents and me. My parents had built a room next to the kitchen with a bathroom for her space. Unfortunately, she had broken her hip and could not walk well.

Dad, Mom, and I were used to a multi-generational living arrangement during the summers. But this was a long-term solution. It made for a much more complex and stressful living environment.

I needed to stay with my parents, as the schooling caused my debt. They graciously allowed me to stay and did not charge me rent. Instead, my "rent" went towards paying the student loan immediately.

Both of my parents had stressful jobs. Mom was a Realtor, and Dad worked as a professional Mechanical Engineer for a large elevator company. They hired someone to help come in and take care of Grandma C during the day and to cook and clean.

The three of us worked in offices, and the caregiver came in her car. This meant we had to jockey around where to place the cars. Mom had the prime spot, the garage, because her car would take clients to see houses. Dad and I were constantly switching positions in the circular driveway. I learned to back up my vehicle but often went over the cobblestones because my backup skills left something to be desired.

I may have driven across the country twice and down to Mexico, but I had a devil of a time backing out of a circular driveway.

Backing over the cobblestones, which was not good, was preferred over driving on the grass. Dad lovingly spent the weekends working on the lawn. They had almost an acre of green grass, and there was not a single patch of brown. While everyone else around us got groundskeepers, Dad did his lawn. The lawn is his lifelong way of entertainment, his exercise, and his enjoyment of being outside.

This sort of frugality, while not mentioned or talked about, was established in me early on. While I had tried to keep expenses down when I went to graduate school, I did not come back with an extra degree. As a result, that year of work went down the money drain, and I also lost some savings. Plus, I lost a full year of working and saving in my 401K investments.

Sasha instinctively knew how to keep the costs down. As we both enjoyed using the kayak, hiking, and bicycling, he found a place that was almost in the middle for the both of us. Ohio Pyle State Park is closer to Maryland and West Virginia than New Jersey, but I had a more accessible drive than him because I had friends living in Pennsylvania.

I brought my tent, sleeping bag, snacks, and mountain bike. There were trails, and we might get onto the Youghiogheny River too.

I had never been to this state park. There were quite a few firsts with Sasha. He was my first and only. It feels incredible to say that, especially as I was twenty-six when I met him. He was and is my one true love. Back then, there had been disappointments with most of the men I met, who were my age and just starting their careers. They wanted to settle down, have 2.1 children, a house, and a summer place.

I didn't want that. I had already been to more states, countries, and national parks than most friends. I wanted someone as adventurous as me, maybe even more. Sasha turned out to be that person.

I fell in love with him in the Outer Banks. He made me feel like the most important and the most desirous person. He reminded me of the Italians in Venice who sang love songs on the canals to the newly-married couples. His eyes expressed their fascination and enjoyment. They reached into my soul and held me close.

When we went to Ohio Pyle, I was ready. I wanted him as much as he wanted me. We might have hiked and biked before the evening happened. We might have even had something to eat.

What I do remember, though, is utter bliss, happiness, and fulfillment that night. I realized waiting this long was worth it with someone you care about and almost loved.

Chapter 4

I Love You

After that weekend, the weeks blurred together until we could meet again. While the tent camping happened in August 1995, the next time we got together was when I went south for Labor Day weekend. Fall truly is the best time for the Mid-Atlantic area, as you still have the warmth of summer, but the fall colors are making their appearances.

Sasha's friends decided to meet up at the Washington Harbor in Georgetown. There was an open-air restaurant and bar where you could go and watch the boats go by. As we walked over to his friends, this man called out to Sasha, whom we did not know, and said, "Hey, you two look very happy together!"

Sasha says, "Yes, I am!"

"Do you love her?" he asks.

And Sasha looked at me, looked into my eyes, and said, "Yes, I do believe I do. Yes, I LOVE Her! I love you, Laura."

That moment was incredible for both of us. It was the first time he had said that to me.

We were giddy with laughter and love, and this man, who saw us together, filled with happiness, said, "Congratulations!" and handed us a bottle of champagne!

We said, "Are you sure?"

"As sure as you are about your love," he said.

That experience, friendliness, and togetherness made the extra weekend special.

From then on, the weekend was non-stop fun with new friends and family. We were a new couple who loved each other.

It seemed only fitting that after I met his parents on our second date, ultimately, he would meet mine. At the time, my parents had Abby, our tabby cat.

Before he came to visit, I told Sasha about Abby. He decided to stay in a motel as he was allergic to cats. Mom and I worked together to clean the house of cat hairs. It did not matter.

Cats sense when you do not want to be touched. Abby instinctively knew Sasha was allergic. She walked right up to him and started rubbing and walking around his legs. So here is Sasha, trying not to be around the cat but to be polite as well.

My parents and Grandma C got to meet him. This was the first man I had brought home since high school. And I knew they liked him.

Not long after that first auspicious meeting of my parents, Sasha invited them to his house, along with Karen and James. Sasha had a townhouse in "Arlandria," although the address says Alexandria.

It was not in the prettiest neighborhood. But, Sasha was in the community he could afford, even with the high-interest rates of seven or eight percent. Most of his friends rented rather than bought, but he liked that he was close to his sister and his parents, and it was in the opposite direction for work traffic.

He decided to make a traditional backyard favorite dinner of lobster and corn on the cob. This impressed my parents and my sister. While it was not the prettiest neighborhood, and the cockroaches were in the street eating leftovers from someone else's bins, my parents understood my love for this man. They enjoyed being with him and knew this dinner's importance to us.

At this point, we started seeing each other every weekend and emailing each day. Then, as the holidays began, I had to decide what to do.

Sasha and his family are Serbian Orthodox. This is an Eastern Orthodox Christian religion. It is a Christian religion similar to Roman Catholicism, except that the Eastern Orthodox religion separated from the Catholic Church in 535 AD. They have priests who can marry, and they do the religious ceremony in the Serbian language. The Serbian Orthodox religion uses the Julian calendar rather than the Gregorian calendar.

My parents raised Karen and me as Catholics. This first year together was easier to plan because Sasha's family celebrates Christmas and Easter on different dates.

This difference made it easy to decide where we would be for each holiday and which family we would be with for the holidays. From the beginning, we celebrated Thanksgiving with Sasha's family and Christmas with my family.

That first Thanksgiving, I had beautiful thoughts of two different traditions. But it turned out not to be the case.

Instead, Sasha got sick and could not keep food down. It wasn't good, and he had to go to the hospital. When I brought him home, the doctors told me he needed a suppository as he could not take anything via the mouth. I think that event hit home for us. Through health or sickness, we would stay together.

By Christmas, I told my parents I would move in with him. Catholic parents with their eldest child, no matter how religious or not they appeared to be, seem to find the living together idea appalling. Yet I did not want to get a place, and I had almost paid off the debt I had incurred. Finally, Sasha said I would not have to help with the mortgage to get rid of my debt.

By January 2, 1996, I had moved in with Sasha, found a new job, and became a Virginia resident. Also, a person in love and actively enjoying my new surroundings. Two weeks later, I brought out the wedding magazines, a diamond-buying guide, and a due date for him to propose. I was my Dad's daughter, and I would not wait to get married or "live in sin," as my parents said, for too long.

Chapter 5
A Whirlwind Courtship with Long Talks

Sasha was a skier. He went to Colorado State University to ski every chance he got. After he moved back, he skied when he could and was still very good. But not like his ski bum days.

I was never good at skiing, instead loving the summer sun and sand. I was on a swim team and water ballet during the summer and swam as much as possible in the ocean. When I lived in Oregon, though, I learned how to cross-country ski. I loved doing that sport. I was not fast, yet the swoosh-swoosh of the skis in the snow made for a peaceful and thoughtful experience and exercise. It also was not as expensive as downhill skiing.

Winter of 1996, we did both types of skiing, going to West Virginia. The outdoors was constantly beckoning us, and away we would go.

During the week, we fell into a routine. While I tried to cook, Sasha was the chef. I had a longish commute working in Bethesda, and his commute was shorter, working in Merrifield, Virginia. He would get home from work and prepare dinner, and in the evenings, we would watch movies from his massive collection and talk. He was as voracious a reader as I was, and the library often saw us picking up or bringing back several books each week.

One of the major decisions for our life together came when we discussed money and children—two critical decisions to make before getting married. We wanted to get our thoughts, ideas, and long life together figured out before we had rings on our fingers.

While Sasha was the oldest child in the family, the name Jevtich was created when his parents came to the US. It was Jevtić without the h, but to most Americans, if they correctly pronounce the word, put an h on the end when they spoke his last name. To fit in, the h was added. There was massive pressure on Sasha to continue the family name.

But Sasha did not want to have children. He bought into the hype that raising a child, from before birth through college, costs at least a million dollars. I believed there still had to be a strong family presence to have children. They had grandparents close by for free babysitting and advice. It would cost much more if your new family were in one state while the family network was in another.

I was selfish. I did not want to share the attention, space, or money with the possible future children. I was not a great babysitter, only choosing to care for children who were well out of diapers and had cohesive conversations.

I always imagined myself as the kind aunt who would take my nieces and nephews on adventures, not as a parent, but as a friend.

But what I feared the most was that I would not be a good parent. I was afraid I would be standoffish, arguing or yelling at them. So that was how I communicated with my parents and Sasha when things got stressful. And I got anxious.

I did not realize it was anxiety at the time. In college and graduate school, I would get these intense side pains. Only a warm hand or heating pad would make them go away. I always associated these pains with my menstrual cycle, even though they happened off-cycle times. I would brush it off. Grandma F thought it was an ulcer, but I was never diagnosed. Others thought it was irritable bowel syndrome, but that was vague too.

I thought I would rather be on birth control pills to regulate my hormones, stress, and pain levels more than without them. But, if I got off those pills, those increased hormones would bring me back to the college days of stress and pain, and I did not want that again.

I also felt, at the time, the only reason...and it is a sad one to say, but the only reason to have children was who could take care of you when you are old. My parents were doing this for Grandma C. Aunt Tina and Uncle Joe were taking care of Grandma F. Neither one of the grandmas would die in a nursing home as they were cared for by their children.

My family was going through this at the time, and Sasha's grandparents were cared for by his Aunt Mica and Uncle Fay in Boston. These examples of our families caring for their parents were the only reason I thought about having children.

Horrible thought, you might be thinking, and I felt guilty about it. And vowed to save money instead, just in case I had to go into assisted living.

As I write this, I don't know what people might think, yet I remember the guilt of saying the words aloud and remembering my thought processes. I remember Mom's responsibility of caring for Grandma C and not her own. And I remember feeling I did not want to put someone else through those feelings.

We decided that having a child was not for us. We would let our sisters, brothers, and cousins have the kids, and we would be the benevolent Uncle and Aunt who did crazy stuff and adventures instead.

The other hard decision was not that hard to make. If we were together, there would be no credit card or loan debt. The only debt that we allowed ourselves to have would be a mortgage. Our credit cards would be paid off each month. We would buy cars that were used or could be paid off quickly. But, most importantly, we would not have knick-knacks that needed weekly dusting.

We both grew up in homes where there was dusting involved. As much as I hated cleaning, I loathed dusting. Why? Well, after the dusting is the vacuuming, and I don't like the loud noise of the vacuum. I could sympathize with the dogs and cats.

If I had to dust, Sasha would vacuum, and I would leave the room. I thought, well, do not bring anything into the home that needs to be dusted. I also was not a collector of anything except books. I did not collect the little kitschy pop culture items. I had my mountain bike, and we got a kayak for me, but the other stuff, homemaking, and household decorating were not me.

Although, as I write, the stuffed animals were different. I had a few, including my panda from when I was a child. The stuffed animals would scare away my bad dreams, especially when stress was high.

Sasha had an extensive collection of compact discs (CDs), Beta, VHS, cassettes, and laser discs. It made sense as he enjoyed music and movies. Everything had a proper place. His furniture had storage, and the kitchen had space for everything we needed.

When I moved in, I still had a little more to pay with the student loan debt. I figured I could pay it off in six months to a year if I was frugal and did not spend it on extraneous stuff. Sasha was able to help in that regard.

Most of the weekends away were still inexpensive. We stayed in lodges or motels that were off the beaten path. We went to West Virginia rather than the Poconos or Seven Springs in Pennsylvania. The gear we got for those adventures was secondhand or built for extended use.

I was doing these types of savings to be debt-free. Sasha was doing it because that is what he did anyway. He was saving, too, for a more significant purchase later that year.

Chapter 6

Surprise! Sasha's 40th and My Surprise

Like I said before, once I moved in with Sasha, Dad asked, "When will the wedding be?"

Of course, we had to make sure we could live together. My family has always said that I hated cleaning, and they were right. I wouldn't say I liked the pungent smells of the cleaners used. Companies would add lemon or other aromas to mask the harsh chemicals. Those chemicals made me sneeze and cough.

It was no surprise then that the main thing Sasha and I would argue about was cleaning. Most of the time, we did not discuss, but when we did, it was probably because I had not put something away or cleaned up. I get about halfway to three-quarters the way finished, and then I get distracted. Finishing was not my strong point.

However, 1996 was a tumultuous year for my family and me. Grandma C went into the hospital in July, complaining of being unable to breathe well. They found out in the hospital that she had pneumonia. Mom, Dad, Karen, and James visited her before attending a baseball game. I did not, as Sasha and I were not in New Jersey or interested in watching sports.

She died the next day. Afterward, Karen told me that Grandma had asked, "Do you hear the singing?"

"No, Grandma, what singing?" Karen asked.

"The singing is going on right now. The angelic voices are beautiful and calming. You don't hear them?" Grandma asked. Karen just shook her head no.

Karen thought she might be hallucinating because she was on pain medication. Or maybe she became religious at the end.

I felt incredibly guilty that I had not been up there to see her one last time. Sasha and I had gone on a friend's boat to watch the fireworks at the Washington Harbor.

Grandma C passed away on July 6, 1996. My Grandpa C had passed away over ten years before. They had a ceremonial plot in Newton, New Jersey, and my parents had the service at a funeral home. Sasha went with me to the funeral. He was uncomfortable about death and talking about it. While death is an awkward subject, bringing it up and discussing it should be done well before you are at death's door. Thankfully, Grandma had planned well in advance.

She had a will made when she sold her house to move in with my parents. She made specific plans for her death, including paying for the burial. This was done at least two years before she passed away. It was easy to follow, making my parents' lives and grief much easier.

Her death was in the middle of my planning for Sasha's birthday. He would turn 40 on July 22, 1996, and I wanted to have a big party for him. I coordinated with Yvonne, and we invited everyone, including Karen and James. His parents, Yvonne and John, their children, Sasha's brother Bo, and about forty other friends said they would be there. We decided to have the party on a Saturday, after his birthday.

I told everyone it would be a surprise party and they needed to park further up the block from Yvonne's home. They had to be there early. His friends and family are not punctual, so I used to suggest they come half an hour earlier than us.

One of his friends, Richard, did not remember the notification to park far away from the house. So when Sasha and I drove up, supposedly to go out for his birthday, he saw Richard's distinctive red sports car nearby. So he said, "Wait, is Richard going to go out to dinner too?"

I said, "That's not Richard's car. It has to be someone else."

He did not believe me and started looking around a little more. I ushered him quickly towards Yvonne's front door before he guessed my intentions.

"SURPRISE!!!!"

Everyone yelled as soon as the door opened. Everyone was excited and happy to see us. While he had guessed the deal, I did not think many people would show up, even if it were only two seconds before. But it turned out to be a great surprise.

Yvonne and Mom J outdid themselves with decorating and preparing food. And the happiness flowed freely. But the bigger surprise came later.

My sister was going to leave, and Sasha told her, "Please stay just a little longer." His brother and family had not shown up yet, and he wanted to wait until they did. He had a surprise for me too. Bo showed up running late because of work. Once Bo got there, Sasha had his friend Leo take pictures with his work digital camera.

He went through this speech thanking everyone there and, especially to me, his love. Then, when he started to get down on one knee, I moved toward him, overjoyed that he was proposing.

He asked, "Will you...." And I said, "Yes, I do!" before he got the words out!

While I surprised him, he surpassed that surprise by proposing to me! After the champagne was poured and passed around, I said, "You know, we need to tell my parents."

We used Yvonne's home phone to call them. Sasha called and asked to speak to Dad. Dad got on the phone, and Sasha asked permission to marry me.

Dad said, "Yes."

Sasha said, "That is good to know, as I've already asked her, and she said YES!" They laughed and offered us congratulations.

Chapter 7

Planning A Marriage in a Different State

I started planning almost immediately for the wedding. It was funny; we had met in July 1995, got engaged in July 1996, and married in October 1997. So we were engaged longer than we had dated.

While Sasha's Uncle Slobo was visiting from France to show his artwork at the French embassy in DC, he said, "Why don't you get married in November 1996? Then we could be at your wedding."

I was scared and said, "ACK, I don't think I could plan that early or that quickly!"

And indeed, I could not. After Grandma C passed away, Grandma F came to live with my parents. The caregiver helped my parents again. However, Grandma F was bedridden and needed more care.

Plus, soon after Sasha proposed to me, James proposed to Karen. They had been going out longer than us but were younger too. As Karen was a teacher, she decided they needed to get married in August, while I decided on an October wedding.

In a sense, we both got married in 1997, the year our parents would celebrate 30 years of marriage. Mom had a heaping amount of things to do to get ready. Karen and I relied on her for most of our wedding plans.

My parents were able to offer both couples equal amounts of a wedding budget. Suppose you spent more than those extras you paid for them. If you spent less, you got the leftover money.

Sasha said that he would be happy with my choices. However, at the time, I was going through a conflict with my feelings about the Catholic Church.

I wanted to get married on a Sunday and have brunch, my favorite meal. It was also less expensive to do breakfast than dinner. However, being married on a Sunday meant not being married in a church. I had no affinity for the church in Westfield. I had not gone to church in a long time.

Instead, my Mom and I found this beautiful conservatory, a glass building with greenery that looked like the outdoors under glass. It would be perfect for a couple who enjoyed the outdoors without the bugs, my favorite saying.

If I was to be married on a Sunday, I wanted to make the weekend longer. First, everyone would travel back either later that day or the next. Second, if we had a paid day off from work, we could spend less vacation time after our wedding. Third, getting married on Columbus Day weekend would be a nod to my Italian heritage. I thought of it as a win-win-win situation.

The issue of no children arose when looking for a priest. I did not want to be hypocritical or lie to a church about children we did not plan to raise. Plus, the teachings of no birth control did not sit right with me.

A friend of Sasha's family, a Serbian priest from Boston, agreed to conduct the ceremony. I asked for the word obey to be taken out and put in husband and wife rather than man and wife. Liberal and feminism by both of us meant equal footing. While the priest was hesitant, ultimately, we prevailed, and that part was taken out of the ceremony.

These different thoughts were going through my brain as we were trying to plan the wedding. I was going up to New Jersey every other weekend. However, two critical events stand out the most.

First, when Sasha proposed to me, he still smoked daily. He always went outside to smoke, as he did not want the smell inside the house. I could smell it and did not like it. Soon after he proposed, he got a massive ear infection. Whichever way it happened, he decided that smoking was the root of the problem and quit. I felt it was the best engagement gift ever.

He never returned to smoking cigarettes again.

Second, I paid off my student loans in 1996, only two years after incurring them. It had come with hard work, caring parents, and Sasha. With just a car loan left to pay off, Sasha gifted me the remaining balance on the car loan. I bought a Saturn four-door in 1990, which would last me for over twelve years. Most importantly, I was going into the marriage debt-free.

We decided during our talks that I would take his name. I did not want to hyphenate Laura Capuano - Jevtich. However, in a quirk of fate, I messed up on my social security form and put in the Capuano rather than just a C. As a result, the marriage certificate also has my name as Laura Capuano Jevtich. From then on, my documentation said my long name without the hyphen.

Figuring out these ideas is important because we are soul mates. We knew we did not need pre-nuptials and separate bank accounts. When we were married, we had joint bank accounts and credit cards and jointly took care of bills. We would pool our money together to create a more significant nest egg, no matter how small it seemed.

This fundamental point may not work for some people when starting a life together. Yet we saw more people getting divorced because of money issues and separate bank accounts than owning them jointly. So, before you get married, communicating these wants and needs early on is the best way to stay together.

As we tried to keep the costs down, we invited 150 people, fifty from Sasha and my friends, fifty from the Jevtich side, and fifty from the Capuano side. Most of my girlfriends and Sasha's friends were at our wedding party. Plus, I had Sasha's sister and sister-in-law in my bridal party, while Sasha had Bo, John, his brother-in-law, and Marcus, his first cousin. We ensured our family and friends would come by putting them in the wedding party.

However, Mom had a devil of a time to cut her list to only fifty people. My family's side is quite large. She kept asking Sasha's Mom if all those people she had would show.

Many of the Jevtich friends, friends of thirty years or more, had abandoned them during the Yugoslavia wars. Yugoslavia broke up during the late 1990s, with different ethnic groups' conflicts emerging. Moreover, the wars had religious overtones. Serbians are typically Eastern Orthodox. Croatians and Slovenians are Roman Catholic, and Bosnians are Muslim.

In Washington, DC, and the surrounding areas, it did not seem to matter where you came from or what religion you were; you were friends. They had become American citizens around the same time. However, once the wars started and people took sides, the Jevtich family was dropped from their friend lists.

It was a mess for the Jevtichs, and I did not understand what was happening. You had friends. You were Americans. You had a different religion, which would make life easier for get-togethers. I did not realize the unrest going on and became angry with Mom J when she could not decide to give up more spots.

My family and the marriage were in New Jersey, meaning more people would come from my side. Most of Sasha's family and friends were in Maryland, Virginia, and Massachusetts. He had family in Europe and Serbia and might be unable to come.

All the stress added up. Grandma F had fallen and broken her hip. She went to live with Aunt Tina and Uncle Joe for a while. But she was a handful.

I do not know if the broken hip or the decreased mobility harmed her more. However, once she forgot how to get home after living in Westfield, New Jersey, for over 50 years, we realized she had dementia.

Grandma F was a fun-loving and generous person. She encouraged me to write my poetry and short stories like she did when she was younger. She could have been in a state or county-run nursing home that she hated, or she could live with her children in their homes. But ultimately, the children made the decisions for her and brought her home.

Toward the end of Grandma's life, my parents brought hired hospice. Mom had the house ready for the weddings and the pre-parties and secured the deposits for everything; she could not do it all. Grandma F was bedridden and heavy, needing two people to help her move. She passed away on June 10, 1997.

This time, the funeral was held in our childhood Catholic Church. She had an excellent mass and turnout, as she had lived in Westfield for a long time.

By July, Mom and Dad had changed the first-floor bedroom and bath into an eat-in breakfast nook with a kitchen bar area. Then, finally, they were ready for the first of the pre-parties.

Karen and I had our pre-parties, the bridal showers, and the registries at certain stores. Sasha washed his hands of it and said, "Whatever you want is fine with me." So Mom and I went to Macy's to figure out what to get.

I knew I wanted Waterford crystal because I had gone to Ireland to see how their crystal was made. I wanted Lenox because there were different pieces. Yes, I had fallen into Wedding Consumerism and did not stop for a while afterward. Plus, Oneida silverware as it had both silver and gold within the place setting. I loved mixing the metals because of the Girl Scouts' song:

"Make New Friends, But Keep the Old, Some Are Silver and the Other Gold."

Ultimately, my sister had her wedding in August. She also had a large wedding party and a large Saturday night wedding. Very traditional, beautiful, and hot. They honeymooned in Hawaii. After they returned, we took a little breather and started preparing for our wedding.

The invitations went out, and we started getting responses from the Jevtich side almost immediately that they were not coming. While the immediate family would be there, including his grandparents, only his first cousin Anouk from the French family could make it. In addition, most of the senior Jevtichs' friends would not be attending.

Considering my parents put a deposit down for one hundred and fifty people to attend, this was a blow. You had to deposit early, even though you did not know how many would be there.

In New Jersey, we were both non-residents, so we needed to get the license in the town we were marrying. You could apply for it up to six months beforehand, but the permit was only suitable for 30 days once you got it.

I had only been with an environmental company for nine months and did not have much vacation time to take off. So instead, we went to New Jersey on a Thursday, three days before our wedding. We had our kayaks on the Jeep and would spend our honeymoon in the Maryland and Virginia Outer Banks.

What became stressful for Sasha was that marriage license. Thursday became a big driving day for him. He had good intentions, bringing driver's licenses and passports to the registrar. But he had to show his naturalization papers because he was a naturalized citizen! OH NO! Of course, who carries that around?

Back down to Virginia went Sasha, and drove to New Jersey to get a piece of paper stating 29 years ago he became a citizen. I was happy Mom had found my birth certificate, and I did not have to go through all that!

Chapter 8
Getting Married, October 1997

Sasha's grandfather used to say, "I want to dance at your wedding." He would say it in Serbian, reverting to the language of his youth. While he had become a naturalized citizen after World War II and learned English, he spoke increasingly more Serbian as he grew older. It did not matter; his eyes were the same as Sasha's, expressive and kind.

On the Friday before the wedding weekend, we got our marriage license. Most of the family and friends would be coming up for the rehearsal and dinner on Saturday.

The Serbian Orthodox priest accompanied his wife and Sasha's grandparents, Aunt Mica and Marcus. Everyone was converging at The Madison Hotel in Morristown, New Jersey.

I wore an off-white chiffon and lace wedding gown to match what Mom wore at her wedding. However, instead of a veil, I wore a crown of flowers.

My attendants wore off-white pantsuits they ordered from a catalog company. The sizes were from petite to women's, and whether you were tall or short, it did not matter; they were the same price. I did pantsuits because everyone was on one form or another budget. Also, my maid of honor, my cousin Denise, hated dresses, and I wanted her to feel comfortable.

My matron of honor, Karen, and attendants included Amy, Darlene, Mary Beth, and Natyna, my childhood friends, Jackie (Bo's wife), and Yvonne, my soon-to-be sisters-in-law. Eight attendants.

Sasha decided to have eight attendants too. So besides Bo as his best man, his brother-in-law John and his cousin Marcus, he had his friend, Todd, who saved him while skiing, his friend, Leo, from the audio-visual industry, and four beach friends, Mark F., Mark W., Gary, and a beautiful woman named Annie. She wore a tuxedo and stood with the men.

Mom, Sasha's Mom, Aunt Mica, and Grandmother wore off-white too. Aunt Tina wore a stunning blue dress, and I considered her my "something blue."

Mom and Dad landscaped their yard in pink, burgundy, and white mums with white pumpkins. The female attendants had bouquets of greens, and Sasha's attendants wore sprigs of greens. Only Sasha, Dad, and Dad J wore off-white roses.

Before the ceremony, we took pictures at my parent's home and the Madison Hotel. Several of my friends and the Jevtich family were staying at the hotel. I had my immediate family at the Westfield house and the rest at the hotel in Morristown. This also reduced the cost of a limousine to drive everyone to the hotel.

But first, panic at the rehearsal dinner.

Since The Madison Hotel was a typical wedding venue with fall weddings, there was one wedding in the ballroom on Saturday night. We rehearsed for the wedding on Saturday evening in a meeting room where we would also have dinner. I was nervous because there would be steps in the conservatory. I was afraid of falling or tripping, and the ceremony was unusual.

I remember trying to finish the rehearsal with the people going every which way. At one point, my sister shook me because things were not going the "right" way.

She said, "Calm down, Laura! Everything will be fine."

"How do you know? No one is paying attention, and what if I do something wrong?" I asked.

"That will not happen; remember how crazy things went with mine? Yet we still got married, and it all worked out. Yours will be great too." Karen said calmly.

After that, the rehearsal went as planned, and I was ready for the ceremony.

I think I was worried about the ceremony being too long. So we created programs for everyone to follow the service and know what to expect. While a Catholic wedding usually takes about an hour with its parts, a Serbian Orthodox wedding could take longer. This was why we made sure with the priest that the wedding would only take a half hour. The ceremony and the reception were in the conservatory. After the wedding ceremony, we would walk out for cocktails and appetizers. Once the conservatory was ready, we would return to be presented.

A Serbian Orthodox wedding is done in both Serbian and English. There are certain rituals done to signify certain parts. I put that into the program along with everyone's names and printed it on my home printer. I did the same with the invitations and envelopes. This was one expense I could do at home.

The ceremony is as so: with the most crucial part being the trinity and everything done in threes, in remembrance of the Father, Son, and Holy Spirit.

In the exchange of rings, the rings are blessed by the priest, who holds them in his right hand and signs the cross over our heads. The rings are exchanged between us three times.

The candles, which Mom J procured, symbolized the perpetual light of Christ and that we must shine in virtue and purity with good deeds. We each had a candle, and after that part was over, they were given to Karen and Bo to hold.

During our wedding, while the bride and groom have an active role, so do the best man and matron of honor. They make sure we do not trip, they hold things for us, and they actively take part. At least one must be a Serbian Orthodox, and Bo fit the role.

The joining of the right hand came next, with the priest putting a unique cloth wound tightly around our right hands. It would stay that way throughout the rest of the ceremony. It symbolized joining two to one, united in mind and flesh—the couple's oneness.

The high point of the ceremony that most people remember is crowning. Each wears a crown, which represents the Glory and honor of marriage. We are crowned queen and king in our kingdom and will rule with wisdom, justice, and integrity.

While wearing the crowns, we drink from the standard cup. This signifies sharing the happiness and sorrows of life. We did this three times, and so did Karen and Bo.

Then after drinking the wine, there is a walk around a small round table. We do this with our hands tied together, wedding bands on our fingers, and crowns on our heads after drinking wine. Thankfully, Karen held my long trailing dress, Denise had my candle, Bo held Sasha's candle and my crown of flowers, Denise held my bouquet, and we managed to get around that table three times to signify joy. Our flower girl joined in the second time around the table, throwing flowers at our feet.

Afterward, the priest removed our crowns and wished us a happy marriage. He also separated our hands, presenting us as Mr. and Mrs. Jevtich!

My crown of flowers went back on my head, Sasha swept me off my feet in a kiss, and we proceeded out of the ceremony joyfully. Happily and excited about what the future holds. We danced with his grandparents and especially his grandfather.

It was a beautiful day, morning, and afternoon of dancing, happiness, and good cheer. My sister was right; we did have a great wedding.

Chapter 9
Honeymoon and Shark Attack!

I wanted to see if you read the chapter titles. There were no sharks, the ocean was warm Mid-October, and large creatures were swimming with us.

When we married on October 12, 1997, Mom and Dad wanted us to come to their house for the after-party. But, unfortunately, the Madison only gave us four hours, which meant some people were heading back either north or south, or the New Jersey people were staying put.

It was a marriage of different traditions and heritages. The family's Irish and Italian sides mingled nicely with the Serbian side. Everyone had a fun time.

It was also a holiday weekend for New Jersey. We headed to my parent's home for the party. I know that Sasha wanted to get back to The Madison. It was hard to leave a party when you had not seen people in such a long time. Ultimately, he managed to wrangle me back to the hotel. But, of course, he forgot his sunglasses. We both need prescriptive glasses, so not having sunglasses on the beach would be horrible.

We did not realize it until after we got back to the hotel.

We stopped at my parents before heading out on our honeymoon. John gave Sasha a Cuban cigar for the journey. Even though he had stopped smoking cigarettes, special occasions like this trip seemed perfect for the cigar.

It was funny; I smoked more of it than Sasha. He got lightheaded from the smoking and the swaying of the boat. Maybe even a little seasick. I never had motion sickness. The ferry was enjoyable, and the breezes were perfect. The fresh air was much better to smell than a cigar.

We traveled to Assateague Island National Seashore and Chincoteague. Our friends had gotten us several nights at a Bed and Breakfast at Cedar Gables Poolside Inn. We brought our kayaks to try out our white-water abilities on the ocean.

From Lewes, Delaware, we headed further south, going through Rehoboth and Bethany Beaches—where Sasha and his friends had beach houses. In Chincoteague, the B&B is on the water of Little Oyster Bay. They had a small pool and hot tub.

The room was their honeymoon suite with a private hot tub and special appointments like turndown service with chocolates. In the mornings, there was breakfast. The atmosphere was peaceful, and the scent of the ocean called to us. I know we spent a day at the beach, at a lighthouse, and looking for wild horses. We told ourselves we would be back because we had a wonderful time. But we never went back.

The day we went out with our kayaks was a day that I will never forget. As soon as you passed the breakers (waves breaking), the ocean was glassy and transparent as an ocean could be. We had fun playing on our kayaks, although I started back paddling at one point, thinking I saw shark fins!

Sasha knew better; they were dolphins. Once we got out of the water to dry off, those dolphins played in the waves. We laughed about my paddling backward, but to my credit, I did not have my glasses on and could not see as well as Sasha.

We started our marriage with the same excitement our meeting each other initially brought us. We were having fun and enjoying every minute together. We were indeed on our way to a grand adventure.

Chapter 10
Real Estate: Of Money and Upgrades

Sasha's townhouse was on Dale Street in Alexandria. It was a fine townhouse for one person if you did not mind street parking. When Avitecture decided to move from Merrifield, Virginia, which is close to Alexandria and opposite the traffic, to Sterling, it meant a commute of over an hour.

My job was in Sterling. I was already putting extra-long miles on my Saturn. So, why not move closer to where the jobs were to get home faster and be together?

We started looking for homes to understand what we wanted and put the townhome on the market. Sasha drove the Jeep back and forth to work and was finding more traffic on the road. When your vehicle is a stick shift, it is hard to imagine pleasant traffic situations.

The trouble was, no one was buying. From late 1997 to the beginning of 1998 was a buyers' market. By 1998, when we sold Dale, it was at a loss.

In 1997, economic growth was going strong, people were job-jumping, and the dot.com industries were booming. People were secure in their jobs or believed they could just as easily find another job in another state.

Rent prices were low, and home prices were reasonable. People moved to the suburbs in droves and did not want a one-bathroom townhouse. They wanted greenery and bigger homes. So we got on the bandwagon to move out to the suburbs.

The new housing market was opening by leaps and bounds. The housing starts signify builders building new homes was up almost 10 percent in 1998. The only other years housing starts were higher than 10% were in 1976 and 1977, when they started measuring them.

Case in point. We used a Realtor to sell the Dale Street home. We kept it exceptionally clean, which was not an easy task for me. There had to be someone out there who would see it for what it was, a place for one person, who liked to grill and eat outdoors, had a small car for parking on the street, and enjoyed being close to Washington, DC.

A Realtor came in with a lower-priced offer, and we brought a check to settlement.

At that point, we decided the next house would be bought for well under its value and never bring a check to a settlement. Instead, they would be giving us the money. However, we would not have to wait too long, as no more than six months later, builders threw money at buyers to buy their homes.

Buy A House, Give Me Money, and The Upgrades

What do you mean by giving checks out to home buyers? During 1998, Loudoun County in Virginia was booming with newly built homes. Farming communities became housing communities. A community called Cascades was booming. This suburban area is planned for 6500 single-family homes with five community centers, shopping, and trails. Plus, there was a high school, a middle school, and several grammar schools.

While under construction, the Cascades Parkway would lead to State Road Route 7 and a parkway. Every kind of amenity seemed to be there, with a library, churches, and every shop imaginable just minutes away.

We liked a specific area within the Cascades community called Lowes Island. The builder was MI Homes, who had different models and great prices. Their specials included a $25,000 rebate towards upgrades, a split of upgrades, and a down payment on the house. So a $250,000 home would cost $225,000 instead. This contract was what we wanted, an upgraded home for a lower cost.

We fell into buying the American Dream at the right time. By American Dream, I mean home ownership, upward mobility, and buying stuff. It started with the bridal showers and wedding gifts and kept going. So when we assumed a mortgage through MI Homes, we felt we had real credit and buying power.

We had an ace up our sleeve, though. Our brother-in-law, John, and his family were home builders. They built a few homes in Cascades, but not in our section. It did not matter, as we made sure John saw the plans. He looked them over and made some suggestions.

We also made a few changes to the plans, especially with the bedrooms, bathrooms, and pantry. We wanted to enter the house via a hallway, not into the kitchen. How else could we remove our shoes and put away coats if we did not go through a hallway?

We made sure there were ceiling light fixtures in every room. We switched the dining room with the living room. We wanted an open floor plan with ceiling fans throughout the home.

One of the main innovations we made with MI Homes was the gas fireplace chimney in the great room. The venting went out to the side. Since the area above would be wasted space, we told them to make a cut-out above the fireplace for our TV monitor. We were among the first to ask for that, and now it is a standard feature in most new homes. Plus, at the time, and because it was a new community, they brought in cable lines and Digital Subscriber Lines (DSL) that came through the phone lines.

We were pain-in-the-neck buyers, visiting the lot daily to watch the progress. Finally, on a sweltering weekend, we pulled the speaker wires into the house before the drywall went up. We had eleven speakers, something an audio-visual designer wants to have in his home.

We thought this would be our forever home and made it the way we wanted.

We closed on the home in July 1998. And the buying spree began: furnishing the house, adding a deck and a natural gas grill, a hot tub, a dining room table for ten, a kitchen table for four, and an L-shaped couch for six people. There were only two of us. We used Sasha's furniture from Dale for these two guest bedrooms for everyone from New Jersey to visit.

We decided the basement would be unfinished. We had a front-loading washing machine on a pedestal, which Sasha made for me. And racks and hanging rods to dry the clothes. Our large bathroom had a walk-in closet for both of us that we put in ourselves.

And Sasha, bless his handiness, set up the garage with pulleys and racks for our mountain bikes, skis, kayaks, and tools. And we were able to get both cars in as well.

We were pains in the butt to the builder, going every day, making sure that everything was done correctly, complaining when it was not up to our standards, and taking pictures for the studs and our knowledge. These skills would help us later in life, over twenty years later.

Chapter 11

Of Interest Rates and Accumulation

When I think of how much we spend on our household furnishings, furniture, and small appliances, not to mention the display to watch TV, equipment to listen to music, computers, and everything else to make a comfortable home, I want to tell our past selves to STOP, do not do that!

Hindsight is 20/20, of course, and we cannot go back. I could return to our credit card statements or bank accounts to see how bad it was, but we were never in debt. We paid the credit cards every month. Sasha paid the bills. I invested our savings. Back then, I winged it. He could invest more in his 401K because he was at his company longer. I kept jumping jobs.

When we bought our home, the interest rate for a 30-year mortgage was seven percent. This percentage was through a lender from MI Homes. It was called George Mason Mortgage Corporation (GMMC). Once we had closed on the home, though, the loan was sold to Countrywide Home Loans in 1999. When we got the notification, we said, "What! So where do we pay now?"

When we bought the home, we did a 5-15-80, which means five percent (%) down, a fifteen percent loan, and an eighty percent loan to avoid paying Private Mortgage Insurance (PMI). First-home buyers must pay PMI if they do not have a full 20 percent mortgage payment. Therefore, our 15% loan rate was much higher than the main one, at almost 7.5%. The main one, which had the bulk of the mortgage, was a rate of 7%.

We put every extra dollar into the larger interest-rate loan until it was paid off by refinancing in 2001. Then the entire mortgage was in one place and one loan. When we did this, we also got a lower interest rate.

The credit card rates were two to three times higher than the mortgage rates at 15 to 18 percent. Since we always paid them off each month, they considered us to be low-risk, and we had a higher credit rating. We kept getting offers for more credit cards and higher charging amounts. We declined, keeping one credit card through our bank and an American Express card.

However, we believed in the hype of using our home equity as a low-interest credit card. So, instead of charging to a credit card, we bought large ticket items through this home equity and paid them off over a few months.

When we bought the home in 1998, the ways to get a mortgage were messy. Less than a year later, our mortgage was sold to Countrywide. This company had offices in Virginia, but its reputation was not as good as GMMC's. So we decided in 2001 to refinance and lump both mortgages into one and move away from Countrywide to a new lender called MortgageIT. Unfortunately, after losing billions, Countrywide Mortgage went out of business on January 11, 2008.

MortgageIT then sold our loan to Wells Fargo somewhere around 2004 to 2005. When we did a refinance and home equity loan with Wells Fargo on October 31, 2005, our house appraised at $707,000! It was the absolute height of the market in our area. For a home bought in 1998 for $279,000, this was an unbelievable jump in price. Sure, we had added value to the house with extras, but still, it was a three-bedroom, two-and-a-half-bath home! We did not ask for that much when the time came.

During the early 2000s, the interest rates were not as high as in the 1980s but nicely manageable in the five to seven percent range. The interest rates for CDs and 30-year Treasury Bonds were 8.5 percent in 2000. Those percentage numbers started to go down at a time when people were using their homes as banks. I did not know about Treasury Bonds until 1999.

Instead, we bought, as everyone else did in the late 1990s and early 2000s. Yes, purchasing and buying some more is the mantra. So buy stocks, invest in dot com companies, and work until you reach 65.

Do whatever you can in your community, have your parties, and buy all the dishes, silverware, and glassware. Buy this and that doo-dad that will make your life easier as you make the dishes from Martha Stewart and Rachel Ray.

1998 was a crazy year for us. We sold Dale Street and bought Rhyolite Place homes, I changed jobs three times, and we furnished the house. We found new friends and were keeping up with the Jones, although not as much.

The outdoor activities we enjoyed became watching our home being built, stringing wires through the skeleton of the home, and having parties at our house. Our swimming in the ocean became sitting in the hot tub.

By October 6, 1998, I had decided to have my 30th birthday at home and invite my work "friends," the family from New Jersey and Virginia, and friends around the neighborhood. Sasha cooked on the grill, and we had an excellent time.

Two weeks later, I was laid off because they "did not have enough jobs to keep me on." In addition, my friends were leaving to get on the dot com and computer bandwagon. But I was not ready, or was I?

Chapter 12
Before Jumping Ship, Look Both Ways

1998 might have had severe highs and lows for me. By 1999, I was doing some crazy soul-searching. We were still newlyweds, and Sasha enjoyed his job while I was floundering with mine. However, I did get another job almost immediately, cleaning oil spills on military bases. Since there were several spills in Maryland and Virginia, there was available work.

This time, the company found work for me in Kentucky. With all the traveling I did in college and grad school, I had never been to Kentucky. I thought of horses and whiskey but not military bases in Louisville. What was weird was that it was a naval base.

I thought, "Okay, a naval base in a land-locked state." That is OK; I was outside and working.

This time, I was the only woman on the job. We were looking for petroleum oil and gas that had leaked into the groundwater. Kentucky has karst or limestone geology and topography with natural gas deposits. It meant no smoking near the drilling rig. Trying to tell the country boys not to smoke next to their rig was like telling a cowboy not to chew tobacco. The attitudes and slights of the crew happened every day.

Going to work meant leaving our new house, friends, and husband for a ten-day trip that started on a Sunday night. We would fly USAir coach as they were the cheapest out of Dulles Airport to Louisville, Kentucky. I would bring my newly laundered jeans and shirts to be worn under Tyvek or Carhartt suits. We worked in many cold weather conditions, including freezing temperatures, which made cleaning equipment much more strenuous, demanding, and harrowing.

We stayed in an Extend-a-Stay hotel, where they cleaned our rooms every other day. They provided breakfast but not lunch or dinner. We had a per-diem for each day's food, hotel, and gas for the trip to and from the site. After going to restaurants, I grew tired of that life. Especially as most of the crew wanted to go to Hooters. I went once to experience it. The food was overpriced, and I was not enthused.

After that, I decided to pack a lunch. I went to a grocery store and started doing that. I found a second-hand bookstore and bought some books to read. I occasionally went out to eat at dinner, but I was usually alone. I was lonely and missed Sasha terribly. I was missing those parties and weddings while I was out of town.

We would fly back on a Thursday morning after packing Wednesday night. Sometimes there would be delays and other such nonsense, and we would get home late on Thursday. This was supposed to be one of our four days off every two weeks, but it never happened that way. So since Sasha worked on Fridays, I decided to give back to my community.

I taught women in a transitional home center how to use Microsoft Word to create resumes and cover letters. Volunteering every other Friday in a one-on-one session, I felt better about my choices. It was a rewarding experience and something I had the knowledge, skills, and patience to do.

While on the weekend off, Yvonne had a party with some of the Serbian family friends, and I was introduced to Julie. She had decided to catch the dot com ride and urged me to do the same. She suggested learning more computer software programs like Word, Excel, Publisher, and others to teach the software to students.

This started my lifelong learning of software. I had a natural knack for understanding how they worked as I created documents and flyers and did photography manipulations.

By May 1999, my soul searching was complete. I found I could not move forward as a Geologist. I did not have the Master's Degree that companies wanted, nor was I interested in cleaning or remediating nuclear waste or asbestos. Instead, my thoughts were of a future with lung cancer (asbestos) or whole-body destruction (nuclear). Yes, my thoughts ran wild, and my dreams were vivid.

The other significant experience that made me choose computer training over geology was because of a book. The book led me to other books on frugalness and simple living. The book was called *Your Money or Your Life, Transforming Your Relationship with Money and Achieving Financial Independence*, by Joe Dominguez and Vicki Robin. The book was published in 1992, and I picked it up at the second-hand book store in Kentucky and started looking at life differently.

Yes, we had spent money on a brand new semi-custom-built home. Yes, I was traveling consistently and not enjoying myself. I also did not understand the financial markets with the employee 401K and Investment Retirement Accounts (IRAs). It was in a portfolio somewhere.

While learning software, Julie recruited me to start working for myself as a software trainer. She had several huge contracts that needed trainers. She started me off with $150 per hour. This included training for companies. I taught email systems like Outlook and Netscape. I wrote technical manuals for the US Patent Office on specific software and Microsoft Office suite for office workers who lost their secretaries. I thought I was on my way.

Chapter 13
Being Childless in a Child-Centered World

Before we were married, Sasha and I discussed children. He had brought it up first. He asked me to think long and hard about not having children. He already had a nephew and two nieces, and he felt that bringing a child or children into this world would stop us from having adventures. He instinctively knew the cost of raising a child, as did I.

Even though I made between $25,000 to $45,000 during my rush hour career days, and Sasha got into the six figures before he retired, our income might have been fine for us, but not enough to have a child. It was not just monetary, though.

While I knew and read books about parents making sacrifices to have children, Amy Dacyczyn from *The Tightwad's Gazette* comes to mind. She managed to have six children; her husband made $30,000 a year. When she started sending out a mailed newsletter, she became the breadwinner, and he became the house husband. They worked as a team and ultimately created and had a beautifully paid-off home with a large family and financial independence. However, they also lived in rural Maine. I knew friends who lived in rural areas and made it work. I knew it was possible.

We lived in a suburban area of the Washington DC metro area. It is an expensive place to live, with good schools and semi-high property taxes. There was also another reason for my resolve not to have children or a child. I could not just have one. I knew people did. But I was raised in a two-child home. Sasha was raised in a three-child home. Then there was the way we were raised.

My parents had verbal arguments about many things. There were criticisms and shouting between myself and my Dad. The Jersey shore dinner would be as follows.

A typical dinner had at least one argument. Dad was at one end of the dining room table, and my Uncle Joe was at the other. I sat next to Dad, with Karen, Denise, and Stephen going down the line to Uncle Joe on the one side and Mom, Grandma F, and Aunt Tina on the other. The light was not quite in the center of the table. Dad always complained he was in the dark most of the time.

Dad and Uncle Joe worked in Northern New Jersey while we lived in Avon-by-the-Sea during the summer. They both had long commutes. Everyone sat down at the table at dinner time. Aunt Tina and Grandma cooked, and sometimes Mom did too, but the children were in charge of setting the table and washing and drying the dishes afterward.

We were often at the beach during the day, at the community pool, or back and forth on our bicycles to home again. The Dads would be back home around 6:30 pm. Remembering it now, I know the adults had cocktails before dinner and usually a beer or wine at dinner. We had our milk glasses and were told we had to drink our milk.

We would sit down at the table. Mom, Aunt Tina, and Grandma brought in the platters of food. The food would go around the table, each deciding how much to put on their plate. Of course, there was always the ability to have seconds.

But something would happen. Dad would say, "Laura! Hold onto your fork properly," ...or "Eat your vegetables!" or "Pay Attention!"

(because my head would be in a book). I might have responded or not, and then my Grandma would say, "Stop picking on her!" Then Dad would get angry, Mom would get upset, and my sister would spill her milk.

The milk would spread fast as we did not use tablecloths. Instead, we had placemats, and the milk would spread far and wide to the other side of the table. We'd jump out of the milk spread, throwing our napkins at the widening liquid spread. Unfortunately, we could not move too far, as the room was narrow and long, and invariably someone would bump their elbow or head on a sidewall, wainscot, or railing.

At that point, chaos would reign, and someone would get the sponges or paper towels and clean up the mess. At that point, dinner was over.

I'd escape to the bathroom because my stomach was in knots. Karen would hide her vegetables under her napkin. Denise would get started on the dishes, and Karen would dry them. I would come down in time to put the dried items away.

Remembering this time in my childhood, when I was figuring out my future with Sasha, did not make me think, "Oh, I want to have children!" Instead, it gave me the opposite response. I did not want to be the person who got angry, the person who had to come between, or the person who had to clean up the messes. I did not want to be in that situation at all.

And that is why I decided not to have children. Sasha had his reasons, and I had mine. We realized we had found the perfect partners to spend a happier life together. We knew there would be arguments, but there would not be a third-party suffering the brunt or the aftermath of those arguments.

Chapter 14
The Scare and The Happiness

Being self-employed while trying to learn software is hard. Finding clients and billing while setting up classrooms after ten years working for private environmental companies was next to impossible. I was not yet ready to be a boss, especially during the latter part of 1999. Julie strayed away from the training industry and instead created a dot com company. That meant her clients went with more accomplished and successful trainers. I needed more structure while still learning software.

Leaving jobs that cannot take me higher was a recurring theme for me and many in the computer industry. However, it caused stress in my marriage. Even though I trained over 1000 adults of different levels and stood and spoke to large audiences in the corporate world, I considered myself an introvert. I did not have the confidence to make friends outside of work. I was not confident about finding clients to stay self-employed for long.

Instead, I went to a company where I could teach adults and get a steady income. I found it with ExecuTrain. They were in Vienna, VA, a mere thirteen miles from my home. Yet it would take almost an hour to get to them each morning and an hour to get home each evening. I had entered the rush hour of careers. Everyone was in their cars headed to the Beltway. Nevertheless, I did enjoy it at first.

They had this unique way of "helping" us learn the software. Let's say you were to teach Beginning Word, a one-day class. That one day is about six hours of class time. They gave us the Trainer's manual and a day to learn the material. The next day you would teach it to a room full of adult beginners. The beginner and intermediate classes were one day, while the advanced classes were two days. After only two days of learning, I taught Advanced Microsoft Access. Talk about stress; yes, I had that.

I call it what it was, a stressful job for a perfectionist. However, I was learning so many programs that would become the basis of my lifelong learning process and help me in my future endeavors.

2000 looked great; I was secure in my hectic learning and training courses. Sasha was promoted to senior designer, and things were looking good in our extended family. We would spend time on our back deck, eating outside and Sasha cooking on the grill. Karen and James lived in Bethesda, Maryland, my parents in Westfield, New Jersey, and Sasha's parents in Fairfax, Virginia. We visited family all over Interstate 95 and I-495 (the Beltway).

The scare was for December 31, 1999, Y2K scare. Everyone feared banks, computers, and electronics would revert to the number 1900 rather than move forward to 2000. I saw trainers jumping ship to work on the issue. Everyone partied hard on December 31, 1999, and prayed for a few numbers to flip to zero.

We woke on January 1, 2000, and looked at our bank accounts. Remember, this was 2000. Most people did not have online banking back then. Sasha was an early adopter. He has done online banking since 1993! Our bank statements and bills were paid, and all our banking was online.

When we woke up that morning, we looked. No change except that the bank was closed, and we waited until the next day to move money. Nothing changed to zeros except the cameras. Most people forgot to change the setting of their cameras to the correct date, and we forgot. And for the paper checks we did have, we crossed out 19 and put 2000.

While I was learning and taking part in a new career, Karen and James decided the time was right for a child.

The Outer Banks has unique connections to the Capuano clan. So what better place to tell us she was pregnant than at a beach house on the Outer Banks? She invited the soon-to-be grandparents on both sides of her and James' family, our Aunt Tina and Uncle Joe, and Sasha and I.

I remember celebrating the news with Champagne, except for Karen, who had sparkling cider. But the best memory of that weekend shows our adventurous spirits. We were excited that Mom and Dad brought their Jeep. The Outer Banks was perfect for driving on the beach, and we asked the family to come out for a ride.

Mom, Dad, Aunt, and Uncle went in their Jeep, and Sasha and I went in ours. Off we went. We had already tested this Jeep on other adventures, but my parents had not. They followed us on a relatively easy trail with a few water crossings. The most adventurous was the last water crossing to a beautiful, remote beach.

There was no way to check the stream crossing, and Sasha decided to gun it and go. The water went over the hood of our Jeep for just a few seconds. Finally, we reached the other side and looked back at them. I could see his determination of Dad to follow and the surprise on Mom's face as the water rose so high.

Once we got to the beach, everyone had this thrilled look and talked about an exciting adventure. We remember that weekend when Karen told us the news of us becoming Aunt and Uncle to her firstborn. It celebrated pregnancy and the excellent water ride in a Jeep.

Chapter 15
Heartbreak and the Start of Anxiety

I have always had anxiety; I did not realize what it was then. But then, vivid dreams in kaleidoscope colors with nightmares were commonplace. Hence, my many stuffed animals scared away those bad dreams as a child.

I started having bad dreams again towards the end of 2000 when learning new software and setting up classes, especially with angry customers, worried me. No longer doing fun classes in software I enjoyed, I was almost exclusively doing work in databases and convoluted Excel spreadsheets. People were angry about the prices when all they wanted was a secretary. The company had some weird practices that charged people who made less. They were billed through the state or federal government and had expensive billing.

As I was not part of the billing, I did not know how they got their contracts. I just knew I was not long for this job.

Thankfully, I found a training department through a real estate company. They were growing by leaps and bounds in the early 2000s. Real estate was a booming business, and the towns within Northern Virginia were growing fast.

Working within an Information Technology (IT) department with many people working for Realtors was fun. Our training department was small, with only three trainers. We wrote manuals and then taught classes at headquarters or offices. We had twelve laptops that needed the software and updates, plus a projector and cables.

This office was even closer to me. There was not that much traffic, and it was down a pretty road that was newly constructed. I listened to NPR in the mornings and whatever rock stations were coming home.

I loved driving to and from work. My car was sporty enough that it had some horsepower to be zippy and take the curves well. I enjoyed helping senior Realtors not be afraid of computers. Mom said I had the patience of a saint. I felt sympathetic to these women; they learned much information about Real Estate and passed those tests. Then they had difficulty getting listings or selling properties because they did not know how to create a flyer.

Sasha and I were planning a trip out west, and this would be the first time in a while for a more extended vacation. I finally had two weeks off in June 2001, and we decided to take advantage of Sasha attending a major conference in Las Vegas. InfoComm was the trade show for the integrated audio-visual industry. Typically, the show would go back and forth between Orlando, Florida, and Las Vegas, Nevada, in June, as it was cheaper in both places. Hot and dry in Las Vegas and hot and humid in Florida. Which one would you pick?

Chapter 16
Of Fun and Free Fall

I bought my first travel log and journal for the trip. We packed for the road trip, a hike to Havasupai Reservation to see the falls and experience Las Vegas. What kind of adventures could we have?

I remember we went out in our gray Jeep. Sasha had sold the red Jeep a while back as a means to us both driving across the country.

We headed west on June 7, 2001. Before this trip, I wrote in journals without prompts; this was the first time writing in a travel journal with prompts. It had places visited at the top with a date, then space for lodging, daily meals, transportation, entertainment, and miscellaneous expenses, and then a place for comments, notes, and observations. In the middle third, there was an open-topped envelope for receipts. And the pages for the Daily Diary of Activities. Then purchases bought during the trip, interesting people, and unique places.

I tried to schedule happenings; typically, we traveled by the seat of our pants. We had two places to be at specific times, but that was it.

We drove twenty-one hours, with a few stops, from Cascades, Virginia, to Oklahoma City, Oklahoma, and stayed at a Hampton

Inn for $59 on June 8, our first place to sleep. They had a good breakfast, a nice bed, and a big room. Since we were in Oklahoma City, we had a nice steak dinner with baked potatoes, salad, wine for me, and a Bud for Sasha total of $30. While I had read the YMOYL book in 1999, I had not started writing down every expense.

Back at that time, those are reasonable prices. I still hope to find a restaurant with a $15 steak dinner. I even wrote down gas prices; $1.34 per gallon of regular gas in eastern Tennessee.

When we traveled through those first twenty-one hours, I wrote that Sasha drove at night and I drove during the day. We got great gas mileage but encountered rough roads in Arkansas. The scenery was not beautiful on Interstate 40. I could not sleep in the Jeep to save my life. I might have napped, but deep sleep eluded me.

Once in New Mexico, the roads and scenery started to look promising, and I did not want to miss a thing. As a geologist going across the country, I loved figuring out the geology as the scenery passed.

We got lost in a Native American reservation. As we headed down a dirt road, we were glad we had prepared for the trip with water and snacks. This trip was the first time we bought silver jewelry on the side of the road. Earrings and a necklace of silver bear with turquoise and hematite stones; the jewelry was beautiful.

We got into Las Vegas on June 11, 2001, and spent two nights at the Mirage for $81 each night. The amenities, a large bed, and a room were well-appointed. Unfortunately, they did not have breakfast for hotel guests, which is how Vegas works. Instead, there are different restaurants inside each hotel and casino, and you choose what flavor you want for the morning and evening. This first part of Las Vegas was a fun time for Sasha. His conference would be later in the week.

We were complete tourists. We took a gondola ride in Venice for $25, drinks by the pool for $20, breakfast in a café $23, and dinner at Olives with a show at Bellagio (Folies Bergère) for $150.

Sasha had to be at the convention and classes soon after. So he took what he needed for the day, and I was to move us from Mirage to Treasure Island (TI). The Mirage was on our dime, but TI was on the company's receipts. I had an early breakfast and went back to bed. I was not sleeping well. Insomnia is a pain when there is so much to do.

I moved us over to TI but was unhappy that the walkways and moving sidewalks were not working. The beauty of those casinos and their "freebies" drew me in. Even though Sasha could have the evenings as his own, that was not the case during the conference. We saw shows and other events on the exhibitors' dime.

I saw fascinating casinos during the day, ate less expensive lunches, and then met Sasha for fun evenings hosted by exhibitors. This schedule set us up for fun for the rest of the trip. We would get up early, walk all day, and sleep less.

Our first real foray into a Native American reservation to visit a unique place had good intentions. We left Las Vegas for Arizona at 7:30 am, which was late. We got to Kingman, and I took over the driving. We parked at the top of the Havasupai Hilltop. We were going down at the wrong time, 1 pm but could do nothing, as we had a reservation at the bottom for that evening.

The entire walk seemed like we were on a sloping beach. Finally, six miles down, we saw some trees and this unbelievable blue, crystalline aquamarine blue river. The last two miles were the hardest as we were close, but not. We got to the lodge at 6 pm, exhausted. The restaurant had closed; we went to the store and picked up salty snacks and Gatorade. Some people who were hiking out gave us their food too.

I awoke at 5 am and watched the morning come across the courtyard. A horse munched on the grass while I was reading.

The square and town looked empty, yet there was a church, a community building, and a school—Nature's beauty of crickets, mules, and horses.

We decided to sleep and eat until at least 4 pm, when we would go to the falls. It took us a while to get down to the falls, but we stayed for several hours and returned up in the dark.

We left around 4:30 am on June 18 to hike out of the reservation. It took us five hours to get back up to the top. As much as I wanted to enjoy the experience, I felt unwelcome. That experience was a first for me. I realize they have a love/hate relationship with tourists. Imagine you have a way to make good money, but it means letting strangers come onto your land. I was sympathetic to the resentment.

We got to Flagstaff that night and saw my friends Ann and Ed from graduate school. We had gone to their wedding in the late 1990s, and they were on vacation and camping. So it was thrilling to catch up with them that evening.

Chapter 17
Summer of Fun in 2001

On June 19, 2001, we visited Grand Canyon National Park for the first time together. As a special treat, we got two nights at El Tovar Hotel. $130 a night. Dinner was $92 in total. And the service was impeccable. Young adults from Eastern Europe came on a visa to work in the national parks with Xanterra as their employer. So we almost had every meal there.

Grand Canyon on the southern rim is at 7500 feet above sea level. Flagstaff is at 7000 feet above sea level. Even with us being in good shape, I had altitude sickness. There was a slight pain in my chest, and I started walking slower. I know we took a bunch of pictures. A helpful hint for anyone with a fast walking partner, take many photos to slow them down. Then, your mind focuses on that view rather than how you feel and de-escalates your stress levels.

The shuttles at the park were great. You can hop on or off, see what you want and then head back to the hotel. We planned to hike along the shuttle trail to Hermit's Rest on our last full day. Remembering it now, we thought we would both be able to walk along the path, but I got tired.

Again, the altitude bothered me.

"Let's meet up at Hermit's Rest. I will hike, and you take the shuttle when you get tired," Sasha said.

That was the plan.

It did not turn out that way. We were supposed to meet at Hermit's Rest at 7:30 pm. Sasha got tired about two-thirds of the way and took a shuttle. I was at the building while he was at the entranceway. They are two VERY separate places. We missed each other completely. I started to worry, going up and down the trail looking for him. He went back to the room, thinking I had gone there. When I was not there, he called a ranger to say I was missing! I stayed at Hermit's Rest until the last shuttle out and then called the room at 8:30 pm.

We had been so worried about each other. Finally, we fell into each other's arms and had a late fish and shrimp dinner. We felt we deserved the meal after a day like that.

We left Grand Canyon the next day to the Eastern side, called Desert View. Again, we walked around, checked out the Watchtower, and saw the sights.

We continued east to Four Corners, getting there late in the day. They usually charge, but we did not have to pay because it was almost closing. So we did the iconic arms stretched in two states while our feet were planted in two more states and took pictures.

Then we got to Cortez, Colorado, and found a room and a brewery. The next day we felt refreshed. The worry and elevation passed us; I was feeling much better. I felt fine going up and over the passes, even walking around towns at higher elevations than Grand Canyon. I had acclimated to the elevation by this time. Being young and in love made whatever I felt go away so I could enjoy the trip. With our last full day of fun behind us, we were prepared for the long drive back the next day.

This type of traveling is very familiar to us. We already knew there were some states with long stretches of nothingness. In Pagosa Springs, we picked up cherries, peaches, and grapes for nutritious snacking. We managed to get west of Louisville, Kentucky, when we were too tired to drive on.

The next day we did it again. We got through Kentucky to Virginia, getting home at 6 pm. We unloaded the Jeep on Monday, June 25, 2001. At least I had another day to organize everything. In my diary, I wrote, "Great Trip, but I do not think we will do this long a road trip again." Hahaha!

The summer of fun and adventure was discussed at work and within the family as we settled into our routines. Yet I was not sleeping well, having insomnia, and waking up hot. There was too much going on in my brain.

I worried about going to sleep. I took PM and sleep aid pills to put me out. My dreams had always been vivid and kaleidoscopic. Most of the time, there were nightmares or dreams of indecision or fear.

I would wake up sweating, wondering why is this happening. But, of course, I knew. I worried about work. I worried about my relationship with Sasha.

Even after a fun-filled trip, we argued. I yelled and cried; who knows about what? His parents never seemed to yell at each other, yet that was how my family and parents spoke in heated moments. Our arguing styles were not the same.

I started going to a therapist in the summer of 2001. The doctor had prescribed Celexa, of 10 to 20 mg a day. Yet, I had decided not to take it or was adamant about not taking pills. There was a mark on your insurance, and your employer was notified if you took pills for mental health, depression, or anxiety. And I did not want to myself labeled as such.

When I went to the therapist, we figured I was anxious, not depressed. So I read the book *From Panic to Power* by Lucinda Bassett.

With the book and the therapist, I started writing in a journal, a Mead spiral-bound book. But I needed to write down my ideas, thoughts, to-do's, and things I was worried about. And I started to get into a hobby, dollhouse creation.

Sasha saw that by me getting into a craft and going to club meetings; I was able to do more than work. I needed a creative outlet. So while I was not into decorating my house, I decorated something small.

But it also was another thing to feel guilty about.

Guilt seems to wash over those pages within my journal during August 2001. I am mad at my friends and worried and stressed and feeling guilty. All of this before September 11, 2001.

Chapter 18
Where Were You When The Sky Cried?

I was going to work; Sasha stayed home because of a cold. So I was running late and listening to NPR when they said, "We have gotten reports of a plane flying into the World Trade Center Building from a suicidal or terrorist hijacked plane. Please wait for further information."

I heard that both planes hit the buildings, and while at work, a plane hit the Pentagon at 10 am. Everyone at work was stunned. People were crying and watching the little TV someone had brought in. Finally, someone suggested giving blood at the blood banks, and many people went.

Instead, I sent out an email to my family and friends to make sure everyone was okay. I knew a few people who worked in Manhattan. Dad was stuck in Minneapolis, Minnesota. I was so worried about him. As the planes were grounded, he ultimately got a car and drove back to New Jersey.

I wrote in my journal about doing a bunch of needless worrying that week, but I wanted to make sure everyone I knew was ok. You see, most of the phone lines said busy or network down.

I started having bad dreams over the weekend and decided to stay away from the news and work on my dollhouse instead.

However, everything overwhelmed me, and I could not tune out my co-workers.

The first day after the stock market closed from the attack, on September 17, 2001, I bought stocks. Sasha said it was probably the worst time to buy stocks, but I said, "We are in it for the long haul, so what difference does it make?"

He shrugged and said, "Alright, you are the finance person."

The Dow went down 600 points that day.

I started the journal to write about the different lessons in the book. The therapist asked me to write down memories from my childhood. I wrote down eight of them in the journal.

On October 7, 2001, we went to war with Afghanistan.

Right around this time, my birthday on October 6, and our anniversary on October 12, 2001, I did a bad thing with my leg. I had a sore on it and started rubbing it until it bled and became more prominent. It was a way to transfer my worries and thoughts, which felt good. When I was younger, I let my dog lick my wounds secretly. The scars would be raw, and they felt good. But, of course, my parents disapproved, and it was done in secret. Afterward, I would put a band-aid on it and leave it alone.

This action only seemed to happen when I was anxious. Around this time, when everyone else was worried too, I was thinking about work, about a database that was difficult to do, and so I started rubbing the sore. When I forgot to put a band-aid on the sore, Sasha saw it and flipped out.

We argued, and he said I was harming my body and psychotic. I said I was not, and it wasn't a big deal. But he did not listen, and we went to bed angry. The following day we got into another big argument. I was so upset I tried calling the therapist to get an appointment because I could not deal with Sasha. Sasha, in turn, called my Mom to say he was worried about me. She said that she would call me that night.

That day I was able to figure out the error with the database. The therapist called me at work, and she helped me understand that I was not insane, but I needed to work on my stress management skills. Mom called me at work as well as at home that night.

She said, "Sometimes, while you might want to tell Sasha everything, it might not be a good idea. He loves you so much that he gets frantic and afraid when he gets worried."

When we came home that night, Sasha and I talked some more. I told him about this database, what the therapist said, and that we must exercise more to eliminate the excess emotions. After that, we made up, and things returned to normal for a while.

I still got the twinges to rub and scratch my wounds. I had to learn to ignore the feeling and do something else to take my mind off touching them again.

I ended up the year on a fabulous note. Even though we had gone to war, Sasha and I worked towards our goals of an even better marriage. I created a website for my dollhouse and organized my clothing, time, linen, kitchen, and craft area.

We spent the week between Christmas and New Year going to museums in Washington, DC, and eating out at fabulous restaurants. I wrote my goals for the year and the next several years. But how was I to know that they would change so much?

Chapter 19

Sales Through Technology

We started the 2002 year happy and continued with happiness for a while.

Who believed that we would finally be part of the American Dream? The house was in a fast-growing community, with two cars, two jobs, and consumerism. We were not called citizens, we were called consumers, and the markets expected us to buy, buy, buy! I traveled consistently for work, driving up and down Interstate 95 to go to offices to train Realtors in Virginia, Maryland, DC, and even up to Delaware and New Jersey. I spent more time running to my car and lugging computers for work than exercising on the tennis court or at the gym.

We were doing well financially and seeing our nieces and nephews weekly. Our visits with family on both sides increased. I was learning so much about technology, marketing, and websites while also learning to keep my stress levels at an even keel.

We started going to New Jersey more often, even with Sasha being unhappy with the traffic along the I-95 corridor. Karen, James, and Brenden, their two-year-old son, had bought a summer home in Avon-by-the-Sea, a dream for Karen. She wanted summers at the beach like we had when we were children. Sasha and I spent many weekends up there, visiting with my side of the family in the summer. We were surrounded by children, although our parents had stopped asking about us having kids. They knew the score.

In 2002, another niece was born on the Jevtich side. Jacqueline Jevtich was born on September 11, 2002, a year after the disaster. Jackie had had a C-section scheduled and decided on that day. At the time, it seemed weird, but now, so many years later, it makes it easier to remember her birthday.

I was disappointed, though. Jackie did not ask me to be Jacqueline's godmother. Each time she had a child, Jackie asked her sister. Karen had asked Colleen, James' sister, to be godmother for Brenden, and I felt weird that I had yet to be asked. Yvonne's kids might have godparents, but as Serbian Orthodox, they did not have a religion per se, not like the Catholics of my family. Stephen and Dany's kids did not do any religion or have "godparents." We were aunts and uncles and cousins.

We put tons of miles on the Jeep and Saturn, went up and down the East Coast, and spent money. We bought, worked, and played with family. Our friends were our neighbors, our families, and our co-workers. We moved into 2003 with nary a worry in the world.

The goals I had set up in 2001 were looking good. We started the new year with happiness, good prospects, and happy family outings. However, I did not realize that 2003 would end with a cease-and-desist letter from a former employer. Would my handling of stress work or not?

I wrote in my journal a scary thought. Although it was not dated, I am sure it was close to the Fall of 2003.

I wrote, "Things I am having problems with - we need to know who will be our department's manager. Will it be me or Sheila, someone who came in a little after me? She has more experience, calmness, and tact, important qualities for a manager. But, on the other hand, I tend to tell it like it is; I want things done quickly, efficiently, and without a wait-and-see attitude."

I wanted Sheila to get up to speed as soon as possible. Veronica, my boss and friend would leave for California in a week. I was worried and upset. I knew I would not get the manager position, but I wanted it to be with someone I had an alliance with, not someone new.

In the end, Sheila did become my boss. Unfortunately, she also was the one to fire me. Veronica had mentioned something to me on this very subject before she left. She said that Sheila had her way of doing things and to watch my back. By my birthday, 2003, I was out of a job I had held for almost three years, the most extended position in geology or computer training.

Dad was going through a similar story. Only the year before, he was let go because of ageism. He was 62 and only three years from retirement. Instead, they gave him a messed up reason for them letting him go. He had a retirement party with another co-worker and went out in style. My parents were a little worried about mortgage payments on their home and thought they had to sell it. So instead, he went into business for himself and sold back his services to his former employer for triple what he was paid as an employee.

He had some suggestions for me as well. Instead of trying to find another job in training, why not go into business? I had the database of Realtors, which I had developed and worried about back in 2001. Within that database were the Realtors who had taken classes from my former employer for the past three years.

I created Sales Through Technology, LLC, within a week of being let go. And I got the business cards, a website, and promotional materials set up within the month. But the first quarter as a business had the cease-and-desist letter from my former employer. They thought I was moving into their turf and wanted me out. So I sent them a letter back, with the help of Dad, and they did not contact me again.

Instead, I used my training and marketing skills to sell myself and my services. I was no longer worried about how I did in a class, as I mostly did one-on-one training or helped as an assistant. At the time, the Real Estate company I worked for had made their website of homes with the Realtors' names attached to the listings. However, it meant the Buying Agents did not have a way to garner more clients. The way around was to have a killer profile page and a website. And I could help them achieve it. By the second quarter of 2004, I had reached a five-figure income, became part of the Dulles Area Association of Realtors (DAAR), and was on my way to becoming President of the association's affiliates.

I was learning about technology, coaching Realtors without being called a coach, and making $100 daily or more for a couple of work hours. I was on my way to becoming a serious entrepreneur and small business owner with more friends and an enjoyable life. My third career has started, and it was the best one yet.

By the end of 2003, we went up to New Jersey to celebrate Christmas with my side of the family. And Karen and James had more good news. She was pregnant with a second child. They knew it was a girl. And I would be her godmother. So things were looking up for 2004.

Chapter 20

Refusal of the Call

In 2004, Sasha was 48, and I was 36. He was noticing some changes in the audio-visual industry. I was oblivious to his turmoil, although I did hear his complaints about clients more. We were also a little unhappy about our couch potato lives. Since meeting less than a decade ago, we have been much more active. To be active now meant driving to a place to hike, swim or even walk.

We supposedly lived the American Dream but questioned what that dream entailed. It was out of reach.

Our friends were our neighbors, family, and work friends. Most of my closest friends still lived in the state I grew up in, and Sasha's friends were the same. And two-week vacations were not enough time to see the country how we wanted.

Sasha was unhappy with his career. His clients were not listening to his suggestions and ideas and not buying from his company. As a consultant, I knew his tactlessness would not help and would further alienate him from his clients. We had been married seven years; the seven-year itch came to mind, and we had our home for six years. I had started getting more clients and increasing my sales over the previous year.

While I was happy with our semi-custom home, I did not feel like I had the same friendships as in high school. Not having kids in a neighborhood full of them made meeting other women hard. A few women were in the community with similar circumstances, but our interests seemed far different. Finally, I found a book club with a friendly group of women.

While Sasha was going through this career turmoil, he saw disturbing events in his industry. First, his close friend died from a massive heart attack at 40. He left behind a devastated wife and a couple of children.

Then, four of Sasha's AV industry friends died that year of lung cancer. One was a vegan in prime health, and only one had ever smoked. They were his age or younger. As he had smoked cigarettes for over ten years, I knew he was worried.

My office was in a loft on the house's second floor. His desk and a second office were in the basement. So there were two floors between us. I had no idea what he was working on in the basement.

Most nights, we would sit in front of the TV to watch the news and eat dinner. We even had those TV trays to have in front of us. I reflect on that time and think how funny we must have looked.

Sasha turned off the TV one night after the news and stated he wanted to talk to me about something. He seemed so serious at the time. I do not remember if we were in front of the TV or not at this point. However, I remember his blue eyes silently and seemingly pleading with me to be understanding and patient.

He first started by saying he had been researching this for a while. I honestly do not remember, nor does he, how long he explored options. Maybe he saw that I was successful at marketing and websites for my clients. Then, he talked about selling our house and moving to Colorado.

Back then, I did not know a soul in Colorado. He had gone to Colorado State University in Fort Collins. The pace of work is vastly different from the East Coast, especially in Washington, DC, and New York City metro areas. Colorado, you work to have fun on weekends and create long weekends. I had experienced similar mentalities in Portland, Oregon. On the East Coast cities, you work and buy stuff. You took your two-week vacation and were happy about getting those two weeks. We felt this in comparing the two lifestyles: "work to play" or "work to buy."

He talked about creating his own business and consulting businesses in Colorado. He also thought about living in a cabin or an A-frame house, the kind you see every Christmas season, with snow around.

I was not thrilled by this idea. Everyone I knew was on the East Coast. Even my friends from Portland had moved to Virginia.

He then switched gears somewhere along the discussion and said he had done other research. I know now when he researches something, he studies. He finds the angles, pluses, minuses, pros, and cons and sees others who have done something similar and everything in between. When we were dating, I thought he knew everything. But that knowledge came from research and reading different articles from numerous sources.

His other research was to get a truck camper. A truck camper that you put on the back of a truck. A truck that we did not have. I did not know anyone with a truck. I knew farm people and landscapers had trucks, but I did not know anyone with a truck camper.

I initially hesitated to do such a radical idea as buying a truck and a truck camper. It meant getting a wildly expensive vehicle at the time, 35 thousand dollars, and breaking our rule of not owing any debt except our mortgage. And then buying a camper that costs more than the truck when we did not have the cash saved seemed reckless.

While the Colorado thing seemed scary, the truck and camper idea was not as bad. Karen and James had bought a summer house in Avon, New Jersey. They were doing well. While we did not make as much as they did, we still had a beautiful home. A vacation home might be a stretch, but getting a truck and camper was something we could swing. So I decided to join in on the research and get a better understanding of what we both wanted and needed.

Chapter 21
The Journey Begins

I decided that if we were going to do this, to buy a truck and a camper as our vacation home, we needed to read *Your Money or Your Life, Transforming Your Relationship with Money* (YMOYL) by Joe Dominguez and Vicki Robin. We worked on all the steps, made decisions together, and forgave ourselves of lousy money choices. Using the book together, we figured out what we owed and owned and if we were making a living or dying. This vital information and knowledge about money led us to believe we could embark on this adventure.

Your Money or Your Life became our bible. We spent time gathering the information. I read YMOYL in 1999 when I was working in Kentucky.

The first step in YMOYL is to recognize your past relationship with money. So we called Social Security Administration and visited the building to get our income history.

The First Step: Making Peace with Your Past does just that. How much have you earned in your lifetime, and what do you have to show for it? We went through each room of the house and put a value on every item. We estimated the home was worth $700,000. We were only a little off when we had it assessed in 2005; they estimated $707,500! Our furniture, art, clothing, jewelry, computers, silver, dishes, crystal, motorcycle, cars, tools, everything down to the can opener and cookie container were "worth" $89,438. Our fixed assets were worth $789,438. Liquid ones were the cash on hand, savings, checking accounts, 401Ks, and IRAs, which were lower, at $256,923.48.

We found out through Social Security that I had earned $408,231; Sasha (twelve years older) made $1,088,433. So our only liability was the mortgage at $329,883.80.

From those numbers, we figured the net worth: Liquid Assets + Fixed Assets - Liabilities = $716,477.68. Again, a plus sign was good. That was our net worth if we were able to liquefy everything.

Of course, we did not. We were still figuring out how to transform our money.

The Second Step: was to figure out our actual life energy and hourly rate for work. Mine was a little harder to figure than Sasha's as I had an hourly rate and billed clients on a fixed rate. Sasha's life energy and hourly rate were easy as he was salaried. His hourly rate before YMOYL adjustments was $45.19 per hour. But after adjustments for commuting, meals, clothing, decompression, escape vacation, and illness, it went down to $27.03. Mine went from $20 to $11, as I worked from home with only a few forays to clients.

The Third Step: the most important one of the book that I took to heart was tracking the money coming in and out of the household. While I did not start in 2005, by 2007, I had created a template in Excel with spreadsheets that worked. Whether in a house or an RV, I tracked what we bought and our income from whatever sources we had. I nailed it.

The Fourth Step: happens after the first time we tabulated our expenses and income. There were three questions, and you would use a plus sign (+) for positive, a minus sign (-) for negative, and zeros for neutral. Each life energy hour was worth a rounded figure of our two adjusted hourly rates of $32.

When we went back into our monthly tabulations, we asked ourselves these questions:

1. Did we receive fulfillment, satisfaction, and value compared to Life Energy spent?

2. Is this expenditure of Life Energy in alignment with our values and life purpose?

3. How might the expenditure change if we did not have to work for a living?

Each category and line item total was divided by Life Energy to get a number. The most oversized line item was our mortgage. We figured each month we were spending 50 Life hours to pay it, just for the interest. The principal was 10.8 Life hours. We also added an extra $1000 each month for extra principal pay down, which was 31.25 life hours. Let's say we gave negative symbols or minus signs to those questions about our mortgage.

By this point, we were into saving money. I was doing these calculations on my computer, so Sasha could not see them.

The Fifth Step: seeing progress, showing income and expenses on graph paper with data points and line graphs. I did this for a while, but we had such wild numbers that I could not make the graph work.

The Sixth Step: saving money and different things you could do. This step meshed with The Seventh Step, to earn more income while saving. We started to sell items we did not need, like Sasha's CD collection, which became digital files. We figured out that I could sell books on Amazon.

Back in 2005, the Amazon sellers marketplace was vastly different than today. Then, they gave you money for every book for postage plus whatever you earned. Considering media mail costs much less than that, you made more money per book sold.

The last two steps help you learn and understand money, compounding interest, and treasury bonds. The Eighth Step discusses the crossover point, where your investments earn you the same or more than your expenses. The Ninth Step talks about financial freedom from work. Finally, you can go and find happiness.

While we did not jump in with both feet to sell everything in 2005, we decided we could afford the truck and the camper while still taking vacations and enjoying life. As a result, I changed my financial mindset.

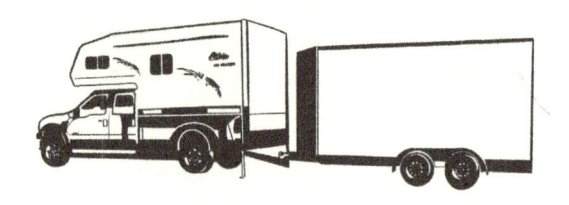

Chapter 22
How To Buy Big Ticket Items

While I did not start tracking or writing down every penny coming in or out of our household, I did so for big purchases. I also read and learned more about money, finances, stocks, bonds, IRAs, and 401Ks. I suggested to Sasha that he change his 401K allotments to be less in stocks and more in bonds, as he had everything in the stock market. Since I had my business, I moved my 401K into an IRA and added the maximum amount for each year I worked. These steps and claiming 10% of our house as my office space helped with our federal income taxes.

I also decided to create a personal website. It was first on Blogger as I did not want to pay for hosting or a domain. March 27, 2005, was my first day writing on the website.

I worked hard for clients using Microsoft's Frontpage to create websites and 1and1 dot com (no longer around) for domains and hosting. Finally, I decided on Blogger because it was free, but I found out pretty quickly that it did not have enough space for pictures.

Photography will always be the bane of existence for me concerning our website. Each time I uploaded a picture, the website wanted two, a thumbnail and the actual image. But the internet speeds were never as good while traveling as the house ones.

The old website of 2005 was cute, with signposts, yellow background, and a grass lawn on the bottom. The hosting company would be my first affiliate, and our site was Laura-n-Sasha dot com, Laura & Sasha's Excellent Adventure.

How could we afford a truck for $32K and a camper for $35K in one year? We bought the truck on the lot of the Ford dealership in our town of Sterling, Virginia. There was an end of the year sale in 2004. We used our home equity when we found out how much our home was worth. We thought we were rich!

While doing YMOYL in late 2004, we discovered our home had almost tripled in value since we bought it in 1998, only six years later. A home equity loan, with its high-interest rates, was still lower rates than a credit card but higher than a mortgage. You could get checks with the home equity to buy whatever you wanted. It was considered "easy money," and many people around us used it as a piggy bank.

Thankfully, we had cash for the truck but were short, and the sales were happening until January 1, 2005. So we pulled the plug and wrote two checks for our Ford F350 Lariat, one from the central bank account and one from the home equity.

The following month we paid off the home equity loan plus interest accrued from that one month. We were in the green again. We returned to that home equity loan three months later to buy the truck camper. We would not pay it off until we sold the house almost two years later.

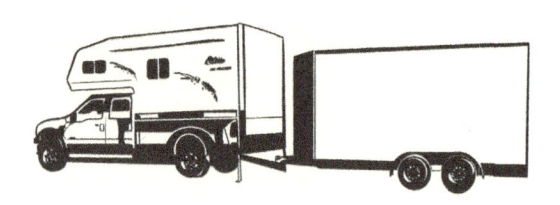

Chapter 23

Preparing to Buy Our Vacation Home

Before we could buy our truck camper, we researched on a forum called RV dot net. While Facebook started in 2004, we were not aware of it. So instead, we had forums where we could ask questions. I participated in several forums, including Simple Living, Backwoods, and RV dot net.

We found a community of like-minded individuals willing to help us learn for free. We realized what we needed for the truck, such as airbags on the tires and Rickson wheels, from RV dot net. We also knew that I would want to write while Sasha was driving, and we set up a Jotto desk to hold my laptop and internet card and have the GPS on the computer. I did not realize the pain of using the GPS until the first day's drive.

I installed the Delorme GPS for my Dell laptop. It came with this dongle connected to the computer and went to the farthest reaches of the dashboard. This way, you could use the satellites to help you.

On March 27, 2005, we headed out. We were going to Colorado to pick up a truck camper, which is a recreational vehicle (RV). People who RV are called RVers, and to use it as a verb, such as RVing. My log was as such:

Day 1: Sterling, Virginia, to Greenville, Illinois, crazed GPS with the laptop. We got on the road two hours late. I set up the GPS and tried to figure out our route; I was directional-challenged. First, it stated we were going to Chicago, then we would not use highways, and the system would make these random straight lines as though we were crows flying toward the sun.

I was going to lose all my hair...

Ultimately, I figured out the system. What was interesting in the log was I wrote down the weather, the amount of internet signal (I called it bars and put that word into the website), and the external temperature. Because, as people who live in RVs know, temperatures inside and out are essential. You tend to watch the weather more when you are camping or RVing.

The other words or acronyms I used during the trip were above sea level (ASL). As a person used to being on a coast, going up and down in elevation was a novel experience. I would mention it because the Delorme system had it. And when our ears would pop at 500 or 1000 feet above sea level, I would let Sasha know the elevation.

When we first stopped in Maryland, the diesel prices were $2.34 and gas $2.11. The rain and fogginess of that first day made for bad internet and GPS, with a rebooting of my computer. But we made it to West Virginia by 1:35 pm. We got on the internet to check diesel prices as we went along. This was before GasBuddy.

During the trip west to buy the camper, I talked about having internet service or not on my T-Mobile device or cell phone with Cingular (now AT&T). That first long day, we saw rain and a fight between a Suburban and an 18-wheeler truck. The truck eventually won with no accident.

We stayed at Best Western the first night because they had a refrigerator and free internet access. At $60 a night, our first day is full of numbers: $2.30 for a gallon of diesel, Interstate 70 (I-70), and low temperatures outside. The internet I had in the truck was from cutting-edge technology of the time, a T-Mobile Sony Ericson card that went directly into the laptop. The fast 56kb was the same as dial-up and was considered a great deal at $30 monthly in 2005.

I kept writing each day on the website. Day 2: March 28, 2005, Greenville, IL - Brighton, Colorado. "*Men and Women Ordering Food.*" We went to Ethan's Place because the hotel did not have breakfast. We both ordered omelets, I asked for no hash browns, and Sasha got a spicy omelet with hash browns. They got our order mixed up, with him getting my omelet with hash browns. He started to put salt and pepper on it, and I looked at my omelet and said, "Where is the ham?"

He said, "You should just order what is on the menu."

I said, "I should order it how I like it."

Whenever I think back to that moment, I think of "*When Harry Met Sally.*" But, of course, at $13 for both of us, with tax and a tip, it was a little hard to quibble.

We tend to be the talk of the truck stop whenever we stop for diesel. So we go into the lanes that the truckers go, and as we are filling up, they ask about our 19-inch wheels, unusual for this truck, giant flares, those things around the tires we both put on and how is the 2005 running, stuff like that. So we are "*The Talk of The Truck Stop.*"

After a long search, we found a dealer in Henderson called Five Star RV Center. They had Snow River truck campers. We asked them to add a solar panel on the roof, which they did not do until they had the cold cash. Nevertheless, we were looking forward to meeting our camper.

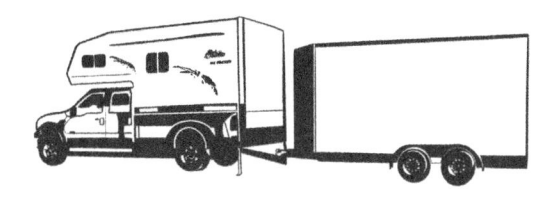

Chapter 24
Lessons Learned

- Being directionally challenged can be frustrating. However, it does not need to be stressful as long as you have time.

- Walmart was a great place for RVers until Walmart wised up and kicked us down to the curb. Use Amazon, grocery stores, or local stores if you need something.

- Time is what separates vacationers and tourists from full-time (FT) travelers and FT RVers. When you have time, it does not matter when you get to a place; you are there for as long as you and your money allow.

- If you stay at a campground, make sure to plug into their systems, their energy, their water, and their sewer. You are paying for it. You might even use their bathrooms and showers rather than your own. Why pay for propane usage when you can use their electricity?

- Boondocking means without hookups: without utilities of electricity, water, and sewer. Usually, it means you are in beautiful places, but not always. We boondocked at Walmarts, truck stops, and rest areas.

- March in Colorado elevations can be snowy and cold. Plan to have blankets, duvets (comforters with a cover), and flannel sheets. Do not try to buy them at a Walmart at 2 am. No one knows where they are hidden.

- Having your internet can save you money and frustrations.

- You can tire even without exercise when you put on and take off layers, go up and down in elevation, and ride on bumpy roads.

- Naming and re-naming your photographs makes it easier to sort them later. Putting in the metadata of dates and times helps too.

- A campground is only as good as its workers. If the workers are happy, then the campers will be too.

- Make sure to put a table or chair in the middle of your RV spot so no one takes the spot.

- Trying out local restaurants can be exciting.

- Buying from a reputable dealership with good communications is critical. We called Five Star several times after we bought the truck camper, and they were helpful.

- Having a rest day between hiking and activity days lets your body rest and gives you time to check out the area.

Why did I like Fruita, Colorado, so much? We stayed there almost the entire trip. We thought we would go to Dinosaur National Monument too, but Colorado National Monument and the town around it held us too close, and we wanted to explore it more.

We did three hikes in the Monument, one we called The Mighty Hike as it was a strenuous, seven-mile hike one way, which we did not finish. It would be best if you always had a reserve to make it back, and we needed it on the hike from hell. I created my ratings for hikes: no butt, half butt, and full butt for those steep rocky downhills. I thought some areas looked so bad; one slip, and we would be meals for a mountain lion. I swore I would never watch another nature show right before hiking; they made for countless nightmares.

The other hike we called the Downhill Hike, as we got a ride to the top and put our truck at the bottom. It was the Monument Canyon trail. The man who took us said he would call the park ranger if he did not see us by 5 pm. We thought that was very friendly. This hike was a favorite, and we took over 75 pictures. For the geologist in me, I kept thinking of the ancient environments that made those rocks.

Maybe I liked the town so much because there were wineries. Sasha did not mind going from winery to winery and checking them out with me. Seeing elk penned up was funny and made us feel like the suburbanites we were as we took many pictures.

The reason was that everyone was so friendly. Everyone seemed to like our truck, ask about our truck camper, and enjoy our company as newbies. We just had fun.

We gave ourselves three days to travel home, partly because of the Kansas winds and partially because we were not used to driving with a camper on the truck. Finally, we came home on a Sunday with enough time to unpack, have dinner and watch a show before heading to bed. We were hooked on this way of vacationing and looked forward to meeting others.

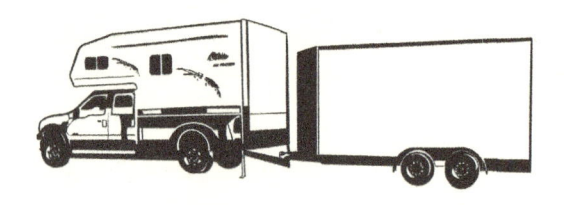

Chapter 25
Idyllic Life Fraying

In 2005, before we went on and after coming back from our trip to get the camper, we spent quite a bit of time with our growing family. My sister had Lindsay in 2004 and honored me with Godmother and Aunt. Jacqueline Jevtich was the last child born of the Jevtich family in September 2004. So now we had eleven nieces and nephews; from my sister, there were two, Sasha's sister and brother, each had three children, and three from Stephen's children. Since Karen and James had moved to New Jersey to live full-time, their children and Stephen's children were together more often.

We would take trips to New Jersey, and they would come down to celebrate the children's birthdays. We loved having family in our home, especially as the outdoor deck was perfect for large gatherings.

In June 2005, we celebrated Mom and Dad J's 50th wedding anniversary. My parents and the whole Jevtich family attended. Also, I got my friend Amy to take pictures of the night and the people coming as I was making a scrapbook for them. My parents stayed with us over the weekend.

July was full of adventures, going to the lake with the Batal family on July 4, 2006. We opted to stay in the camper rather than sleep in their home. It would be the first time we slept in the camper rather than someone's home, but not the last.

When we brought the camper up to New Jersey, we showed the kids, and they loved it. When you think about it, a small RV like a truck camper makes perfect sense to a child. Everything is small—a dinette, perfect for four kids, a small kitchen, and a big bed. Even the toilet and bathroom seemed unusual.

By July 22, 2006, our entire family celebrated Sasha's birthday. It was an excellent time, never to be repeated. Soon, in the future, there would be two divorces that would pull the families apart with devastating results. But we were unaware as we enjoyed our new toy and our adventures.

Looking back, our life seemed idyllic. We were surrounded by family and enjoyed being with friends. We traveled more now with the camper. Yet there were problems too, not seen in pictures or did I write down much during this time.

We went to Atlanta, Georgia, buying a motorcycle for me in January 2006, a truck camper rally in April, and out west with my parents in Sedona, Arizona, in May.

We also picked up a utility trailer. This trailer was the kind that you can completely customize on the inside. I have often thought of Sasha as an organizational guru as far as a garage is concerned. Our home garage was perfect, with everything having its place, and the trailer was no different. We had space for extra water, gasoline, and diesel. Sasha's motorcycle and our outdoor shower contraption, a Blue Tote, chairs, a tool chest, and an outdoor screened tent could fit in the trailer. Sasha mapped out where everything would go, made a spreadsheet on the weights, and realized our truck could pull and stop the trailer.

Safety first; this was our motto as we saw RVs on the side of the road. The roads were littered with potholes, or people drove too fast, and blow-outs were common. Depending on how quickly you go at the time, a blow-out could rip your entire side of the RV. Also, it was expensive to get a new tire, especially for our truck tires. Therefore, we took it slow.

My business was going well, with many new clients popping up, wanting websites and web pages to describe the areas they served. I was rarely needed for marketing or creating newsletters. Much of my work was moving online or in my office rather than face-to-face. I was the President of the DAAR Affiliates, and we planned get-togethers and meetups with Realtors. The Realtors were begging for inventory as there was never enough, and prices were increasing, higher and higher. The loan officers devised creative ways for anyone to buy a house—no one thought of the future bubble or crash.

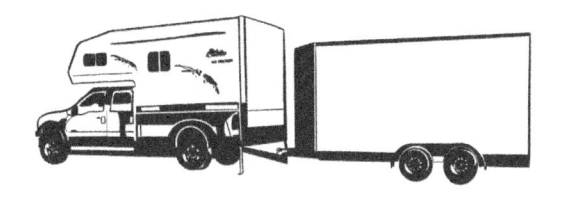

Chapter 26
Sabbatical 2006

All our traveling in 2005 and even more at the beginning of 2006, Sasha still had vacation time on the books. Since I had my own business, it was easy to take a vacation whenever possible. So by July 2006, Sasha would accumulate six weeks of vacation time and decided to ask for it all at once.

We would go on a Sabbatical from work. We wanted to experience western living, and living in a truck camper seemed the perfect opportunity.

Now, Avitecture had never had a request like this before. They understood somehow that he needed this vacation or sabbatical. Once they had given their OK, we planned when, where, and how. We decided for September and October, the perfect time to go west, with warmer temperatures, but not too hot, schools and colleges in full swing, and more campground spaces.

There were several places Sasha wanted to go in Colorado. I left the planning to him and moved my business online. I would only work on websites, updating and making them fresh. This time we had several different mobile internet and cell phone systems, so I could still work when needed.

We started on Sunday, September 3, 2006, in the evening, taking the entire Saturday to dry out the camper. When we picked up the camper from storage, we had mistakenly left the vent open from the last time, and some areas were wet. We parked the truck with the camper on top and had the trailer and truck blocking our driveway and mailbox.

We had enough with the US Postal Service and got a PO Box. We received tickets to move the truck because it was too long between the two mailboxes. Our postal person was too lazy to get out of their vehicle.

We also noticed the eye rolls from our neighbors, like "there go the hicks, getting out their camper again." One of the houses was for sale on our block, and the neighbors had asked us to move the camper, complaining that it was sitting outside our house too long!

"Look, Lady, we are moving as fast as possible!" I said.

It was a little nerve-wracking.

Saturday was the dry-out day, and Sunday was the packing day. After that, we would start the trip at 7 pm, driving and calling our parents to let them know we were leaving.

After stopping at a Flying J to get diesel and water, Sasha turned down a dead-end road. He had to go over a curb, not just with the truck but also with the trailer. I hopped out to help direct. The experience was slightly scary, as we had just started the trip and did not want a flat. Everything turned out fine, but what a way to start.

We decided not to go too far that first night, only going into West Virginia. We stayed at their welcome center. The center said no overnight camping but did not say "no overnight parking," so we parked, not camped. I am not sure about the thinking. Did people put up tents?

When we woke up, we realized we had parked near a prison. Quite promising for our first night, we laughed and kept going west. We made it into Illinois by Labor Day Monday the next day. I drove the truck with the trailer for the first time that day and got used to being a Jersey girl "driving with the traffic" to a Virginia woman "who forged her way." Even though we had cruise control with the truck, you cannot use it with the trailer. Instead, I learned to slow down and enjoy the ride.

We stayed in Colorado State Parks during the trip, boondocking on Federal lands or at welcome centers or truck stops. However, your memories of a place or campground do not mean you will have them again.

Case in point: In 2005, we went to Monument RV Resort, and they said we could take the camper off the truck. In 2006, they said, "No, you cannot!" They were very snide and snippily about it. So we decided to take our business elsewhere and stayed at the state park across the street—pink bathrooms, to be damned.

The other lesson I learned during the sabbatical is that I am not a motorcycle person. I hate to shift gears with my feet or hands. So why did I not tell Sasha this when we bought the little red motorbike for me? Well, I wanted to please him. I wanted to be adventurous, but I was scared too. When you learn to do something active when you are young, you do not have far to fall. So when Sasha was figuring out what was wrong with my Honda 110, I put pink, sparkly butterfly stickers on my helmet.

Sasha rode his motorcycle and found Grand Valley PowerSports, where we could trade in my Honda 110 for a 2006 Yamaha All Terrain Vehicle (ATV) Kodiak. We left our house keys with a neighbor, Kristina, who could go in, to the exact place where Sasha had the title of the motorbike and FedEx the title to the store.

The financing was fabulous because of Sasha's credit rating. We could buy for no money down, zero percent financing for six months. We would pay for the ATV when we got back home. But, for now, I would be riding for free!

As much as we enjoyed State parks like Lake Pueblo, Taylor Reservoir, Cimarron, Fruita, Island Acres, Bangs Canyon, and Little Sahara, we enjoyed boondocking in open spaces more. The ability to have no one else around, and use your solar, water, and sewer for as long as you can, seemed perfect to us. We managed to stay in one spot near Grand Junction, Colorado, for a full 14 days without having to move the rig. Of course, we did need to get water and empty the black tank, but boondocking was the best.

We found bliss in boondocking. Some state parks did not have utilities, which is okay with low prices. However, they can have some fantastic places, like Little Sahara State Park in Oklahoma, where people ride on the dunes.

On our 9th wedding anniversary, October 12, 2006, we rode, then went to Breaux Winery for an event with DAAR. We decided not to go home after the event but to keep having adventures. So we stayed at Green River State Forest for the weekend of riding. On the last day, we visited Prince William Forest Park, a National Park Service unit. They were looking for volunteers to work at the visitor center, and an idea popped into our heads.

We made it home at midnight. We had to work the next day. And we had the decision to make.

Chapter 27
Choosing Frugal and Selling All

We came back from our sabbatical renewed. We assessed what we wanted in life and started working the steps of Your Money or Your Life. We discussed different possibilities and looked at the pros and cons. The idea was to sell the house and everything in it and move into our truck camper. We would go from 2400 square feet of the house to 24 square feet of the truck camper.

We realized time was short, and home ownership prevented us from leading the kind of lives we wanted to live. We had become couch potatoes, eating in front of the TV. We did not have children, and we wanted to travel. So many people TALK about traveling; we wanted travel to be our focus. For example, we had to stay home on weekends to stain the deck and mulch the landscaped beds. This example crimped our active traveling kind of lifestyle.

We realized that by doing the YMOYL steps, we paid over $3,000 a month for the mortgage, property taxes, utilities, lawn care, storage, newspaper, maid, insurance, Home Owners Association (HOA) fees, and maintenance. These expenses were before we did any recreation or fun. We loved the house, deck, hot tub, and community but wanted more.

We decided that if we did anything, we would rent a house or apartment in a different county in Virginia, where we could keep the truck camper, trailer, and toys. Sasha would continue to work for a few years.

Or, I could get a volunteer position in a state or national park where we could live. We learned that by giving them 32 hours of my week, we could get a campsite with full utilities. It would mean a further cut of working for myself though that did not seem like a hardship. No longer was I the President of DAAR Affiliates; I designed and maintained my clients' websites. I started playing around with Google and YouTube, and people subscribed to our newsletter and videos.

We talked about it with our families. Finally, I discussed this with Mom, a Realtor in New Jersey, and she suggested staging the house.

My parents were also talking about selling their home. They wanted to be closer to their grandchildren, and Karen and James had sold their beach house in New Jersey and moved to Richmond, Virginia. My parents wanted to be near and be in an area that was great for seniors. Even though Dad turned 65 in 2005, he kept working with his own business. This allowed them to travel.

She suggested that instead of picking a Realtor to list the home, we sell it ourselves and pay a Buyer's agent three percent. After the marketing I had done for Realtors, it made sense to do that and more.

However, our parents were not too keen on us selling our home. They called us homeless. I said, "No, Houseless. Home is where you park it." A favorite saying of full-time RVers.

We started purging and selling our stuff almost immediately. As we went through the YMOYL steps, I felt I could kick my former self as we bought so much stuff. Stuff I rarely used but thought I needed. But, of course, clothing was the biggest issue. I was rarely in a suit anymore, nor fancy clothing.

I started volunteering eight hours a week at Prince William Forest Park, a national park in Dumfries, Virginia. This park was near Sasha's parents' home and off of I-95.

We were on our way to making an actual living by getting out of the semi-custom house we had built to enter the truck camper fully. The time we decided on the list on the Multiple Listing Service (MLS) was approximately two months. We did a soft open in December but listed it as For Sale By Owner (FSBO) on January 2, 2007.

Most people I worked with were unhappy that I had decided to do an FSBO rather than list with them. But, at the same time, it costs only $399 to list our home on the MLS, and a Realtor costs between $15,750 to $18,000 for three percent of the listing of our home.

I also found that the real estate market was slowing in 2007. Whether the Realtors I worked for were finding it harder to make money or they had figured out how to do my work themselves, I do not know. People were not paying on time. They were paying late for my services. The time was right for a change.

Starting in 2007, I tracked every penny coming in or out. I did the first year in quarters and wrote blog posts showing expenses and budget. After that, I added the costs I had with my business and housing expenses.

Yikes! $23,064.65 for three months. This amount of money was formidable. We knew that once the house was sold, our huge mortgage and upkeep would be gone, but how much of an uptick would we see?

January expenses: $4,401.80
February expenses: $4,059.04
March expenses: $14,788.93

Chapter 28

Selling the House and Everything In It

When we put the house on the market, Sasha started listing his music and DVD collections through eBay and Amazon. During this time, Amazon paid you to sell stuff for them, and we took full advantage of it. PayPal and eBay made small commissions. In January, February, and March 2007, we sold over $5,000 of items. I could make good money selling our stuff online rather than doing my regular work.

I spent time making sure the house was always available to show. My Mom helped stage it, especially the main bedroom and bathroom. Then, we took our stuff out of those rooms and moved into the guest bedroom and bathroom.

I took pictures of the entire house. We prettied up the landscape and had cleaning people into the house twice a month. Then, I created a website called 47651RhyolitePlace dot com. It had floor plans, pictures, and virtual tours. Once sold, I put the prices for every item listed on the estate sale in those pictures. There was also a features list with a bulleted list for every room.

My organizational and time management skills were at the highest levels. I was stressed and doing too much, volunteering, working, selling, creating, and shipping our stuff. Not only that, I was having trouble sleeping. I was so hot at one moment and cold the next that I decided to see the doctor. They performed some tests and suggested I go for my first mammogram. I was 38, but they believed I was pre-menopausal. April was turning into a significant high and low period for me.

Low because they found a lump in my left breast, we were starting a new adventure, and I was also scared something terrible was occurring to me.

Here I was, usually very healthy, paying for my health insurance through my small business, and they had found a lump when they did the mammogram. A mammogram that the insurance would not pay for it. For some reason, I had to pay for it out of pocket.

No one in my family had ever had breast cancer. They needed to do a biopsy to see if the lump was malignant. But I had to wait for this invasion of my body. An offer had come in on Easter Sunday, April 8, 2007. It was a little lower than we wanted. However, to get it higher, they wanted a fast turnaround to close on May 5, 2007.

It was a mad rush to sell everything and get my health in order. Stress was at an all-time high. Finally, we could move into the RV spot meant for the volunteer visitor center worker on the same day as the closing.

We asked for help from my parents, especially my Mom, to figure out pricing for our items. We even sprang for an advertisement in the Washington Post for an estate sale. My parents, Aunt Tina and Uncle Joe had run an estate sale business. While there were estate sale consultants in Virginia, we did not need them. Instead, we wanted my parents as the extra eyes and Sasha and myself to do the selling.

Many people have asked us how you can sell all your stuff. What about the photo albums and mementos? We scanned everything that we could. Our wedding photo albums went to my parents, as did the crystal glasses and silverware. My sister got the family silver, and my parent bought our dining room set.

I removed most of my clothes, costume jewelry, and makeup as I did not need those items. There were some books we kept and a few stuffed animals that were cute, and we gave our James Bond DVD collection to my Dad. I felt no attachment to the stuff we bought. And that is what we tell people. Leave your emotions at the door, enter the next room, and price everything. Someone will always need it more than you.

We went into the closing, packed everything, sold our final artwork from the wall, and started our new life on May 5, 2007.

Chapter 29

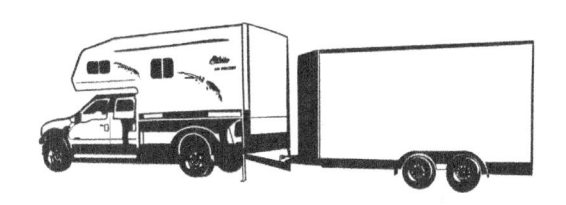

Living in a National Park

Starting in May 2007, even though we were living in our truck camper, we still had not completely separated ourselves from working for dying like YMOYL states. We were still working, me at my small business and Sasha at his industry and company. I also took on another task to create the Laura-n-Sasha dot com website (which is no longer hosted online). I made it in 2006 using a hosting company where I was an affiliate and suggested that hosting company to my clients. I would get a sliver of a commission. The company was relatively new out of Pennsylvania, so I was confident they would be around for the long haul.

One of the web benefits at the time was Google Adsense. Most websites did not have ads or banners or anything else on them. They were there for you to read; you could go to YouTube to watch homemade videos, and when you had Adsense and YouTube, you could make money on your site. In addition, Amazon affiliates paid you when you suggested items on your website. But to do this, we needed a physical address. Why had I not done this when we had a house? Sigh.

We transferred our mailing PO Box from Sterling to Dumfries, Virginia. We had to go to the post office to pick up what little mail we received. I went to the Park Superintendent and requested a letter stating we were living onsite to get Google's Adsense to work. It took time and effort to make this happen, but in the end, Adsense and YouTube paid almost every year the same amount as our hosting and domain name costs. And that worked well for me.

Sasha's commute to work got longer. When we lived in the house, it was 15 minutes. When we moved to the Park, it was 45 minutes to an hour, depending on traffic. He did not drive the truck. Instead, he took my car. My work days were Monday through Thursday, and we hiked in the Park on Saturdays and Sundays. For such a small park, they had massive amounts of hiking trails.

An essential step in YMOYL is to have a wall chart showing your income and expenses. I took this a step further and showed our expenses on the website. Each category, things bought, total amounts, and how my pleasure and life energy we had to use to have each part.

I wanted to show people this lifestyle was possible. By showing how we were not paying for a mortgage or any extraneous stuff, we could enjoy life and that others could too. But, unfortunately, most people thought us nuts! They might have thought us wise when we sold at almost the peak of the housing market, but they could not believe we would stay in such a small space.

However, one of the main points they missed is not something you can show in a picture of how we lived outside of the RV most of the time. We lived outdoors during the spring and summer, hopping onto I-95 to see our friends up north or Karen and James to the south.

We got gym memberships once it got too hot to hike, and we took showers there. We spent time in libraries near the park, using their WiFi and reading books. We did not have a TV in the camper and enjoyed reading. I learned more about bonds, interest rates, CDs, and how to apply for federal government jobs.

I found banks wanted a physical address for you to open an account. It took a concentrated effort to get bank accounts, but I persisted. I opened accounts with Pentagon Federal and the Department of Interior credit unions. Both had high-interest rates for laddering their CDs, from five to eight percent for one- to seven-year CDs. Once I felt comfortable with the 30-year treasury bonds, we bought those for long-term savings.

Our friends, especially Mary Beth, Leo, and Karyn, visited us in the Park. Even Sasha's parents visited to see where we were living. My parents drove down in July to take us out for Sasha's birthday. Most weekends, we visited family or friends, and most evenings were spent next to a fire toasting marshmallows, talking, or reading. Most of the time, we did similar things as before, but with a slight difference, no TV, no house, and the great outdoors as our backyard.

There were three months of expenses, and we happily found them moving down.

The quarter showed five weeks in a house and eight weeks in our RV. The writing was on the wall for the business. I knew that I needed to close the business.

$13,014.84 for the quarter
April expenses: $7,010.63
May expenses: $4,840.07
June expenses: $1,587.88

Chapter 30

Too Hot! Feeling Burned

August was sweltering, and the AC unit turned on when we got into the RV. Even though we plugged into electricity, we were as frugal as possible. I still worked at the visitor center, but this would be my last month working. I was disappointed I could not extend my time there, but the Superintendent had a policy about no volunteer overstaying their visit. This rule would be a hard lesson for me to learn.

The month was also quite buggy, and the National Park Service does not spray for insects. When you live mainly outside the rig, it can be hard to deal with bugs. However, our routines were to work Monday through Thursday at our respective jobs, go to the gym to work out, take showers, and get home around 8:30 or 9 pm to have dinner, read, and get to bed.

I knew August was tough for me, not because of the heat but because I argued with a co-worker. While I was right about whatever it was, he felt he needed to be in the right. He was also a paid park ranger while I was a volunteer. It did not matter that I had been there longer.

The other disappointment ran to a failed presentation on a rainy night. I was supposed to present a ranger talk about the Great

Depression. I had PowerPoint slides with a projector ready, but it rained and got the projector a little wet.

I was applying for jobs through the NPS and governmental system called USA dot gov. I applied to any position within the GS4 (high school degree needed) to GS7 (master's degree or employment history) for a park ranger, visitor use assistant, geologist, hydrologist, or any other position I could find. In addition, I became certified in online classes through the Department of Interior Learn program. And Sasha and I took the First Aid and CPR class together for another reason for hiring under our belts.

What probably depressed me the most was shutting down my business. I knew it was necessary to move forward with this new lifestyle. I was sick and tired of constantly having to hound Realtors for my money. I still paid money to run the business, and little cash flowed.

I sent termination letters to my clients in July, and most everyone FAXED the signed letters back. The business had a good run for almost four years, and I achieved an increase in profits every year.

You know when something ends, and you are unsure what will happen next? That was me.

The last bit of uncertainty happened in August. I went in for a biopsy of the lump they had found. Mom came down for that and was there when I woke up from the operation. They had taken it out, tested and ultimately, I got the news that everything was fine—no cancer. Mom explained that maybe the family history was that we had cysts, but not the malicious kind. So at least, I got relief there.

We checked out our families' homes before moving to the woods. Then, we went to Richmond to visit Brenden and Lindsay while their parents were gone. My parents also came over, and we became Aunt and Uncle.

I loved how organized Karen was, with a little book of places to go, coupons, cards, and directions. Impressive, to say the least, as they only moved down to the area in late 2006. Karen seemed to know everything about the place already.

My Cingular phone was a high-end smartphone, and I wanted to return to a regular one. In 2007, the cellphone company charged for email and text messages. It costs money if you take a picture and want to text it to someone. Because I bought the phone with the service attached, they had locked the phone. So we went to the Cingular store and asked the shop guy, "Can you please unlock my phone?"

He looked at us like a deer in headlights, saying, "What do you mean, unlock a phone?!" He proceeded to show us how to turn it on. He was clueless; he was of no help. We decided to wait until my contract was up in September and get it unlocked.

I was so glad August was over. And Sasha got word that the project he was working on could be done remotely. He did not have to go to work except one day a week, on Wednesday. We could go to the library together.

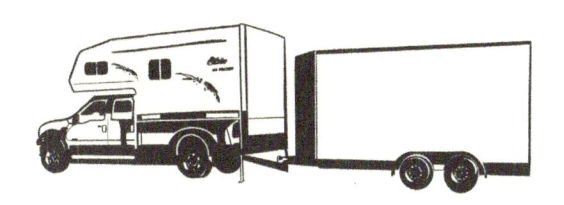

Chapter 31
Into the Woods

The fact that Sasha only needed to go to work one day a week was perfect as we were moving from our spot off the highway into the park "up the mountain." We would get the campground host spot at Prince William Forest Park. This move added 15 minutes on the park roads going 25 to 30 miles per hour.

Living in a Park was a new experience for our family and friends. If they wanted to visit, they had to pay $5 on the weekends. During the week, there was no one at the booth. Or seniors who buy when they turn 62 can get America the Beautiful Senior Pass, and they show the card and get in. When I worked at the visitor center, seniors came in on birthdays to get their passes. I would wish them a happy birthday. It was so much fun.

Once they paid or had their pass, people would either go to the visitor center or take the Scenic Drive loop, which takes them to hiking trails and the campground. There are many ways to camp at this park. An RV campground run by a vendor on one side of the park. A tent or small RV campground that had three loops and 100 sites. A backcountry hike in an area with six rarely used campsites and five historical cabin camps with heated or unheated cabins with separate entrances and fees.

We decided to keep the camper on the truck. We wanted the stability and height to give us access to the slow internet and cell phone coverage. The campground was for boondocking, although there was water at some sites and bathrooms that I did not have to clean.

I was onsite on Fridays, Saturdays, and Sundays. I cleaned the sites on Mondays or Sundays when they left. I received full hookups, a radio with a charger, and the use of a Utility Terrain Vehicle (UTV). It was a Kawasaki Mule. I was there to empty the fire pits at each site. I ensured the fire was out and dumped the coals on the outskirts of the camping site.

Each day, I went around once in the morning and once in the evening. I ensured they paid, put their license plate on a sheet, and marked their campground slips.

My first experience being a campground host was on Labor Day weekend. The campground was full, but not completely. Only seventy sites but many questions and exciting people.

In the third quarter of 2007, we were finally clear of the house. My business completely closed in October.

Quarter expenses: $5,812.65

July expenses: $1,745.95

August expenses: $1,843.89

September expenses: $2,222.81

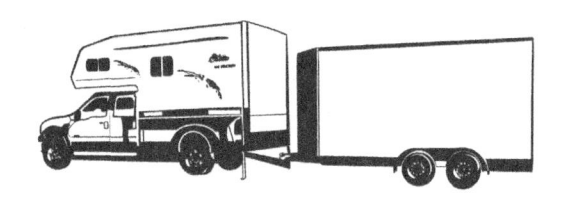

Chapter 32
Old Hand Camping Host

By October, I had become an old hand as a campground host. The Mule was working, and I would zip around doing my host responsibilities. We would go to Stafford County library to read and relax, and Sasha would work. I read so much then and put the list on the website. We would get DVDs to check out on my laptop.

I started a new hobby, growing sprouts in my kitchen window. I started with wheat grass, lentils, and beans, moving to radishes, clover, and alfalfa.

Sasha said, "These are your little children. You put so much care into them."

I said, "No! It was not like that. I certainly don't eat children!"

The sprouts worked for the salads but not for the oatmeal creations I did. I loved creating different types and watering the sprouts. I could not garden in a National Park, so sprouts were my best way.

Many changes occurred in 2007 with my family. In ten days, my parents sold their home in Westfield, New Jersey. I went to New Jersey to help celebrate Brenden's seventh birthday with my family and sort through my childhood stuff. I decided not to keep much, and Karen and I said goodbye to the house. We both had our wedding pictures taken there. It was not our childhood home but our young adult home. My parents outdid themselves to make it look beautiful.

Both of my parents were nervous and excited to sell. Dad had never moved out of the state. He grew up in New Jersey, went to high school and college in New Jersey, and spent most of his adult life there. His ancestors had a long tradition of living in New Jersey.

During the first year of selling, they decided to have fun and got an apartment in Avon—a year-long lease, to enjoy the summer.

The campground would ultimately get fewer people in it, only those that wanted to freeze in a tent. We asked for and moved into a cabin within the only cabin camp of Prince William Forest Park that remained open during the winter. These cabins had heat. They were historical buildings that people could rent during the winter.

Sasha and I moved into the Cabin on November 7, 2007. I checked people into cabins on Fridays and checked them out on Sundays. I was available to them on weekends and made sure they cleaned the area before they left.

We were back in a house, a house without internet. We paid extra to get dial-up; we could not always be on it. It was the only line to the outside world. We had the extras of a house, including a washer and dryer, and very few expenses.

The people who rented the campground were usually fans of Dungeons and Dragons. We would see young men and women drive up and look very goth, with dyed black hair, black clothing, and boots. The first time they came was very nerve-wracking, with screams at night. No one was allowed to bring real weapons, only wooden swords and colorful feathers or ribbons instead of arrows. I would go around after they had left and find colorful ribbons or other things not belonging in a forest.

At the beginning of the week, I would go with Sasha to the library. He worked on his job, and I read and surfed the internet.

However, we ensured we had time to visit with family and friends. November was the last hurrah with the camper before we winterized it. This meant we blew out the water in the pipes and put in antifreeze, resulting in no pipes freezing. We went to North Carolina, where Yvonne and John had a beach house. They had invited us and Mom and Dad J down for Thanksgiving.

Yvonne and John had bought the house next door for a rental and stated we could stay there. The rest of the family would be in the other place. We did not use it for sleeping, instead only to shower there. We slept in our camper instead. That way, we did not have to pay to clean it up later.

We decided to take the week off before Thanksgiving and spend time playing with the ATV and motorbike on the trails of the east. We went to Uwharrie National Forest for the trails. We found rocky trails that took some time to get used to. Several were hard, three black diamond ones and one with a cross. Yes. Someone had died on one of the trails. We looked at it, walked down to where the cross was, and we were amazed that it was considered a trail.

A regular rider told us what happened. A group was in a Jeep. While they were taking their time going down, they overturned, and everyone died. So we decided NOT to try that trail. Instead, we did several others. Sasha was an expert on his motorbike. Me, I was happy with the non-rock situations. However, I seemed to jam my thumb when I went on the bumps.

We stayed there during the week, and no one else stayed over. People were in the forest for day use. Then we went to a winery to pick up local wines for Thanksgiving. I tried them, and Sasha tried the ones I liked the best. We found that both Virginia and North Carolina wineries asked you to pay for the tasting. I am not a fan. I would buy a bottle after tasting several for free.

We had a fabulous Thanksgiving with the family and decided to go north early. So we went to Busco Beach in North Carolina. This is a motocross lover's dream, with different sandy trails.

Excellent trails for beginners and experts, and many families here enjoy the park. There were dunes, lakes, and mud holes galore. We spent Saturday night boondocking and enjoying the trails the next day.

We headed north, got some great BBQ, and pulled pork from a local eatery. North Carolina has some tasty treats and fun trails.

By December 2007, I was an old hat at getting the groups in and out of the cabins. Finally, we figured out our weeks and what we were doing with our plans and ideas for the future.

I started sending resumes for volunteer work in Northern Virginia to campgrounds for the following year's summer season. We discovered another volunteer couple was coming to the spot we had last May.

I got a call from Kings Canyon in California for a full-time temporary position starting in January and going until May. We figured we needed another year. So I had to decline the job.

While groups came in during the weekends in December at the cabin camps, all the holidays were during the week. My parents visited us in December to see where we lived, and they liked the cabin.

We tallied the expenses for three months, a little over $1500 on average. Nevertheless, we felt thrilled about the new year.

Expenses for the quarter: $4,522.09

October expenses: $1,198.31

November expenses: $2,346.09

December expenses: $1,119.12

Chapter 33
The Great Recession

While hindsight is 20/20, we pushed this year to save some money. We were determined to make the dream of changing the money mindset for Sasha. We tried to keep our expenses as low as possible. We preserved 58 percent of our paychecks in 2008. It would be a year of highs and lows, feelings hurt and restored. We bought a motorcycle for Sasha this year and sold my ATV as I did not use it.

In January 2008, I learned the drill by volunteering at Prince William Forest Park. I felt sad that they did not ask me to return to the visitor center as a Visitor Use Assistant volunteer, nor did I see an option to work there as a park ranger.

Like everyone else in the new year, we set health goals. That year we re-upped our Federal savings accounts, which pay extra health insurance benefits for people who can. You put money into a health savings account and may earn interest, but it must be used by the end of the year. Sasha had plenty of sick leave available, and I set up appointments.

January was tough for me for health and also for jobs. I tried hard to find something in Northern Virginia where I could work and live. But there are not too many places. Most state, regional, and county parks only want you to work for a month. Many people wanted to volunteer; we wanted to stay in one place for six months or longer. The indecision and delays from the National Parks hurt me and lowered my self-worth.

During that low point, I bought Workamper News. Workamper is a job site for people with RVs who work for campgrounds, parks, and other vendors for their site and pay. They emailed the newsletter on January 7; I had Sasha download it at work as it was a large file.

I called Candy Hill Campground in Winchester, Virginia, on January 8. They were very interested in talking with me in person. On January 9, I met the owners, who hired me on the spot. Total boosting my morale and self-confidence. I should have researched them first.

That was the trouble with Workamper News. While they had reviews of the campgrounds, no one could post horrible reviews about the campground managers. Hindsight is 20/20; we did not know this back then.

Would it have mattered? I got the experience of being a work camper. We lived in an area of Virginia with lush vegetation, history, and easy-to-grow farms. Unfortunately, we did not understand nor respond well to the hypocrisy or racism of the campground.

I would work as a workamper, someone who works for a campsite. You give the owners your time. Any extra time worked would be paid. I would not clean bathrooms but work in the office, greeting new campers, setting up reservations, and selling items in their camp store. I would learn a new computer system called Campground Manager, similar to Microsoft's database system. I stated I could work for them starting April 20.

Less than a week after I committed to this campground, I got calls from the National Park Service for seasonal park service jobs. After that, I received a call for almost every job I applied for.

We were not ready to leap. As much as I wanted to work for the NPS, I wanted to do it when we were both ready and could enjoy the experience together. So I had to decline them all.

At least I knew that the time frame would be typically in March or April when I would get the calls. So Sasha and I made a plan. One more year, if we could save, we would devise a plan for Sasha.

On our website, I decided to show each month of expenses, to give others ideas on doing this lifestyle too.

January expenses: $1,816.38

Chapter 34

Cabin Living

Why is it that when you are enjoying something, it ends sooner? And when certain events are more challenging, do they take longer?

Such was the case for us during the last parts of winter 2008. We were reading like mad as we hardly watched television. I went through series quickly, usually reading five books a week.

I was learning to make more food with a crockpot. The winter season is the best time for crockpot cooking, with soups and stews galore. In addition, it uses less energy, even though we do not pay for utilities.

In 2006 we went to a truck camper rally. We could not return in 2007 as we were selling the house, but we decided to go in 2008. This time they asked me to do a talk, "The In's and Out's of Full-Timing in a Truck Camper." I was excited to do the seminar. No one else, not a single person we knew in the RVing world, had ever lived in a truck camper. Most could not comprehend what we did. They thought us nuts or that we would immediately be getting a divorce. We wanted to show them that living in a truck camper was possible and stay married.

We were impressed by the number of RV shows during the winter. We went looking at toyhaulers. These are RVs connected to a truck in the middle of the pickup bed. They were fifth wheels because the "fifth wheel" is the arm connecting the bed to the camper. It was a fun, recreational activity that got us out and learning more about the RVing world.

Since I got a job as a workamper in Winchester, Virginia, a fifty-mile one-way commute would be a daily thing for Sasha. We decided he needed a little fun with a motorcycle: a Suzuki VStrom1200. He used that to travel back and forth to work. It would be a big bike with some serious protective gear.

In February, we decided to get the VStrom when we went to Florida at the same time as my family in March. We would go to Disneyland with Lindsay and Brenden, and the trip would be great for everyone. Sasha and I would fly down together, stay with the family for a few days, and then he would ride the motorcycle back up to Virginia. I would fly back alone to Dulles International Airport. Great plan, right?

I bought the three tickets in February. Both sets of parents flipped out. They thought us crazed. The questions had the gauntlet of "What if something happens to Sasha? What will you do?" "What contingencies are in place?" "How would you live?" "How would you SURVIVE?!"

We decided that for the trip to Florida to happen, we would need to finish the packing before we went. We also needed to get the truck camper on the truck because I could not do it alone. I had heard of single people doing it, but I did not have those skills.

We did a bit of shouting when it was time to put the camper back on the truck. There was always shouting as you had to speak over the diesel engine. How it worked was like this:

Sasha would line up the truck as best he could to be straight ahead of the camper. He would get out of the truck and use the Happy Jacks (a remote connection to a motor to lift the rig). I would go to one of the legs. This entire process was not something you do during windy days. Imagine your house going up on these spindly legs, maybe an inch thick. Up and up they go until you get to the worn-out line in black that states, "DO NOT GO FURTHER or the house will collapse," or something like that. At that point, you scream, "STOP!!"

You do these jacks on four legs, hoping they are roughly the same height. And high enough that the truck can slide under without hitting one of the legs and toppling the camper to its side.

Then Sasha gets back into the truck. I direct him with my hands to move either left or right, slow or stop. It is impossible to hear over the diesel engine with the window down. At this point, all wildlife has left the area.

Even though I know he cannot hear me, I wave my arms and shout to go left or right, STOP, let me check, turn the wheel, move an inch, or yell an obscenity. Usually, we lose our voices by the end.

The camper would be back on the truck. Occasionally, we had to do something strange to make it work. There were very few dents in the inside wheel wells or camper. More often, it was my dented feelings more than anything else.

These actions are why we did not take the camper off the truck. But, when we had to, we did. And we knew we had arguments getting it back on.

Once we decided on something like getting a motorcycle or putting the camper on the truck, other things fell into place. Good too, because March 2008 was hectic. Every day and weekend, there would be people in the cabins. While I thought the fall was busy, March was even more so with Spring Breaks, early risers, and late-night revelry.

When I was not volunteering, I was working on my Laura-n-Sasha website. In 2008, I put ads on the sides of the website. At the time, Yahoo had ad placements, and their payout was $50 each time. Google's Adsense was $100, and they did not allow other ads to be placed on the same page. So I had to develop a system to have even months with Google and odd months with Yahoo.

I made sure we were not charged for another month at the gym. They tried everything they could to make us stay and pay them, but we told them we were moving out of the country, and they stopped bothering us. Yes, out of the county, but they did not know that.

I was searching for higher interest rates. The Federal Reserve started decreasing interest rates to deal with the Great Recession, and my IRA money had to be put somewhere to make more. So I opened an IRA CD with the Department of Interior Federal Credit Union because of the great rates. And put the money into five-year CDs as they were the longest available.

An organization whose business model preys on the new camper and RV people managed to scam us. Camping World, the company that sold us an AC/heating unit, could not fix the heating element part. They would also still charge us for trying to fix it. No, this was not happening. It took a while, but I was not charged.

Sasha was looking forward to the trip to Florida. He would ride his Fabulous Accessorics, Really Kool, Likely Expensive (FARKLE) Suzuki Vstrom 1200 back from Florida, driving through Blue Ridge Parkway. It would not be a fast drive. But, it would be an enjoyable and beautiful scenic drive through the countryside. We would not be together, but I would be with my family, which would be fun. Seeing Disney through children's eyes meant memorable experiences later.

February expenses: $2,473.01

March expenses: $7,172.13

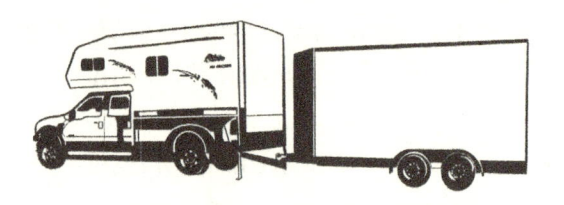

Chapter 35
Truck Camper Rally

With too many vehicles on our site, we ultimately moved the truck across the small street. The trailer moved next to the camper, and our car and motorcycle were under the camper's nose. We would open our door to see cows over the fence. We were in the country now!

I found the job at the campground easy to do. The computers used Microsoft products, and I felt confident I could learn the Campground Manager system. So easy by the second or third day of working, they decided I could close the store and office by myself.

However, it did take me a while to notice some strangeness within the campground. After two weeks of working, one worker quit, and another was fired. I worked double shifts to get in the hours before the Truck Camper Rally. I worked at the campground until we were ready to leave. Then, my fussy computer started acting up while creating the seminar.

We got to the Tall Pines Campground that held the truck camper rally in North Carolina. We had four days off and made the most of those days at the rally. We came with a freshly cleaned rig and saw quite a few friends from two years ago.

My computer started acting up when we got into the campground. I worried it was going to crash. It was freaking me out, as I had not done backups, and we planned to wipe the computer clean and restart it later. But I could not do so if I could not turn the computer on.

There were over a hundred people at the rally, the biggest one yet! We got name tags, and Sasha was meeting people he only knew from the online forums. While the computer was getting glitchy, putting me into a tizzy, I powered through and continued to enjoy the weekend. We went to a Friday night crab fest, with Karaoke and dancing.

My morning seminar filled me with dread. The computer was going in and out, working and not working. There was no screen to project the PowerPoint. So they brought in an inflatable one. Then my computer goes DEAD. I had the files on a USB drive but no laptop! Finally, someone allowed me to use their computer, but they did not have PowerPoint, only OpenOffice. While OpenOffice can see and use PowerPoint files, I had to learn to use the software in 15 minutes.

While this was happening, the tent was filling up. My seminar became the best attended and most packed class. My heart was in my throat. I was sweating bullets and had not drunk water in a while. My voice came out as a squeak. Thankfully, my brave and hardworking AV and IT crews got me ready to go at 10:30 am for the seminar.

Everyone sat in rapt attention. I gave the seminar, had a Question and Answer session, and had hearty congratulations and applause soon after.

The rest of the rally went well, and we were home, ready to step into spring with the new knowledge and friendships of the truck camper community. I got a new battery for my laptop and backed up my computer.

After such a whirlwind and getting used to campground living, we were ready for the tourist season.

April expenses: $2,595.70

Chapter 36

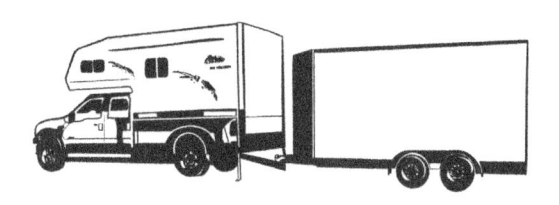

Festivals and Full Timing

The biggest festival in the area is the Apple Blossom. It is a spring festival celebrating the apple orchards surrounding Winchester, Virginia. Apples are a big deal here; some vendors and visitors visit Candy Hill Campground yearly. They have a trolley to get you to the event. What did I like best about the festival? They wore pink and green. My favorite color is pink, and I like apples.

We were getting used to living in a campground. It was different from living in a National Park.

May was the month for some deep thinking. Sasha would take motorcycle rides on his day off. He investigated areas where we could go riding. And he was not having much success. So we sold my ATV. I also played computer games. Sometimes I got caught up in a contest or book that I would do nothing else.

We had both parents visit for Mother's Day at a French restaurant. We knew Sasha's parents would love a French restaurant, and it was a brunch, which I knew my parents would love. So they returned to check out our campsite, and they could see the cows in the distance.

By mid-May 2008, the Truck Camper Magazine came out with our interview. We were Truck Camper famous for at least a few months after that, and with over 1000 hits on our website in one day, we felt fabulous.

We had an online guestbook, and the questions started piling up. People asked us how we lived small in a truck camper.

A truck camper is not for living inside of it. A truck camper is living an adventure. It helps you get to where you want to go, lets you sleep in comfort, has the necessary toilet and shower to stay clean, and has a kitchen inside so you do not feel like a cave person to cook. If it rains, you are fine, not soaked in a tent, lying on the muddy ground. No hotels nearby? No problem, bring your truck camper to the beach. Are you tired of hiking all day? No need to drive home exhausted and sticky. You have the truck camper to the rescue. You still spend more time outside than inside. If you had to spend time inside, it is time for a larger rig.

A question often asked is, "What is the deal with following the sun?"

What we wanted to do, once Sasha finished working, was for me to get an NPS job for the spring, summer, and fall to work in a northern state. Sasha would work as a workamper close to one of the parks. We would live where he works to get the site for free. Because we would be in lower temperature areas, no AC was needed and therefore no high energy costs.

Work hard and save money. "Make hay while the sun shines" idea. Then, as winter starts, we would head south and not use as much propane heat. You stay for a while and use less gas or diesel to explore. Work in the summer and enjoy the winter. That was the plan.

Someone asked about insurance: health, vehicle, and homeowners. While we no longer had homeowners insurance, we had vehicle insurance. The camper was uninsured. Sasha got health insurance through work, and I paid $134 as I was not yet 40 years old.

We loved going to the library in Winchester. They had many beautiful books to read. Expenses went down with less exploring.

May expenses: $1,294.48

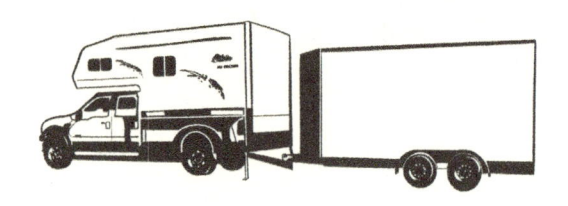

Chapter 37
A Summer of Weird Weather

Have you ever heard of the two-hundred-and-fifty-dollar tomato? It goes like this. A newish gardener goes to the library to find ways to garden. She finds a book called Square Foot Gardening and reads it from cover to cover.

She says, "Grocery prices are so high. Let's grow our own!"

He skeptically replies, "How much work do I have to do?"

She gushes, "Hardly anything! I need your strength and carpentry skills," while batting her eyes and looking doe-like.

"OK," he sighs, "I'll help."

They head to the gardening and lumber stores to pick up wood for boxes, three parts to make the soil in large quantities, metal for the covering, thin wood to mark the squares, trellis, plants, and seeds. The total comes to $229.24 plus two books on Square Foot Gardening by Mel Bartholomew because she did not want to get the library books dirty—$ 22.76 from the used bookstore. Total of $250.00, and the tomato tasted pretty good.

While I grew more than tomatoes, the Winchester weather we experienced had weird highs and lows. So whenever I could, I went to the campground pool to cool off. Sasha got us pool noodles so we could float in the water.

One of those pool days happened in mid-June. I had gone to work after a relaxing morning at the pool. The temperature outside was 98 degrees Fahrenheit and the day was fine and clear. We had looked at the weather forecast, which mentioned storms, so we brought in our awning and ATV.

Around 3 pm, the temperature dropped from 98 to 70 degrees at work in less than 15 minutes. At the office, we heard thunder, BOOM - CRACK, and felt a vibration, and we ran over to the pool, telling everyone to get out!

"But we don't see lightning, so what's the big deal?" they whined.

I said, "If there is thunder, there is lightning somewhere! So GET OUT!"

The wind started picking up, and we returned to the store to bring everything inside. Then came the rain, so much that you could not see the outside driveway. Finally, I heard Jeremy say he saw a tree go down. Then the lights flickered, and Sasha called from work.

I picked up the phone and said, "Hi Honey, I think we are dealing with a tornado...." The line went dead.

Sasha was frantic, trying to call back on the office landline. That line was dead. We believe lightning hit the transformer, which crashed down. Finally, he was able to call on my cell phone. I told him that Jeremy and I were fine, the storm was still going, and we would assess the damages once it was over.

By the end of the storm, the phone calls started. Some people called for reservations; people said they had no power, and others called to say they were fine.

The storm finished in thirty minutes from when it began. Back to a sunny day, Jeremy went out to assess the damage. There were several trees down in empty spots. But no one or rigs were hurt, and we felt lucky.

The garden was thriving with hardly any work. It was so humid it seemed to water itself.

The insects we saw near the camper were interested in my dehydrator and its heavenly smells. July was fruit picking month of blackberries, blueberries, and peaches, and I made sure to dry at least half of everything we picked. We ate dried fruit in our oatmeal and hoped picking and drying would cut down on the grocery prices.

The month of July was filled with family. A weekend with Yvonne and the kids, and the pool was filled with fun, laughter, and great food. We watched Ally and Kristina lip-syncing, and their swim meets. They were taking after me to swim in races during the summer, something Karen, Denise, and I did during the summer growing up.

The best weekend was celebrating Sasha's birthday on July 22. Instead of gifts, he wanted to go to Luray Caverns. It was relatively close, and my parents stayed at a Courtyard by Marriott with Karen, Brenden, and Lindsay. The day was hot, muggy, and rainy.

Since Luray Caverns is not a national park, they can charge whatever they want. We did go on a tour, but the woman who gave it did not speak well. So we did not pay much attention to her. Instead, we took pictures, some of which looked good in the dark light. I felt like a real geologist with the stalagmites, stalactites, and lakes that went for acres underground.

We went to lunch with everyone discussing the caverns and enjoyed the company. My parents, Sasha, and I had so much fun together that we did not want the day to end. We went on a ride on Skyline Drive in Shenandoah National Park. They had a convertible, and we had 360-degree views. We touched the clouds multiple times that day. The conversation flowed, and we had a fun-packed day and evening. We went into August looking forward to the cooling weather.

Parts of my garden were doing great, with the rain we received. Looking back, it seemed to rain every day, which cooled the temperatures. But unfortunately, the tomatoes and peppers did not ripen, and the squash flowers rotted. Instead, the cucumbers and herbs were growing like weeds.

Hiking during this weather can be challenging, as we sweat massive amounts and drink Gatorade and water while driving home in the air-conditioned car. Then finally, we change out of hot and sticky clothing to jump into the cool and refreshing camp pool. We could only imagine doing this every day.

August was filled with car trips to New Jersey and seeing friends and family. It had been a while since I saw my girlfriends, who lived in New Jersey and New York and had weird times of work or play. As my time was more flexible, I would go up to see them. We did realize, though, we are not morning people. Getting up early to get on the Pennsylvania Turnpike and tough it out with traffic is not a fun day.

Around the middle of the month, the temperatures were no longer in the nineties. We still had the AC on to take the moisture out. We also had an oscillating fan on the counter to keep the cool air moving in a small space. There were several places where I put Sasha's birthday cards on the wall. Sasha had a card that played music when the card opened up.

While I was at work one morning, Sasha got up and started surfing the web. Suddenly he hears, "I'm Sorry, So Sorry," in a soft, whispery voice.

He looks around, thinking, "What in the world is that?!?"

He turns off the iPod and radio and completely unplugs it, yet he still hears it. He reboots the computer, thinking there is a virus, and then thinking he fixed it, he hears, "I'm Sorry, So Sorry" again while the laptop is off! He thinks, "What evil is this?" that a computer virus could work while the computer was off. Once the computer comes back on, he runs a complete virus scan. Finally, he comes up to the office with his bad news.

I tell him the "So Sorry" music comes from his birthday card! He was sitting next to it and did not realize that when the fan turned toward the card, it opened and closed, so he only heard a few words and not the entire message!

A good laugh for the day.

June expenses: $2,002.11

July expenses: $981.88

August expenses: $1,297.94

Chapter 38

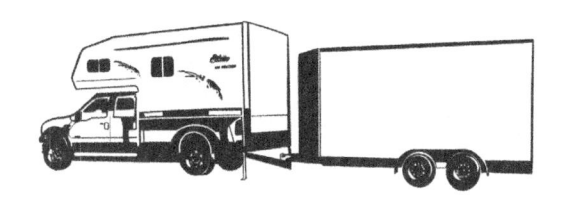

Weddings and Birthdays

My friend Mary Beth married on the shore of New York at Breezy Point in Queens. She got married before a tropical storm. This is life on the east coast. You plan for adventure, and nature makes its voice heard.

Mary Beth had our old gang of high school friends come to her wedding, and we got to see everyone, including some people I had not seen for several years. While we wanted to stay longer, we were worried about flooding and headed back to New Jersey, where my parents had rented an apartment. Returning to New Jersey took twice as long because there were multiple accidents from impatient drivers swamped by flooded engines. We were thankful that we brought the truck.

We took off the week, from the Friday before Mary Beth's wedding to the Thursday after, to spend time with friends. Then we went to an RV show in Hersey, Pennsylvania. This RV show is second to the Florida show in size. All the other shows pale in comparison. This Pennsylvania show had seminars and acres of RVs to check out. We spent two days and a night at an expensive Day's Inn. We decided to drive back early rather than stay another night.

When we returned, my garden was messy, and I spent the day pulling out what did not grow. However, considering this was my first time gardening, the season turned out reasonably well.

We never got many red tomatoes, but we had cucumbers, jalapeños peppers, chives, nasturtiums, marigolds, arugula, carrots, radishes, and lettuces. They grew within four months, and some were still growing strong.

Since the campground pool closed on Labor Day weekend, we searched for ways to exercise. We went with Valley Fitness Club, called "The Club," as it had country club amenities at gym prices. However, they had a pool and classes, which made it more expensive.

In October, it hit home that Virginia might be for lovers but not for RVers. Or at least not for people with more than one car.

When I tell people I changed my money mindset when I was 38, I wasn't lying. I was adamant about a simpler lifestyle, one not filled with things but with experiences, family, and friends. I wanted to spend time with my family for my 40th birthday.

I am sure people re-access their life when reaching a milestone. My life was good. We were saving a bunch of money. I was in charge of the finances and investments, and taking care of a home that was only 24 square feet was easy. But I was not fulfilled working at the campground.

As a workamper, I had to work 12 hours a week to pay for the site. But I was asked to work another 12 to 18 hours each week as they kept losing workampers or people from the town. I was paid minimum wage for hours worked.

While I realize they were trying to make money, they employed some people who needed background checks. We found out after the firing one man was a sex offender. He did not live onsite.

I received my volunteer pass to the National Parks in October 2008. When you gave them 500 hours a year, they gave you a volunteer pass. The work was rewarding, and the benefit moved me towards getting a job with the NPS, my ultimate dream. Yet here we were, at a campground where the owner charged you a quarter for a book of matches when you got firewood.

And the owners were young, younger than me, yet had weird friends that were older. Maybe they thought that Bud, who spent money and time at the campground, was a good person, but he was a racist.

Bud was talking to another worker in the campground office and telling a story. No, I cannot tell the story as I was shocked by the word he used to describe a Black man. Without thinking, I said, "Please do not use that word around me. I will not stand for it."

They looked at me like I had grown horns. I just looked at them. Then I turned away and went back to work.

When I told Sasha about that experience, he said he was proud of me but also scared. He pointed out that Bud open-carried a handgun around the campground. The fact that I talked down to him and possibly hurt our stay at the campground made for a couple of tense days.

The owner was there as well and saw the interaction. His wife talked to me afterward and suggested I not speak to Bud anymore. I told her he could not use the foul word.

My hours were cut while he was in town. That gave me an excuse to find another place to volunteer during the fall. I started volunteering at the Museum of Shenandoah Valley (MSV) at their historical house and vegetable gardens. I would give house tours in the afternoons and help pick vegetables in the park on Friday mornings.

My birthday celebration was at Shenandoah National Park, and Mom got rooms in the Lodge. We started the vacation with a picnic lunch and a hike. I was impressed with little Lindsay, only four years old, who almost hiked to the top. Brenden was great, hiking to the top of the trail and climbing on rocks. He had never done this type of hiking before, and we were proud of his ability.

We had a celebratory dinner that evening. The following day we had a buffet breakfast. Then my sister and her family had to go. So we said our goodbyes and went for another hike with my parents. We walked and hiked with them to the waterfalls. The weather was perfect, the streams were running, the waterfalls were cascading, and I could not have asked for a better birthday present. This is simple living: being out in nature, enjoying the day, and being with loved ones.

Winter came early to Winchester, much quicker than we thought. With punishing rains and freezing temperatures, can we survive the winter with Sasha driving 100 miles round trip on the motorcycle?

September expenses: $3,385.26

October expenses: $1,535.05

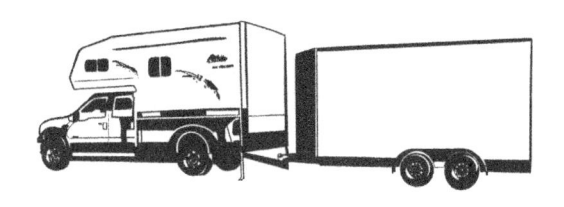

Chapter 39
Gods Conspiring Against Us

A workamping couple came into the campground at the beginning of October 2008 with a massive rig. This 40-foot fifth-wheel with a mid-sized truck is similar to an 18-wheeler truck, only with a smaller cabin. They moved into one of the largest back-in sites. They had one vehicle, and you could hear them each time they went anywhere, as the engine was loud.

They had managed to stay ten days before they quit, deciding they did not like workamping. I don't know if it was that or other reasons, but they left a gap for the rest of us to fill.

By mid-October, my garden finished for the season, and by early to mid-November, there were no more apples to pick. So I went into hyperdrive, drying the fruit every day. We smelled like apples for the first two weeks of November.

Midway through November, Sasha got a flat on the motorcycle. It was raining, and he had to get it towed to work. I called the tow company for a flatbed tow truck. Sasha arrived at work hours late and dripping wet.

The next day my computer died. I went to work with Sasha in our Saturn, and while I loved the idea of a MacBook Pro, I did not get one. I was tied to Frontpage, a Microsoft program for designing websites. So instead, I picked up a Dell for $399. It did what I needed, and backing up consistently allowed me to save my work.

Two days later, I went inside the camper after work to a wet floor. This incident was the last straw, having come home twice to a damp floor. But this time was worse, as there were two inches of water. So while I went to dry the carpet out and put down bleach to kill whatever grows in the wet, I called Sasha.

We had to figure out what to do—this month had been tough. We kept turning off the water each evening to avoid frozen pipes. We had winterized the outdoor hoses, putting heating tape around them and a light near the pump to keep it from freezing. Putting on layers to walk over to the office and always having a raincoat was getting more challenging, too.

I worked to figure out where we would live. If we could find one, the prices for furnished apartments were high. Sasha asked around at work, and a co-worker suggested we sublease with him and his wife. They are moving into a new rental in Lansdowne near Sasha's work. With three months upfront, the rent of $500 worked for us. It is a basement room with a bath, unfurnished.

I gave Candy Hill Campground our 14-day notice that we would leave after Thanksgiving weekend. We stayed with my parents in Williamsburg for Thanksgiving and enjoyed being with them again.

My website in December 2008 did not have dates as we were busy figuring out what to do. First, we brought the camper to the house to get everything we needed. Then it went to a dealer called Outdoor Express RV to fix the slide-out leak. We told them we were not in a rush to fix it sometime this winter.

There was no furniture in our basement room, which I did not call a bedroom as there were no closets nor a walkout. We pulled the bed from the camper, used laundry baskets and thrift store drawers for our clothes, two camp chairs, and a table for a desk.

We feel like we are back in college. At least we had an entire refrigerator to ourselves. We used the kitchen and the laundry.

Even though we were living in the basement, the smoke permeated every inch of the home. The wife smoked in the house and put her ashes in dishes in the kitchen. Yuck! I closed my mouth and escaped to Panera Bread down the street to apply for NPS jobs.

We spent more time together at Sasha's work in December. We decided I would get a volunteer gig in January to get me out of the smoky house and keep applying for NPS jobs. We figured if I could get a park ranger job, we could have Sasha retire from his career. We felt we had saved all we could in this area, and it was time to live the dream. We knew that would happen and a job would come soon. We had to be patient.

December expenses: $1,537.55.

We spent $29,997 for the year and saved over 60% of our income and investments. Sasha was happy we figured out an end date for his working career, and I found a volunteer job that would allow me to work with children at a children's museum close to where Sasha worked.

2009 was going to be a great year; we were sure of it.

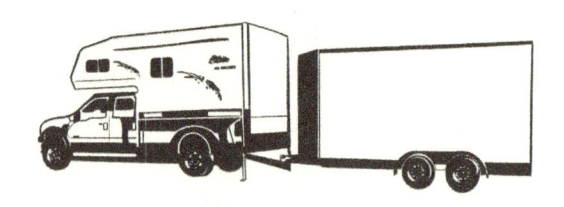

Chapter 40
New Start in Frugal Creativity

January 2009 was the start of the NEW Everything. Even though we lived in a house, we had lived in group homes; this experience was different. We did not like the experience or respected the people we lived under. They were slobs. I am not a neat person, but when you live small and have less stuff, everything has a place, and you put everything back in the SAME PLACE.

Yet that was not happening. Everyone worked at jobs; instead, I looked for a National Park Service job.

I also worked on our website and created a "Frugal Grocery Shopping List" that I gave to family and friends for their email addresses. I updated the regular prices every quarter, letting people know which store had the best prices. No processed foods, as we did not eat them. On one side were the foods, and on the other were household items. I created the Shopping List in Excel; the foods were by type and were color-coded: dried, canned, refrigerated, and frozen.

Within the sheet, I had the price, the unit bought, the price per ounce, and the price per pound or gallon. That way, if the store has a 6-ounce can of tuna (yeah, right!) with a four-pack of three-ounce cans, you could figure out which one was the better deal.

In January, I started to notice size differences. While the can of tuna was the same, the amount within it changed to five ounces instead of six.

We were eating out more because of the uncomfortable living conditions in the house. We did not have a place to cook or eat meals. The kitchen table always had stuff on it, and the smell of smoke made us gag. So instead, we bought food for Sasha to have at work.

Once the camper was fixed, we stored the trailer and camper on a farmer's property. We joined this new social media site called Facebook in December because Bo had suggested it. It was fun to catch up with people there. We knew this was the wave of the future.

It can be hard to get out when you are stuck in a spot. Such was the case with the suburbia house. Our fixed camper was stored onsite for free for the past three months. But now they wanted us to pay for the repairs and to get it off the site. So we had to find a new campground where they charged $900 a month plus utilities or have our rent in suburbia go up another $50 to $550 a month. We decided on the latter.

We became a one-car family, putting the camper on the truck and having the trailer on the farm. I would drive Sasha to work, then head to Panera Bread or Corner Bakery for lunch before heading to the library or my volunteer position at Heritage Farm, a children's museum. It was a fun workplace, and I helped them with their email database. I also got to show people around.

The National Park Service has over 10,000 seasonal positions each year nationwide. Unfortunately, not every one of them is available. Writing hundreds of applications was not uncommon, especially when you do not know precisely how they want you to apply. Those hundreds of applications might only net you a few jobs offers for a seasonal job.

I got my first job offer as a Park Guide (GS-04 or Governmental level 4) with Alibates Flint Quarry National Monument and Lake Meredith National Recreation Area (two parks in one). They stated they would complete the paperwork in two months, putting us there around the end of April if everything goes through. We were getting excited about this new chapter.

My second job offer came in March for a Park Ranger Interpretation GS-05 from Cape Hatteras National Seashore in North Carolina. This was a higher level than the one in Texas, with better living conditions. For example, the Texas one did not have hookups, while the North Carolina one had an RV village for employees and volunteers. The cost for the spot onsite was $160, amazingly cheap, and if Sasha decided to volunteer, it would be free.

I told them they needed to get me the paperwork before the Texas job. I had accepted the Texas offer but was waiting on the paperwork. While a background check was necessary, the Chief of Interpretation rushed the paperwork. I got it a week later via FedEx and sent the forms back the same way.

They offered me the job. She asked if I could come on March 30th, a Monday, but I said, "No, I could not do it that fast."

Instead, I could go the first week in April. Then, I would hop right into training for two weeks, learning about the history of the area, the geology, and interpretation.

We also told the folks at our rental that March would be the last month staying with them. We would stealth boondock rather than pay for a couple of extra nights. So I got the camper ready, putting almost everything back in their places while Sasha was at work. The only thing left to do was the bed. So we put the bed into the camper on March 31, 2009.

Sasha sold the car in April and rode his motorcycle down when he retired. So we will be off on our grand adventure, me as a Park Ranger Interpretation and Sasha as a retired man of 52! We looked forward to April.

January expenses: $1,240.64
February expenses: $4,412.51
March expenses: $3,376.19

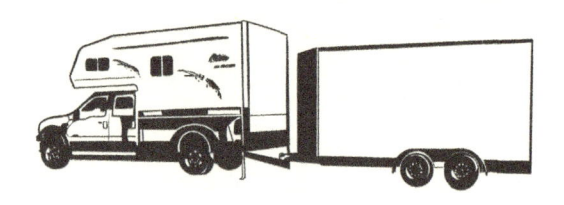

Chapter 41
Sasha's Retirement

This was the month of separation, April 2009, when we came together for our goal of full-time living in an RV. Sasha considers this month and year that we became full-timers, but I think of May 2007, almost two years before. Then, we found we could save money so much easier when I volunteered or workamped for living space while he worked.

The month of living alone while he finished his work and retirement from his industry was hard for us. We moved out of the wretched basement room and smoky house and back into our beloved truck camper on April 1, 2009. It was clean and fresh as we headed to an undisclosed spot a street from Sasha's work. We managed to be in that spot for a few days before heading down to Cape Hatteras for the weekend.

Stealth camping, RVing, or anything to do with living in a vehicle can create problems in suburbia. As soon as there is even a hint of someone living in a car, the police get summoned. Thankfully, that did not happen to us, but we did get a knock on the door asking us to leave.

We moved to the Sterling Walmart. We headed out the next day after saying goodbye to Sasha's parents. At Walmart, no one bothered us, and we felt safe. We did not unhitch. That particular Walmart was a 24-hour store.

We headed to a Flying J truck stop that evening and stayed there as it was an easy on, easy off spot. The next day we drove until we could go no further. We stopped at an abandoned gas station with a vast side lot. Just behind the fence was a trailer (not an RV) park. We woke to the birds chirping.

As we went further into North Carolina, the internet started acting up. I hoped to have WiFi at the office. We arrived at the park on Saturday and got the camper and trailer set up. We also got the hookups done. As we set up, we met the people parked next to us, Pam and George, volunteers who worked at the lighthouse.

On Sunday, we got the covered gazebo set up. It has four sides of gauze; we have more shade and eat outside without the bugs coming in. Sasha also showed me how to empty the black and gray tanks, as I had never done that before. After that, he decided to stay until Tuesday morning to hear about my job.

We walked over to the lighthouse and down the beach and thought we had found paradise. The water was perfect, so clear and blue.

I went to work that Monday, and Sasha was the perfect home husband. I made breakfast, and he cleaned up, made the bed, did the laundry, and folded and put away the laundry. He worked on his motorcycle to get it in tip-top shape for the ride back.

I had training in Manteo, North Carolina, for the paperwork, which took three hours. After that, I went in with two other returning seasonal park rangers. After the paperwork, we had safety training and then headed back south. On the way, we checked out the Bodie Lighthouse and checked in with the Chief of Interpretation, Laura S.

After training, I walked to the camper and told Sasha about my day. We had a nice dinner and enjoyed being together. I awoke the next day, probably anxious to start training and say goodbye. I got breakfast ready, we ate together, and I headed out for my training. Sasha cleaned up and left. He would go as far as my parents and stay over that first day.

I loved the training. We had two weeks of intense interpretation training with several other seasonal rangers. There would be twelve seasonals at Cape Hatteras, although we never got to that number except for about a week as rangers quit or moved to higher positions elsewhere.

This separation meant two households. Sasha stayed with his parents for the duration. As a retirement gift, he also got himself a MacBook Pro and gardening supplies for me. I gardened with potted plants. We looked forward to Sasha's retirement and return to me.

Once Sasha left, we called each other every day. We also talked to family and friends so much that we upped the number of minutes used for our cell phones. And once he returned for good, we got a WiFi router with a card to get a 5-gigabyte Verizon system.

When you think of retirement from a company, the people are old and gray, but Sasha was neither. He would turn 52 that summer, and his hair, while cut short, was not gray. He was the reason we could take awesome adventures and leave work behind. His working at a six-figure job allowed us to quit jobs we no longer enjoyed. We could choose to work in lower-paying jobs that we would WANT to work rather than HAVING to work.

As long as we made fifteen thousand dollars a year, our investments would earn us enough to pay for our expenses for the rest of the year. We tended to make more than $15,000 a year combined, which allowed the interest income to be less.

Sasha's retirement party was at a local restaurant, with speeches and well-wishes from everyone. They knew of his love of music and gave him a special iPod engraved with his name on the back. He managed to sell our Saturn for $3000. And for retirement, he could decide to volunteer or not this year. He walked the beach during the day while I was at work.

We decided that come May; we would learn as much as possible about the area on my days off. So on weekends, I was not thinking about programs. The programs are talks, and park rangers give them to the public to help them feel something about the park. So I created eight programs: History of the Lighthouse, Geology of the Barrier Island, a kid's program about a drop of water, The Graveyard of the Atlantic, Pirates!, Snorkeling, Cast Net Fishing, and a night walk.

New park rangers got an allowance of $400 for the uniforms. The uniform includes socks and boots, and I had several uniform changes. I wore a bathing suit under my NPS tee shirt and swimming trunks for the fishing and snorkeling, a short-sleeved NPS shirt and shorts for lighthouse duty, and a Class A summer uniform for the museum and shop duties.

On my days off, we went to festivals and shopping on the mainland and got a weed whacker to cut the high grasses around our spot. Sasha was getting bit by something, and cutting the grass around us made sense. We also got a bug zapper because, well, there were bugs. We lived in a maritime pine forest.

When not going to festivals or shopping, we went to the beach. We got a little cart to put our stuff into and walked to the beach. We checked out Ocracoke one weekend, and the beach was beautiful, with shells as far as you can see. You had to take a ferry to get there, which was serene.

May was a glorious month, yet overwhelming with the programs I designed and learned to do in front of people without notes! Summer started on May 22, 2009, with programs in full swing. I did not do my programs every single day but within two weeks. I completed them at least once or twice a month. There was one program I was most worried about, the Night Sky program. I had no clue about the stars; I knew the stories.

We kept our expenses low the first month together, even with eating out and attending festivals. We looked forward to when Sasha would come out of retirement and volunteer in June.

April expenses: $3,491.82

May expenses: $2,743.65

Chapter 42

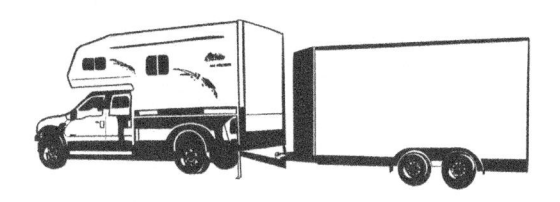

Sasha Volunteers

I am amazed at how people walk around in flip-flops as though they are authentic shoes. Flip-flops do you no good on hard steps as you climb a very tall lighthouse. Nor are they great even on hot sand, as sand can still burn your feet. However, they are one step away from bare feet, prohibited in the lighthouse or museum, nor at any program. You have to wear something.

You can get away with no shoes, only in the water. There you can go barefoot or wear water shoes. I wore water shoes, especially during snorkeling, to show people sea life under the waves.

Sasha would walk with sneakers every day on the beach. And people would ask him why? He found that question unusual, as he saw the same people daily fishing from their trucks. Some would put chairs and coolers, and others put their trucks close to the water and put their lines out.

Towards the end of June, Sasha figured he had enough of "retirement" and decided to volunteer at the maintenance department. He would mow the massive grasses along the roads within the park, paint curbs and parking lots, and weed-whack the edges.

In a sense, we had a role reversal. I had volunteered to save on rent; he would do the same.

Our bills might have been lower if we had just eaten blueberries, peaches, and prawns that month. We did not eat out as much, yet the prices were still crazy high. This would be the first month we would pay extra for Sasha's health care through COBRA. Having a seasonal job with the federal government does not mean the federal government pays for health insurance. I still had to pay, and insurance was going up again. We always hoped the next month would be cheaper, but it never was.

We had a beautiful ocean up to and during July 4, 2009. The coolest of aqua blue colors and see-through waters. We went with several other park rangers to the beach and swam. We saw dolphins surfing the waves. We had a grand time outside with everyone on the beach. Someone had brought a corn hole game, and a frisbee was flying about. We were able to enjoy the beach with the other rangers.

Of course, not every ranger was at the beach. The returning seasonals and others who wanted to get paid double time, a thing I did not know we could do until much later. Instead, it was a beautiful day off, and the joy of companionship was among us.

On July 5, the ocean changed. Sasha had gotten an inflatable ocean kayak and used it on July 4. When he tried to use it later that week, he noticed the ocean was not crystal blue. Instead, there seemed to be more churning on the ocean floor, and the water looked murky and dark. I can't entirely agree with this assessment, but it could have also been our mood.

You see, July was hot with tons of rain. It always seemed to rain on the weekends, our days off. Sasha had started volunteering 32 hours a week, four days, and had Friday through Sunday off. You begin to get cranky when there is no place to go but the camper.

Thankfully, we had some breaks. One of Sasha's great friends, Todd, and his wife, Kimmy, came down to see where we lived and to go to the beach. We went to The Sandbar restaurant, with great seafood and views.

Then my parents and Karen, Brenden, and Lindsay came down. My parents rented a two-bedroom villa, and they stayed there. It was nice and close to the beach. Dinners were perfect, with sunset views and glorious colors.

We ate at the villa each night. I ensured that my family checked out the lighthouse and went snorkeling. They enjoyed it. We went from activity to activity, and they went to bed tired and happy for the next day's events.

The last night they were there, Sasha brought over our portable grill, and we toasted marshmallows and told ghost stories. I do not know which was best, the stories or the chocolate and marshmallow stickiness on the kid's faces.

We were fans of the Calvin and Hobbes comic strip, and there was a point during the strip that talked about rushing to have fun. Calvin had to do it fast and get it all in before school started again. We felt like that, unsure when we would see the family again.

Remember the flip-flop rant? Well, even with flip-flops, Tevas, or sneakers, sometimes you take them off to walk around the beach. Sasha did that and got a shell stuck in his foot. Because we are in a resort area, the doctors did not take our health insurance, and we had to pay cash: $110 for a visit, $10 for the medication, and $50 for a tetanus shot (WHY?).

June expenses: $1,682.43

July expenses: $2,138.99

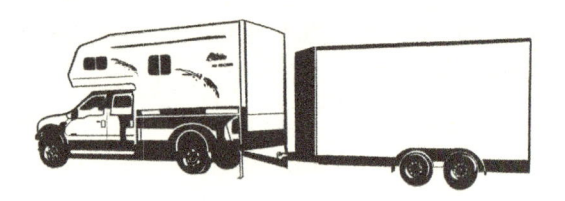

Chapter 43
Hot Happenings

Yes, we did do it this month. We went below $1,000 spent. We barely went out to eat. We did not need to as we saw friends and family, a BBQ with Bo at his party house, and a gourmet lunch with Todd and Kimmy. Their home was a dream, and his garden, oh my, was huge. He said that the pines surrounding us did not help my garden. The pine needles give off a scent that does not encourage other plants to thrive.

When not socializing, we worked hard and fell into bed, tired. I was able to ride a bicycle to work instead of walking. And that was good as could be with a slight breeze. There were gusts of wind when Hurricane Bill came through, just off the coast with rip tides and large waves.

One of the rangers was on the beach, walking her dog along the crashing waves; she got pulled into the water because her dog went after something. She ended up twisting her ankle. She managed to get back on shore, barely breathing, and it took her a while to get back to the house. And that was during her first week on the job!

She was lucky, though. As a Term Park Ranger, she had insurance. The rest of the seasonals did not have it through the federal government. That is why we signed contracts of 1039 hours, one hour less than full-time work. Sure, we worked 40 or 80 hours each pay period. But we did not work enough in a year at the same place to get health insurance. You had to have a permanent or temporary permanent position working eight or nine months with an absence of three to four months to get health insurance and other benefits.

When I asked the other park rangers about health insurance, most said they did not. However, the volunteers, seniors with Medicare, had health insurance. In comparison, we were covered during work times through worker's compensation but not during non-work hours.

We had problems with people staying the entire season. You would think everyone would want to work for the whole 1039 hours, which is approximately six months, but no. So every month, there was at least one or two rangers gone from the total of 14 Park Rangers: twelve were seasonal GS05, one was a term GS07, and the Chief of Interpretation was a GS11. Plus volunteers, at least two sets every three months.

There was a period of calm for a few weeks in August. We had 12 seasonal rangers in place and two upper-level rangers. So our reviews of the programs could commence with extra help on interpretation and teaching to a general audience.

The extra help for interpretation and support on the resumes was significant, especially this month. It was the start of applying for next year's jobs. We also checked around for winter jobs, but they were few and far between. Imagine 10,000 seasonals during the summer looking for winter park ranger jobs of about 500 or fewer. Many of the seasonals went back to their winter positions. So instead, I bought a subscription to Workamper News. We would find something out west; we had to play it by ear.

We would find that while living in a resort area was expensive, we could have had it worse. On the other hand, we could be living off-site, where the rents were higher, but the bugs were lower.

Not sure which way was best, as September saw chiggers, spiders, mosquitoes, ticks, and other bugs.

By the end of August, I realized we had managed to have the lowest expense month of the year. We clocked in at $924.84 for the month.

Chapter 44

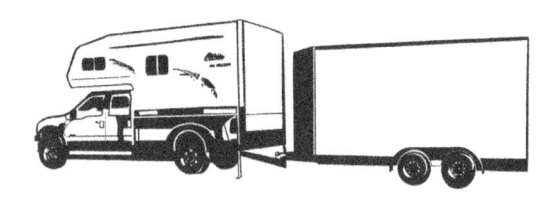

Season of the Bugs

September does us wrong. Sasha had had enough. He volunteered for the NPS, doing great work, painting lines in parking lots and on park curbs. A person drove up and started talking to him. Being the friendly man, Sasha gave directions for something, and the guy gave him a lemonade. When he told his maintenance crew boss about the gift, they said, "And you took it? You drank it?"

"Yes," said Sasha, "Why, was there a problem with that?"

The maintenance people said, "No, but you might want to be careful, as you might get poisoned."

"WHAT?" Sasha exclaimed. And so did I when he told his story.

While not getting poisoned, several NPS people received threats from the locals. A bathroom in the campground had blown up. Several endangered turtles were run over, with tire marks visible on the shells. It seemed the locals were unhappy the NPS was there, closing off certain parts of the beach to endangered species of turtles and birds. They sold bumper stickers of "Plover tastes like chicken" and regularly complained about the NPS in the newspapers. At least one clothing store catering to tourists had a sign stating, "No NPS Served Here."

We became more aware of these feelings once we opened our eyes. Living in a park, you do not see these viewpoints until you start interacting with the local public. Sasha was doing so each time he went out to mow or paint a curb.

Our volunteers also saw these viewpoints. It seemed like we were saying goodbye to another set of volunteers every month. They did their six weeks and then went on to something else. I cannot blame them. Each person worked 32 hours to get a full-hookup site in a bug-infested maritime forest. Most volunteers were seniors who were on their feet eight hours a day. They took their lunch break at 2 pm, after the park rangers. They did the grunt work with none of the fun program perks. They worked four days and had three days off, like Sasha.

And every time we seemed to get a full slate of park rangers, one of them would leave to get a better job. So of the original twelve, more than half would find themselves no longer working for the NPS in three years, and by the time I got out of the park service, only two were still within the National Park Service system.

At one point or another, we had found the place's heat, bugs, and general climate oppressive. We were going online more, and it wracked up our internet usage. But we went online to find a new to us rig, a toyhauler fifth wheel Sandpiper made by Forest River. It had the layout we wanted, a bed in the front, with a slide-out in the bedroom. There was a separate sink from the bathroom, with a shower skylight for tall people. The living room and kitchen had one long slide and a door to the "toy garage" part. Space for storage, a gasoline tank for the toys, and many plugs for being online wherever we sat down.

We bought a fancy hitch in September that would work well with our truck. We would see my family again in September, but it would be a while until we would see them again.

September expenses: $3,976.81

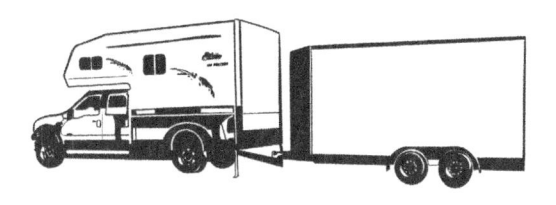

Chapter 45
We Move to New Adventures

The last couple of weeks in Cape Hatteras were long. It seemed to rain all the time, which made cleaning up and storing things hard. We started the road trip on October 14, a day after my Park Ranger status ended, and I was unemployed. This unemployment was considered a layoff, which meant you could get unemployment checks from the state you worked. You had to apply.

It is the dirty little secret that park rangers know but never tell new hires. To work a true-to-life living wage, many park rangers apply for unemployment as soon as they know their end date, as it takes a while for the paperwork to come through. Most states ask for proof of job hunting. Even with experience, you must send hundreds of applications to the National Parks, hoping to get one or two seasonal job offers. Getting those unemployment checks took weeks while you waited to hear back. Seasonals who know they will return to the same park next season can also apply for unemployment. It is the only way to supplement their income while waiting to be rehired.

I learned about the unemployment status and actions I needed to take in those last two weeks. There were no summer programs; we worked in the lighthouse and museum and conducted full-moon lighthouse tours. They taught us how to apply for NPS jobs.

Sasha and I were doing well. While we knew I wouldn't get a winter job, we felt confident we could get a volunteer gig after the road trip west. So we were going to have another grand adventure.

We headed to Post Falls, Idaho, from Buxton, North Carolina, an almost diagonal route across the US. After Idaho, we would go to Washington, Oregon, California, and possibly Nevada. Then finally, we would do the dream, going out west to experience life on the road in a new way, with a toyhauler rather than a truck camper and trailer.

Having the truck camper and trailer was fun, but it became a hassle when living in it. It was too small if we had to stay in one place for an extended time. And let's face it; we bought our truck camper as a vacation home.

But when we went on this journey, living frugally, voluntary simplicity, and working half the year on one person's salary while the other would volunteer was good. What was not was that the truck camper was confining when bad weather struck.

The past couple of months showed us that while we love each other very much, too much togetherness in such a small space is not good. When the bugs are nasty, the rain is hard, or the humidity and heat could make you scream, it is not good to be close to your partner, or you would yell in his ear. I knew he would not like that.

As we readied for the trip, we realized next month would be high on expenses. We were happy that we could keep most of the costs down. We were excited about a grand adventure headed west.

October expenses: $3,094.81

Chapter 46

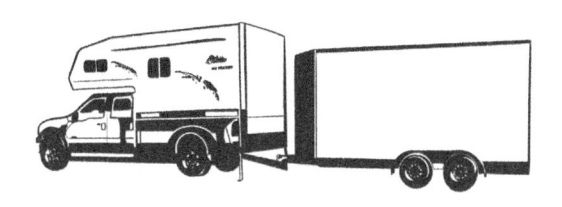

The Grand Adventure Towards Norm

Norm was the person we bought our new-to-us rig, and he would take our truck camper and trailer in exchange. We would give him money as his RV cost more than our setup. But first, we had to get to him. We averaged about three hundred to five hundred miles, depending on the road conditions and weather. The first long day after leaving Cape Hatteras was 439 miles into Tennessee.

Why did I rely on a software program that acts up while driving? I knew how to use the Delorme Street Atlas. So why was it that I kept banging my head on this program? In the end, I had Sasha set it up while I drove.

And just like that, it worked. No matter what I do with software or the internet, a force of nature holds me back. First, I get frustrated to the point of anger and get hyper. Then I cannot focus, and whatever I do, does not work. At that point, stepping away is the only option.

While driving through the Smoky Mountains National Park, the road was uneven, with the road higher than the shoulder. It was drizzling rain, there were a bunch of trucks, and they used this road as a throughway. We went over the white line briefly. It was as though we had gone off a cliff!

Sasha handled it well. We noticed the ABS light came on, and I started to worry. But the truck seemed fine, and we kept going until we came to a truck stop. We took a break, and when Sasha turned the truck back on, there was no ABS light. So I worried for nothing.

We stopped on the second night in Tennessee at a Walmart. Even though there was a sign stating no overnight parking, there were at least six other rigs.

On the first day of being hyper, I had insomnia and a massive headache. I rarely get headaches, but they happen when I am under stress. This road trip was supposed to be fun, goddammit. But not when you think the gods are conspiring against you.

The third day was long, 542 miles from Knoxville, Tennessee, to Saint George, Missouri. We have started to call ourselves the founders of the "Crack Of Noon Club." We did not get up early or start traveling until noon. You would think this would make for long days, but we do not travel in the morning traffic, and we managed to time eating a meal during the evening traffic. I drove 150 miles on straight roads with a bit of rain.

On the fourth day, we went 457 miles from Saint George, Missouri, to Seward, Nebraska. I found an Aldi store where I could stock up on dried milk, hot cocoa, and more. As we go from state to state, they place a sales tax on food. The first time I saw it, I asked the cashier, "What was the deal with the tax?"

She said, "There was a tax on food, as well as on toiletries. It is three percent."

WOW. I can understand putting a tax on alcohol, beer, and cigarettes, even on prepared foods, but these apples? The roll of toilet paper? Why?

I saw between two to five percent sales tax on food. While in resort areas, I understood they want to get as much money from tourists as possible. But in regular places, it seemed unfair.

On the fifth day to Norm from Seward, Nebraska to Cheyenne, Wyoming, we walked out of the camper to winds going around 25 miles per hour. While we went only 423 miles, the winds were more substantial in the morning than later. I drove along relatively smooth roads with little traffic.

On the sixth day, we went from Cheyenne, Wyoming, to Evanston, Wyoming. Another Walmart had signs saying no overnight parking, yet RVs were parked when we woke up. There was also a converted van. It looked like he painted the van with black matte paint and commando-type gear. If he thought he was discreet, he was sorely mistaken.

This part of Wyoming was beautiful but windy. And when the wind was not blowing, the roads were bumpy. Everyone was passing us, including a train in the distance. When you go 55 mph, the faster vehicles make you feel standing still.

Harnessing the power of those winds, Wyoming was full of wind turbines. They were so cool to look at, and under the turbines were oil drilling rigs. Using both technologies, why not?

We traveled to see Bo from Evanston, Wyoming, to Liberty, Utah. We stayed there a while to go hiking. We also replaced a jack on the camper, under warranty, so that Norm will have four Happy Jacks.

We went to Craters of the Moon National Park; it seemed we had the park to ourselves. Unfortunately, there was not a single park ranger around. The lone person at the front desk was a cooperative association salesperson. The campground was small, and I doubted our new rig would fit into those spots.

I had been to this park before when I studied geology. Our field camp had gone here to learn about the park, but it was Sasha's first time. For such a small park, the roads were perfectly smooth. I think they had recently paved them. We hiked a few trails and took some pictures.

We also stopped and got apples and cider at Williamson Orchards. The apples and cider were as fresh as possible and so tasty. I loved looking at the Idaho sky. The clouds looked different, and the sky was so blue. I know many love the ocean and the expanse of the horizon at the beach, but I love the endless road and the sky. I cannot explain it more. It just is.

On October 31, 2009, we would meet Norm and our New Rig.

Chapter 47

Start of New Adventures

November 1, 2009, was when we bought our rig from Norm. He had a scary experience on his first trip in the toyhauler with his short bed 2500. Norm and his girlfriend Lou went someplace high in the mountains. While they drove up without incident, going down, the trailer pushed them to go faster.

The trailer pushed them that way because they did not have a powerful enough truck with brakes for the way down. A short bed 2500 is a three-quarter-ton truck that does not have the stopping capacity of a one-ton truck. To be pushed down a mountain by an RV can make for a "gripping the steering wheel like your life depended on it" moment. His girlfriend told him in no uncertain terms that she would never do that again. As he liked his truck, he decided the RV was too big and put it up for sale.

Their scary experience led to our gain.

We planned to have the rails (the metal connections) installed the day after we bought the toyhauler. Unfortunately, the installation company ordered the wrong ones, which meant another week to get the order. While we waited, before I placed anything in the toyhauler, I started measuring the cabinets and spaces. While the closet was huge, other places seemed smaller than the truck camper and trailer. I had a green logbook show where the food, provisions, toiletries, first aid, kitchen, office, and other supplies. Most everything would be easily accessible and centrally located.

Two large areas near the bathroom held toiletries and paper products. Our books took the place of the TV area in the bedroom. We each had a drawer for socks. I had the large cabinet in the bedroom for my tee shirts and sweaters, while Sasha had more of the closet for his clothing.

We found on our first night that there was a whistling noise. The winds were blowing outside, and we never heard the wind blow in the truck camper, a four-season rig. But the toyhauler was a three-season rig built in California for weekenders.

No matter how much you plan, getting a new-to-you rig means buying some stuff. Sasha bought spray foam to plug between the bed platform and the wall. I went looking for a flannel sheet set and body pillow.

We use a duvet system. A duvet system is a European bed covering method with a sheet covering a quilt or a down comforter. There is no other sheet between us and the comforter. We used the duvet system because it was easier to make the bed. RVs barely have room to walk around. Plus, I gave the duvet a good whack, whack, whack, and the bed is made.

However, my best shopping experience was looking for a light bulb. The light above the dinette had gone out. So I went to the NAPA store. This had to be one of the biggest stores, yet most shelves seemed empty. I knew it would take me forever to find what I needed, so I asked the nearest employee, "Do you have RV bulb 1056?"

He puts it into the computer and says, "Yes, we have five of them."

"I'll take all five, thank you."

He rings up the purchase, another employee gets them for me, and In, Out, Done! Quickest transaction ever.

Not only were we buying things, but we were selling things we no longer needed. For example, those diesel cans were sold when we went to an Old Country Buffet in less than a day.

Our time with Norm and Lou was quite impressive. We spent over ten days getting to know them, their little slice of Idaho, and our rig. We showed them how to use our truck camper, empty the tanks, and put the trailer on and off their truck. We felt great about our purchases and found lifelong friends. Norm continued to follow us throughout our adventures, and we were sorry to hear of his passing about 12 years after our purchase. He was one of the good ones.

Chapter 48

Upgrading the Toyhauler

Once we left Norm's place, we hightailed to get new tires on the fifth wheel. We wanted the best safety, and the tires were old. Once a tire is about seven years old, it must be replaced no matter how often it is used.

We carefully drove down five-percent graded hills of Washington, and Sasha decided we needed an exhaust brake. An exhaust brake is used when going down big hills and mountains, not riding the brakes. It slows down the truck naturally.

We got into Oregon during Portland's rush hour. Beautiful views greeted us as we went to Springfield and Eugene to AM Solar. It took two days to put the solar panels and system in our rig, and we stayed in a motel close to the shop.

We went with six panels, four batteries, and an inverter at AM Solar. We wanted the space to walk on the roof if necessary. From there, we went to Henderson's to get a brake system.

We got a more robust brake system and an exhaust brake put in. They started but did not finish on Friday, allowing us to stay there over the weekend. Not only that, they let us borrow a car for the weekend.

I interviewed with Lake Mead National Recreation Area for a volunteer position that weekend. Little did I know this park would become my longest volunteer stint. But I knew I had inspired them.

Once Monday came around, we got everything done with the truck, including getting a Safety Rig Inspection and Road Performance Assessment. We were good. It was time to go into California, where we would get an external fuel tank put on the truck. This would be in Chico, California, on a Wednesday before Thanksgiving. We got there Tuesday night.

And they allowed us to park just outside the shop. Wednesday, we unhitched the rig to install the external fuel tank. They worked quickly and got the tank done by 2 pm. They allowed us to stay the night, so we would not be in the Thanksgiving traffic.

Since the solar panels were in place and working great, we no longer needed the generator. It was too loud for me. So instead, we found quiet, pleasant evenings in California. We planned to go to Joshua Tree National Park in December.

Every evening, we found a casino parking lot. Different ones allow overnight parking. Some were better than others. So we boondocked and enjoyed our November.

What we had in the toyhauler:

- 104-gallon fresh water tank plus four five-gallon containers

- 32.5-gallon black tank

- 72.5-gallon gray tank; the shower and bath sink in one tank, kitchen sink in another.

- 30-gallon gasoline tank for the generator and toys

- 112 gallon diesel tanks; 38 original and 74 external

- Six solar panels with four AGM batteries gave us 600 amp hours. So the maximum is 50 percent of our batteries.

- 4000-watt generator that can have as many amp hours as there is gasoline and as much as I can stand the noise.

- 240 square feet of living space, and

- 80-square feet of garage space.

November would be our most expensive month since writing down our expenses. We spent a total of $35,655.03. Finally, we were ready to take on the best adventures.

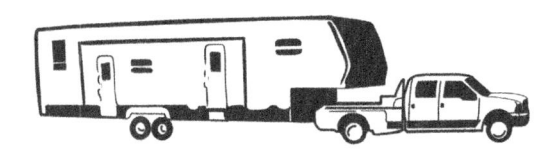

Chapter 49
Whirlwind with National Parks

December turned into a whirlwind for visiting and volunteering in National Parks. We arrived on the southern side of Joshua Tree National Park in November. We set up solar panels to get maximum usage. It took some time doing it, with a bit of yelling, so in the end, I got the rig into place.

While everyone else headed to work the Monday after Thanksgiving, we drove to the Salton Sea to check out Slab City, get diesel, and do laundry without the rig. The Sea was unbelievable, so large and shimmering in the sun. The road was undulating, the air dry and 80 degrees. We were 280 feet below sea level, the real reason for the warmth.

The Salton Sea and The Slabs were different. There is no other way to put it. We never did stay there as we did not think it was a place for us. While it is warm, there are no facilities of any kind. This will be the place if you want to go off-grid and not own land. It is colorful, with Salvation Mountain and RVs painted every rainbow color. Just not our kind of place.

We also checked out the campground at Joshua Tree and the employee housing. There was no way a rig more extensive than 25 feet would fit at the campground. Also, the host site was small.

However, they had a free dump and fresh water stations before you got to the campground. Therefore, you only paid for an overnight within the campground.

We took great hikes in the park. The first was Lost Palms. We brought enough water, and the temperature to do it was perfect. We did not get all the way there and back because we got a late start, but we had gorgeous views: another hike, this time to Cholla Garden. The plants look like light-colored teddy bears you DO NOT want to hug. We did a short walk through the garden.

We were outside of the park for a week and enjoyed every minute. Then, we headed into Arizona and New Mexico on the way to Texas to become Texas domicile residents.

When we headed out of Joshua Tree National Park to go to Buckeye, Arizona, we got on the internet to discover that 13 of the 18 rest stops were closed. They had budget cuts. They decided to make travelers pay to travel through their state. When we finally found a rest stop, the bathrooms had no toilet paper or soap. Instead, we stayed at a truck stop.

We listened to podcasts while driving, including a couple doing technology and one called the RV Navigators. We thought them funny, with four TVs in their RV, four different computers, and four ways of getting onto the internet. It seemed overboard to us.

We found New Mexico had severe winds for December and stayed a day in Lordsburg, New Mexico. There was no point in wasting diesel fighting against 30 to 40-mph winds with 60-mph gusts. We nestled between two large 18-wheelers with our heads into the wind and, therefore, not as cold. We crossed the continental divide in New Mexico, one of the lowest spots in the US.

We made it to Texas on December 9, 2009, where everything seemed big. The welcome center was beautiful, with nice bathrooms, free WiFi, and enormous spaces for RVers. We decided to go slower and come to Livingston, Texas, on a Sunday. We read that any rest stop allows you to stay for 24 hours. Perfect amount of time to refresh and sleep before returning to the road.

By December 14, we had arrived at Livingston to become Texas residents using Escapees RVing Club (Escapees) as our mailing address and domicile. When you do not have a house, you need a place to register your vehicle(s), vote, health, taxes, and insurance. The states at the time we were deciding, with no state income tax, were Texas, Nevada, South Dakota, and Florida, with special conditions.

Since Escapees had been in Texas for so long, they established a "domicile service" that included mail service. We became Texas residents because of this mailing service, cheaper vehicle insurance, and no state income tax.

We did not have to establish a long residency either. I thought a month only needed a week, but we enjoyed being there and stayed two weeks. I took time to apply for jobs, Sasha changed the oil on the truck, and we had a lovely Christmas dinner. We found the health insurance prices went down for both of us, and while 2009 was an expensive year, we did buy a new to us rig.

December expenses: $4,307.40

Totals for the year: $67,302.84, and we went into savings by almost eight thousand. We could only hope that 2010 would be a cheaper year.

Chapter 50

New Decade of RVing

We drove to Lake Mead National Recreation Area (LAKE) in early January. I started volunteering at Alan Bible Visitor Center. Sasha would not be volunteering this time, only me. I rode my bicycle up the nine percent grade hill to get to the visitor center from the volunteer village, around three miles one way. Going up there was hard, but going home was easy; I coasted all the way home.

Thankfully, Lake Mead has walkways and hiking trails. In the winter, some volunteers lead hikes, while in the summer months, all the park rangers are on the lake.

Our friend Richard came out to visit us at Lake Mead. Sasha and Richard went hiking to Liberty Bell Arch but never found the arch. When Sasha and I went with a volunteer to find the trail, we found the Liberty Bell Arch and the river overlook.

The volunteer knew the general way to get there, but part of the trail was not on an actual "path" per se but overland. I wouldn't say I like that type of trail because twisting an ankle on rocks or plants is easy. Also, there were not enough cairns (rocks built up to show where to go along a trail). Western hiking areas do not have trees to blaze the way. Instead, you look down or at eye level to find the path. If flooding knocks them down, it can be hard to find or even know the way to a spectacular site. We would learn this story repeatedly throughout our hiking travels of the west.

This park and year were the first when my parents visited us. Dad had a meeting in Las Vegas. Part of the trip was for business, and part was for leisure. While Dad was at the meeting, we took Mom to check out Fremont Street, free entertainment of glittering lights and neon signs.

From there, we went with them to Sedona, Arizona—a magical place of red rocks and hiking. Two firsts come to mind; I saw my parents on ATVs and using hiking poles. We stayed in Sedona for a couple of days. They went with Sasha to check out the Hoover Dam, as I had to work in the visitor center. We also looked at Calville Bay Marina to see the houseboats, which are no longer available.

On the way out, we stopped by Valley of Fire State Park. It was the perfect time to be there, at 3 pm. The sun was low, red rocks popping in color, and you saw some unique geology and biology. Especially biology. Sasha, Mom, and I searched for bighorn sheep, and there was a small herd maybe 25 yards from Dad. We snapped a few pictures. At least one of the older males was perfect. Most of the photos had their white rumps as they scampered away.

It was a great end to a perfect vacation with my parents.

January 2010 expenses: $1,356.57.

Chapter 51

Future Buying with Boondocking

In February, I found out I got a job at a remote park, really remote. Canyonlands National Park, Needles District (Needles). The Needles was approximately an hour and a half away from shopping and grocery stores. Provisions were a must. I needed to go back and forth two miles with my transportation from the RV to the visitor center. Since I was not living with the rest of the rangers, I had to provide transportation. The rest of the rangers lived in shared housing and carpooled to the visitor center. Not me. I could bicycle, but there were no paths.

Instead, we sold the motorcycle and got Sasha a dual sport, and I bought a Zuma 125cc scooter. I could not use a clutch to save my life. Yet, I wanted a motorcycle experience. I would go ten months of illegally driving and riding a motorcycle-sized bike without a proper license. Do you understand the amount of guilt that caused me?

Here I am, being a Park Ranger, whether as a volunteer or paid and telling people what they can and cannot do in National Parks. I was violating my honor by being on that scooter. The rides were always fun, and I got better at riding in some fantastic places. I always geared up with a helmet, long pants, long sleeves, a jacket, and eyewear. But my driver's license for those ten months did not show an M in the proper place. I always drove below the speed limit because I did not want to get pulled over.

Once we realized where we would go for the summer season, we decided we could spend a little time getting to Canyonlands. We had spent money on provisions in February but started calculating how much we would need for six months of dried goods, and we needed more.

The reason is you cannot eat diesel.

To go from our spot in Canyonlands to Moab, Utah, where they have grocery stores at resort prices, was one and a half hours or 100 miles away. This was not highway driving but curvy, steep, and remote roads. The more we filled our coffers with 69 cents a pound of oatmeal or 89 cents a pound of raisins, the better. By living in a resort area, these items would triple in cost.

Spending now to save later meant less in food tax. Utah charges three percent for any food. They also have a higher "sin tax" on alcohol, whether it is beer, wine, or spirits. When you live in Nevada, you can walk into a gas station and get different alcohol anytime. Utah was not like this, which was a culture shock.

We filled up the different containers for food, diesel, and gasoline, plus filled our fresh water to the brim, along with our extra containers, and started traveling. First, we would go to Searchlight and Lake Mohave. Then, finally, I could ride the scooter under less watchful eyes. I tried to ride it at the volunteer village but got nervous when people watched me.

We went to Lake Mojave and Cottonwood Cove within Lake Mead. There was hardly anyone in the upper campground, and I understood why. There was no way our rig would fit. Instead, we headed to the lower campground. Most of the campsites were sloping downwards. The parking lot was better. There were signs stating parking was allowed but no camping—free parking, good for seven days. Therefore, we parked. We did not have a campfire or anything else to make it seem like we were camping. We had the parking lot to ourselves.

I learned how to do the necessary movements on the motor scooter: figure eights, wavy lines, parking, and getting up to 20 miles per hour in that parking lot. I became familiar with the horn and the turn signals. Finally, I was ready to go up the hill and ride on a more extended trip with Sasha.

We went on the road like we were going to Mojave National Preserve. There was a big hill to get to the main road. I did not dress for a cold ride or have the gear. We turned back around once the shivers and teeth chattering set in.

My celebrated first ride ended with a stop at Cottonwood Cove Cafe. We would be heading out the next day to get to Canyonlands and did not want to rush.

There would be no cell phone communications within the Needles District, so we got Skype. We could only hope for a cheap month.

February expenses: $7,658.62

March expenses: $3,583.29

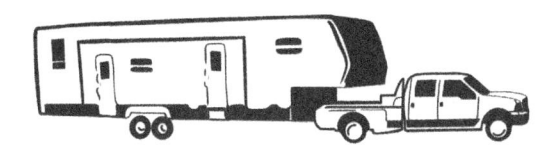

Chapter 52
Cheap Months for Living and Learning

Trying to get onto two concrete strips so the rig would not sink in the sand was scary with maneuvering and shouting. We came to the Needles District within days to spare to set up. It would take half the day to get onto those concrete strips.

We were able to get DSL internet at the site. Honestly, I never understood the concept. The communications came into the park via microwaves. We had radios to talk to each ranger and learned the proper protocols for them, but there were no telephone poles or cell service.

Canyonlands National Park, Needles District, was genuinely remote. We had our waste treatment, water treatment, electrical grid (two large diesel generators), and two large gasoline tanks. We were the only district with water at our campground. Everyone else had to bring their water in via huge trucks like Island in the Sky District. The Maze District uses four-wheeling trucks, and the River District brings the water in on boats.

Surrounding the Needles District was the Bureau of Land Management (BLM) land. Once you get up higher in elevation and into the mountains, you enter the US Forest Service (FS) land. Each one has different resources and regulations.

When you have a National Park designation, the NPS is the most restrictive in the sense that rangers there are to "preserve and protect the natural, historical, and cultural resources." This is their primary duty. We also educate the public. With this new position, I was a protector, a fee collector, and a backcountry permitter. We had four-wheeled "roads" within the park that were rated based on difficulty. Some roads were challenging to drive, and no ATVs were allowed. Horses were fine, but owners had to pack in the food.

We decided for April that we would only go into town once. I wanted to learn as quickly as possible the duties and responsibilities. We took tons of hikes, both on duty and off. Sasha volunteered, but it was not enough to pay for rent. They had never had a ranger live onsite with their spouse in an RV. It was a completely new experience for them. They had no idea what to charge, so they came up with $100 monthly. Instead of taking this out of the paycheck, as they did in Cape Hatteras, we could send a check via bill pay through our bank. Then we did not need to go to the post office and mail the invoice. The bank did it for us.

Our rent was much lower than those that lived in housing. And that is understandable. Beautifully done, almost everyone lives in the housing complex, including maintenance, law enforcement rangers, and student conservation association (SCA) volunteers. The only other people are the hosts at the campground. But the hosts do not stay that long. We could go to an apartment to do our laundry, so it did not cost us anything. Good, as hiking can get dirty.

Because we went into Moab, Utah, only once that month, April 2010 was our lowest month ever, or at least since tracking. Our foresight into buying provisions finally kicked in. We bought new health insurance through the Association of National Park Rangers. It was a pre-paid system for emergency care wherever you need. They charged every six months.

April expenses: $701.99.

Chapter 53

Health Insurance and Dumpster Diving

We decided to go into town only every three weeks, as our fresh food could last that long. Our expenses were high this month because of health insurance. We try to stay as healthy as possible. We drink water and electrolytes because we live in a dry heat area, and you do not know you are thirsty until it is too late.

I had a person come into the visitor center. She looked pale and clammy to the touch. I asked her if she had been hiking, and she said yes. She also told me that she had been drinking gallons of water.

She then slid down to the floor, stating she was dizzy. Less than a moment later, her eyeballs were white, and she fainted. I got everyone out of the backcountry office and went over to her. One of the other rangers working with me called a Law Enforcement Officer (LEO) to come with an IV. I kept talking to her, patting her until she opened her eyes. I asked her if she had eaten anything. She said she had some almonds but did not remember eating anything else.

It was a case of over-drinking water without the salty snacks or electrolytes called Hyponatremia, something I had never seen.

Thankfully, the LEO came, and we brought her to our back office to hook her up to a saline drip.

In this case, she had not eaten breakfast because she wanted to go hiking early with her husband. At some point, she must have told him to turn around and get her to the visitor center. They came in together, and when she fainted, he could not believe it. Most people do not. The usual cases were of dehydration rather than over-hydration.

She was lucky. With NPS, emergency care does not matter whether you have health insurance. You get treated. If she had to go to a hospital, an airlift cost $10,000 or more, usually not covered by insurance.

Over and over, I talk about health insurance because of the cost. We were always lucky, as we have good genes, low stress, and take precautions. We protect our eyes, skin, and heads while having fun. We know our surroundings and carry hiking sticks, first aid kits, and insect sprays. We eat healthy and exercise, with no processed foods. We do not smoke or drink to excess. So why do we need health insurance, and why is it so high?

We did not have preventive care, only catastrophic care. We would be covered if we broke a bone or lost a limb, but not to get an annual check-up. The most important part of this healthcare insurance was that we could use it anywhere in the US. We did not have to reside in just one state. Similar to Medicare for seniors, this was the reason we went with the Association of National Park Rangers health care.

Sasha spent a bunch of time hiking. When he was not hiking, he was motorcycling. The bike allowed him to be on dirt, rock, and pavement. He was losing weight because of the activity. He was working on his motorcycle, and as per his usual practice, he wore latex gloves. This is especially true when working with oils or liquids.

When he was finished using the latex gloves, he turned them inside out to throw them away. He did this at the maintenance yard. His hands were slippery, and when he threw out the gloves, his wedding band went with them.

He did not realize it until after he took a shower. While the ring had been slipping before, it had not come off. When he went to put the ring back on, there was no ring on the counter. He looked everywhere, then retraced his steps.

Typically, a large garbage truck comes into the district to haul away the trash, but for some reason, it was late. So Sasha went Dumpster diving for his ring. Luck be told, he found it nestled inside the latex glove.

Another shower later, Sasha tells me the story. We went to a rock shop the following weekend. I found him a hematite ring that was good for his heart, had great vibes, and could fit while losing weight.

As it got hot in Canyonlands, we headed to Salt Lake City to see Bo and Sasha's parents. They flew into Salt Lake City, and we took our truck to see them. We had a bunch of fun with the parents and Bo. The reason they came to Salt Lake City was for a conference. In Park City, Utah, there were cute shops and beautiful views. It was a great month for fun and doing neat and different things. And fun to see the parents in another place.

June's most expensive cost was converting from a PC to a MacBook Pro, a refurbished laptop with plenty of memory and storage. Nevertheless, UPS managed to find our spot behind the LEO office in the remote Needles District.

May expenses: $1,836.84

June expenses: $3,260.65

Chapter 54

Four-Wheeling in a One-Ton Truck

The first weekend in July was the holiday weekend, and we decided to venture into the mountains. It is Forest Service land filled with tall trees and tent spaces only. We got an air mattress, tent, and sleeping bags at a thrift store in Moab, so we had comfort as we lay on the forest floor.

We hiked in the coolness of the forest and saw some aspen trees. Even though it was summer, we wore long pants for the four-wheeling ride and viewing the shelf roads. Shelf roads are cut into a mountain because there is no other way to get to a mine. When the mine was no longer used, the shelf road remained. They usually led to beautiful scenery.

We noticed something unusual in the sky above Moab when we traveled back. A dust storm, similar to what you see in the Sahara. Above the dust storm were rain clouds. It became a mud storm; the dust on the truck turned into mud and stayed there. There was not enough water to make the dirt come off. So instead, we went to a car wash once the storm passed.

The next trip would be to Torrey, Utah, and Capital Reef National Park. Our truck was 25 feet long. Some switchbacks on those shelf roads are tighter and shorter than 25 feet. We did C turns rather than K turns to not slip off the shelf and go down in flames.

We went to Natural Bridges and Capital Reef National Parks, ate out a bit, and checked out other parks in the area. It was exciting to see Utah's beauty. The geology was terrific, and I got books and maps galore to pore over later. We would find that we could go pretty far when the heat bore down.

August was hot. When red rocks surround you, the stones retain the heat to dispel it later in the day. Typical temperatures were in the 100s. Again, we went east at a high elevation, this time to Telluride and Ouray, Colorado. We ate out more and stayed in a motel called Antlers.

Telluride reminded me of Portland, Oregon, because it is a creative, festival-filled town. Every weekend during the summer, there is some new event or activity. They had different restaurants, outdoor beer gardens, twinkling lights, and shade trees. Of course, we were spending money on diesel, but the little towns and shelf roads were fun and beautiful. The rock and geology, the waterfalls and flowers, made us get out every time to smell, listen and feast our eyes on the riots of color.

We checked out Telluride stores to get gifts for family back home. A geologist living in an RV cannot be a lover of heavy rocks and fragile fossils. But, it meant more pictures to someday share with others.

I created one of my first videos made of still pictures. I used iMovie and enjoyed the process. Unfortunately, Sasha wanted a song by Alan Parsons Project, and while I incorporated it, YouTube stated it could not be a monetized video. While I wrestled with that, back at the rig, raindrops fell north of Moab. The Monsoon season was upon us.

We did not get much rain in the Needles from that storm, but we received water. There was much water rushing through our canyons. Salt Creek, our stream and spring, started flowing significantly more substantially than before. Ultimately, it became a raging, muddy, milk-chocolatey-colored roar of water. Everywhere that dry waterfalls was no longer dry. The water took bits of sandstone and left mud. The storms took the dust and left mosquitos, and high pollen counts. August was a contrast of excitement and disappointment. Of high prices and losses.

But the biggest issue was the truck's transmission. When we parked in March, we felt the transmission got messed up. In addition, the sand we had to push through to get onto concrete strips was disheartening. It seemed to me that the truck "jumped forward" after reaching 25 mph. This was incredibly nerve-wracking during the shelf and four-wheeling driving we had done.

July expenses: $2,565.94

August expenses: $3,388.75

Chapter 55
Sasha and Lockhart Basin, Who Will Win?

Remember the rains of August? As we were learning about desert environments, we forgot about desert flooding. Yet, no matter where I go, as a trained geologist, I see the signs of geology and earth processes at work. Those dry waterfalls of smooth rock? They became chocolatey movements of water when the rains came. That dry creek bed? With just enough water, you have quicksand on the edges and deeper water in the middle.

After the rains fell, Sasha started riding to escape the heat. He was volunteering less and was annoyed that he had to ask for a radio each time he went out. I could always walk over to the LEO office if I needed to contact anyone.

Each time Sasha took a more extended trip, I asked him to tell me where he was going when he was leaving and when he thought he was coming back. I might not know the desert much as others, but I know how to prepare for emergencies.

Sasha was to ride to Moab on a "county" road within Lockhart Basin. The road until Moab is on BLM land. It is considered a county road with county assistance, which is good.

When Sasha failed to call me at 5 pm (I was at work), I talked to an LEO. These women helped me get through my fears and anxiety that evening. They helped me call the San Juan County Search and Rescue Sheriff's department. While I and other rangers within the District were part of the Search and Rescue team, we did not do searches at night. That is why it is good to have a backup.

As Sasha tells it, **The Trip to Moab, or Sleeping on Slip Rock**

"I wanted to ride to Moab from the Needles District. Unfortunately, unbeknownst to me, the road was completely washed out nine miles from Moab, and I had to return the way I had come. This caused many problems, like being unable to contact Laura and sleeping on slip rock under the stars."

I was getting updates from LEOs and San Juan deputies about when they were on the road in their FARKLEd Rubicon Jeep. I was sick with worry and massively painful side aches. **But, again, as Sasha tells it:**

"The two deputies came out. I had a whistle, so when I heard the Jeep, I started blowing that whistle. Their Rubicon was covered with powerful lights, and they could see I had gone down a dry waterfall."

"I remember thinking, Man; I hope I don't have to go up that beast, a gnarly bit of road again. It took the three of us to push my motorcycle back up it."

I got word around 4 am that they had located him. I had not slept. They told us they would help him drive out of Lockhart Basin. I fell into an exhausted, nightmare-filled sleep. **Sasha again:**

"They helped me unstuck my motorcycle on a seriously steep and rutted hill and followed me. I traveled in the early morning darkness, followed by an amazing morning light. When we got to the main road, they returned to civilization, and I headed home to a stressed-out Laura."

"Honey, I'm so sorry; this won't ever happen again!" Sasha cried to me.

I was so mad at him. Happy that he was ok, but angry because this could have been avoided because of a stupid radio. If he had taken the time to sign out a radio, we did not need to call the County. We could have gotten him ourselves.

He only had three liters of water. Typically, you should have four liters or a gallon per person in the desert. He had two granola bars and an apple. He did not have enough electrolytes. He only had lights from the GPS and a cell phone. He had nothing for camping except long pants, a riding jacket, gloves, and a helmet.

He got a word lashing from me. I cannot remember what I said, I was so upset, but it was a low point for us.

He did no more riding in Canyonlands after that incident.

September expenses: $2,667.71.

Chapter 56

Blow Out!

We got into the upper portions of Texas by October 1, 2010, and stayed in a campground to get work done on the RV stairs. Because we have a toyhauler, there are two stairs to go in and out. One is close to the front, and we rarely use that one. The other set was our main stairs, and one of the steps did not work. We stopped in Amarillo, Texas, at a campground with a mobile RV repair man. He stated he could fix the stairs.

While there, we stopped at some delicious restaurants, such as Rudy's BBQ for the beef brisket and The Big Texan for their tasty steaks. The Big Texan restaurant you see on countless YouTube videos. They have great steaks and a food challenge for people crazy enough to eat a 72-ounce steak, baked potato, salad, shrimp cocktail, and the fixings. There was someone up on the stage trying out the challenge.

We headed out of Texas and into Arkansas, where the roads were concrete. Every joint was felt. But those roads were infinitely better than in Tennessee, especially around Memphis, where they have pothole havens. All the billboards in the area say things like, "Buy your new tires here!" or lawyer billboards of, "Had an accident? Get the most from Us!"

We drove on a Sunday, a hot day. We had just stopped at a rest stop, and Sasha checked the tires. He had a temperature gauge checking the tires. All good. We switched sides, and I drove, and he navigated us through Memphis. We cue up the eBook called *Closers* by Michael Connelly. I adjust the seat and mirrors, and we set off.

For a Sunday, there is a bit of traffic, with people driving fast for an interstate of concrete roads with potholes galore. These potholes can have ragged edges. I drove the rig well, going no more than 55 mph. But because the road was so bumpy, I stayed in the middle lane, where there seemed to be fewer potholes, and dropped it down to 50 mph.

It did not matter. There was a high-pitched scream, which I thought was part of the book, two seconds before BAM and POW! BLOW OUT!!!!

Amazingly, I did not freak out. Instead, I pulled over three lanes and stopped on a bridge. I was going slow enough that I found a place to pull over and noticed the mile marker for the tow company.

These were brand-new tires we bought in November 2009.

Because I was going slow, the blowout did not harm our trailer. We called our insurance, and they sent someone out immediately. The guy who came out changed the tire to the spare tire.

We limped to a tire company, not too far from the blowout, and waited until Monday to get four new tires put on. Then finally, we were back on the road, and the spare was back in place that afternoon.

Visiting family, and trying to get home by a specific date, might have been easier if we drove at night rather than during the day. But we did not know nor think about that until later. So instead, we would put our rig in storage once we got back East to stay with family and friends.

October expenses: $3,975.61.

Chapter 57

A Unique Thanksgiving

November was our most fun-filled friends and family month in a while. When you are away, the heart yearns for connection. When you are back together, no time is lost. That was how it felt to me.

This month would be unusual as Mom planned a fabulous Thanksgiving. First, both sides of the family would be there: my parents, Karen and James, Brenden and Lindsay, Sasha, and myself. Then the New Jersey family, Aunt Tina and Uncle Joe, with Stephen and Dany, and Stephanie, Jack, and Daniel. Sasha's side came with his parents, Yvonne, John, and John, Ally, and Kristina. Denise, JoAnn, Bo, and his children were the only people missing.

She would need our room, which was OK with us. Mom and Dad J could stay over at her house. She arranged for the New Jersey family to stay at a friend's house. Yvonne and her family would stay in another place nearby.

We took our rig out of storage and moved back into it. We borrowed my parent's car for the month, so we did not spend too much on diesel or dealing with narrow streets. We would use that car to go up and down the East Coast, meeting with our friends.

We headed up to New Jersey first. Then we would go down to Richmond to see the niece and nephew. After that, up again to Fairfax, Virginia, to be with Sasha's parents and Bo, then back down to Williamsburg. Finally, we visited DC for museums, natural history, and botanical gardens.

Mom cooked, and there were pies and cupcakes from the family. The wine flowed, and the conversations did too. It was a happy, glorious holiday for us. Epic because it was the first time everyone had come together in a long time. It was the last time the children and young adults would see each other. Soon they would be off to college.

We headed back to Lake Mead National Recreation Area (LAKE) in December to volunteer together this time. I got into a specialized class called Astronomy from the Ground Up (AFGU). I was asked back for a second season at Canyonlands, even though I applied to other jobs. I also learned that federal employees (including seasonals) would not get pay raises for the next five years. It would stay at $15 for the entire time I was in the NPS or FS.

While we were headed west, we saw a travel trailer pulled by a truck, maybe an F250. He was driving fast in the left lane. A few minutes after passing us, he had a massive blowout, with a passenger side trailer tire blown. That tire shredded and caused the second tire behind it to shred.

When both tires blew up, their combined force ripped the entire passenger side of the trailer. The truck and the trailer fishtailed before he finally slowed and moved to the side. His rig was totaled, a complete failure. As we drove carefully past, bits and pieces of his trailer were on the roadway, causing other drivers to slow down and move around the debris.

We noticed a part of the bumper on the roadway had half of a NASCAR bumper sticker on it. However, NASC was all we saw.

Once we headed out, we traveled, making only a few stops. We went through the Interstate highways of North Carolina, South

Carolina, Georgia, Florida, Alabama, Mississippi, Louisiana, Texas, New Mexico, Arizona, and Nevada. We filled up the diesel tanks in Virginia, South Carolina, Texas, and Arizona.

Our mileage was less than desired as we kept getting headwinds in Alabama and Texas. We saw our Texas family in Houston, where Kathy and Caitlin lived, and went to a Houston restaurant in Houston, Texas. Then, we decided to travel at night to El Paso, Texas. There were infrequent winds, and we needed to get to El Paso at a specific time.

We pulled into the Motorcycle Training Center in El Paso for the weekend. I would take the classes, written and riding tests, and pass with flying colors. I wore my pink leather jacket with my helmet of pink stickers of glittering butterflies. It was the only place in the country (December 2010) that allowed you to bring your motorscooter to take the riding test. I was finally legal and got my driver's license with the tiny M.

Sasha was nervous as we drove through Arkansas. His being worried about driving was never fun. So while I took the class and the tests, he looked for a new-to-us truck; a Ford F450, a one-and-a-half-ton desert truck. It had never seen rain, and it was a 1999 model.

We went to the dealer in Bullhead City, Arizona, and bought the dually, two wheels on each side in the back, so four tires in the back and two in the front. Six wheels, six tires. The cost of the truck? Nothing, plus they gave us $2,000 more for our old truck! That was the first time we ever made a deal like that.

Of course, our F350 was newer and had upgraded features rather than the 1999 Ford F450. Yet, the older model would be easier to work on. They also gave us money because the external fuel tank was not installed, and we had to install it.

December was an excellent month for us, and we looked forward to 2011. We would work together as roving volunteers and be able to drive a government car. I would take the AFGU courses and be part of a fascinating group of park service rangers learning about the stars with astronomers and NASA scientists. I led Full Moon hikes, and Sasha and I would like more of Lake Mead's trails.

November expenses: $4,815,77.

December expenses $3,453.23

For the year, we spent $39,939.99 and saved only 6 percent. The year 2011 could not get here fast enough.

Chapter 58
Perfect Rig & Truck

The 2011 year was interesting. We felt like we had the perfect rig, with the ideal truck, to have grand adventures. I found a new avenue, not just as a geologist but as an amateur astronomer. My geology background served me well. And it would help to have that degree and the science background when we went from National Park to National Park to Recreational Area. We hiked so much that I wore out my hiking boots and got new ones. I had training on being a better interpretive ranger through the Eppley Institute and only had a few stresses throughout the year.

Even though the new-to-us truck was free, they had stated it came with an external fuel tank. But it did not. There was a fuel tank not installed in the bed of the truck. The $2,000 we got in December went towards installing the fuel tank and a new spare tire.

This year we explored Las Vegas. Sasha found a buffet at Fiesta Station and Casino. They had a Mongolian stir fry, where you could pick the meat and vegetables and sauces, and they would make it in front of you. Entertainment and dinner, for the cost of lunch. We were able to find places like that to go to and spend less.

Alas, the Fiesta is no more.

I took people out on the Tunnels Trail for full moon hikes. We saw stars with my green laser pointer.

I knew that returning to Canyonlands would mean more hiking and responsibilities. So before I left in September, I started helping the higher-graded rangers with money. I enjoyed figuring out the till and where each deposit went in the accounting system.

Lake Mead had a new boss, Michelle, as the head of Interpretation. She was the one who came up with the idea for us to be roving interpretive volunteer docents. We would clock in, borrow a government vehicle, and roam around, looking for people to talk to. I would conduct Full Moon hikes, and Sasha and I would lead hikes on Saturdays or Sundays. Of course, sometimes we would do weekday hiking too.

When we were not hiking or roving, we were in Las Vegas. And when we were not in Vegas, we visited with family and friends. For example, my parents visited us in Sedona, Lake Mead, and Death Valley.

They flew into Las Vegas, and we went to Sedona, Arizona, together. They had gotten a timeshare for a few nights. We decided to go hiking and see Sedona's history, prehistory, and geology. The views and the vibes of Sedona were beautiful. There is no other place like it. Where we went hiking was a perfect loop. There were a few ledges, gorgeous red rocks, blue skies, and green trees. Sasha was braver than my parents and I, going out to the shelves of the slip rock.

I have a reasonable, healthy fear of heights, having fallen from significant heights when I was younger. I never broke a bone but scraped my legs. I have slid down some prominent buttes or cliffs in Montana with only a pick ax to help stop the fall. The ledges in Sedona had no slopes, which meant instant death. Something I had no intention of seeing anytime soon.

One of our most excellent hikes was in Red Rock Canyon with the Forest Service. This was my first time learning that the Forest Service does interpretative talks. We saw plenty of rock art, pueblos (homes) of old, and using the cliff to create a structure. They made bricks with water, clay, and mud. And their rock art showed night sky events. For example, based on European records, a supernova occurred in 1054, and the interpreters believed that rock art depicts the event.

After Sedona, we went back to Lake Mead for a day. We had wanted to show Mom and Dad Liberty Bell Arch. This is one of our more popular hikes, and we thought it would be great to see it together. Also, I wanted to show them the mining equipment left behind after the mining had petered out.

Once a Park becomes part of the NPS system, old junk, if it is 50 years old or older, becomes "artifacts." If it is newer, it is just junk and garbage. Therefore, the mining equipment stayed, but the Styrofoam cup was thrown out.

Mom got reservations for a lodge in Death Valley, so we went into the park via Titus Canyon with an all-wheel drive vehicle. This road goes to Rhyolite, a ghost town. We thought it funny that it was the street name of our old house. The road was one-way after Rhyolite, full of curves, and unbelievable scenery, every color imaginable in the rocks or sky—shelf roads for those that are nervous. Sasha took over the driving, and Dad held on for dear life!

We got into Leadfield and had a picnic lunch. This ghost town had concrete blocks they could not move out, an old mine shaft, and a shack. We got to the end of Titus Canyon and saw more petroglyphs.

The next day we went hiking through Mosaic Canyon, where the colors of the rocks tell stories of long-ago environments. I am a rock whisperer; I talk to the rocks and listen to their stories. I hear raging rivers, quiet bubbling streams, and calming floodplains. As I look and read the rocks' stories, people approach me, asking me to tell the stories. I am a park ranger on vacation.

I loved every minute of this vacation. We had geology and prehistory, the history of Scotty's Castle and its surrounds, followed by more geology of Ubehebe Crater and the shadows of Artist's Palette. An Excellent Vacation where we became Rock Art.

January expenses: $5,562.09

February expenses: $3,362.31

Chapter 59
Drive to Canyonlands and Grand Canyon

Coming into a second year in a remote area, we knew the deal and bought provisions for six months. This time we were PREPARED! We let Michelle know that we would be headed to Canyonlands to be there by March 11, 2011.

I had one more night of sky programs and tried increasing our informal visitor numbers. We did something new for Lake Mead, being on the side of the road near the brand new "Welcome to Lake Mead" sign. We waved to over 100 cars and passengers that day and talked to ten people. But, hey, when you try to get those numbers up, you do what you can.

We entered Canyonlands on March 11, and I got to work soon afterward, remembering what I could and upgrading my evening program. The new truck and hitch did very well in the RV spot and for getting us in place this time. And there was even less cussing and shouting than before.

When I did my evening program, I also gave out sheets to the visitors to count the stars when they got home. Canyonlands, especially Needles District, has some great dark skies, and I hoped it would one day be part of the Dark Skies Parks.

Bo came out to visit us. We had just found out, partly because of the looming government shutdown, that Grand Canyon National Park, Desert View District, was calling for me, well, e-mailing me. They offered me a position as a seasonal Park Ranger.

While Canyonlands was a hiker's dream, it was not a Park Ranger's dream. At Canyonlands, I was a park guide. I still had the same pay grade as Cape Hatteras and the same badge, but a different title and different duties. I worked in fees as much as interpretation. I cleaned up resources when people graffitied as much as giving backcountry permits. It was another job. I did not do as many programs, only a night sky program. At Lake Mead, I created more programs than at Canyonlands.

By the very nick of time, a shutdown was averted, and the next day, the offer came. I could work for them from late April until mid-September. It would be as a seasonal park ranger, with no pay increase but an increase in programs.

Sasha was ambivalent about the move because he loved Canyonlands for the hiking possibilities.

I kept thinking, what if I had not moved to Grand Canyon? Would my life have been vastly different? But unfortunately, there was more at play in Canyonlands with upper management changes. They were trying to push out my boss, Karen, or make her retire, some nonsense, and I did not want to deal with the politics.

What can you do? I realized at the time I felt sorry for Canyonlands that I was leaving. So I stayed through their busiest time of Jeep Week, and then we headed to Grand Canyon.

We left Canyonlands on April 22, 2011, and it would take us a day and a half to get to Grand Canyon, Desert View District. We overnighted and boondocked at Twin Rocks Trading Post and Cafe and got to Desert View at 2 pm on April 23. The original spot was too small for us, and we got a different site. Also, we would not have neighbors on either side.

I had one day before working to figure out where I would work and what the ride would be. So Sasha and I took a ride and checked out some of the viewpoints of the Grand Canyon.

On April 25, I started work, getting to know the people there, and Sasha explored more. And lo and behold, he was able to get a job with the Grand Canyon Association. We were able to figure out our schedules together. We would become a two-income family again, something we had not had for five years.

March expenses: $2,621.43

April expenses: $1,229.87

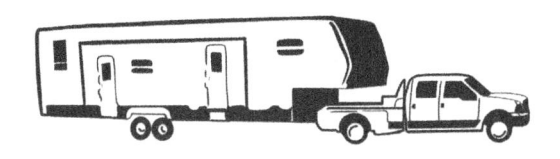

Chapter 60
More Programs, Less Hiking

There was training for new and returning seasonals starting on May 1, and I attended most of the training. But it was nothing like the Cape Hatteras interpretive training in 2009. They were updating the rangers, not giving us training per se. Grand Canyon is one of "The Parks" with 3.5 million visitors annually, so a ranger should know how to do interpretation talks.

They figured you already had your programs completed. I now had four new programs that I needed to create. These were a geology talk, a walking hike and talk, a museum talk, and an archeology walking tour. I would also talk about the Creation of Earth using the myths about the Night Sky during the summer.

Sasha and I spent our weekends exploring the canyon rim. The temperatures were cooler at 7500 feet above sea level, and I felt the elevation change from what we had at 5500 feet at Canyonlands.

We did the touristy stuff, like walking the Trail of Time to see the billions of years of rocks. Then, we checked out the bookstores in The Village, the most visited part of Grand Canyon National Park. Grand Canyon has five districts: the main one is The Village, and Desert View, on the south side of the canyon and to the east. The

North Rim, 8500 feet above sea level, takes a bit of a trek to get there by car, and the River District and Phantom Ranch District work together. The River District is where people travel by boat, and the Phantom Ranch District is where people hike to the river.

The North Rim rangers had a shorter season as they did not plow the roads into the park. However, once the snow came, the season ended.

We only went into Flagstaff once to stock up on fresh foods and milk. And we got to go to a Farmer's Market in Flagstaff, a welcome treat we had not seen since being on the east coast.

We did not realize that Grand Canyon had a mouse problem. While it had a similar environment to Canyonlands, the elevation change allowed small critters to live in their caves more often. So we had to find a solution, and mouse traps were not it.

How busy can a remote park like this get?

May expenses: $2,736.36.

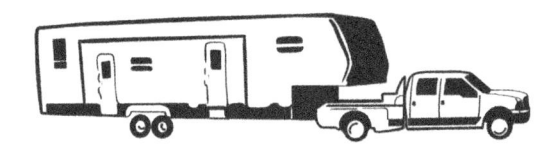

Chapter 61
Mouse Problems and Close Encounters

We lived in areas where we and nature were close. Although we knew bobcats were around, we did not experience them in Canyonlands. But in Grand Canyon, there was a healthy population of mountain lions. Some of their range was very close to where we stayed in Desert View. They are the alpha (top) predators, going after the large elk population. While we had mule deer, elk fed the mountain lions.

The bobcat population seemed to be as healthy as the mountain lions, yet they were fewer in number. This is because bobcats hunt smaller creatures, like ground squirrels, mice, and rabbits.

On June 2, we had a health scare. Sasha went to the Flagstaff Hospital emergency room as I was working. He had a sore throat and had recently cleaned the rig of mouse droppings.

He told this to the emergency care people at the Grand Canyon Village. They urgently said, "Get yourself to the hospital quickly! We suspect hantavirus!"

Hantavirus has similar symptoms to the flu, coughing, sore throat, etc. Sasha did not have hantavirus. Just a cold, not even the flu. It happened at the same incubation time as he cleaned mouse droppings. People that get hantavirus are archaeologists working in caves in the dust and without sunlight. The UV rays destroy the hantavirus.

That was not the case for us. Good sunshine almost all the time. But we still had a mouse problem. Sasha was sick, so I took matters into my own hands. I found the solution, bobcat urine in a can, Critter Repellent: Shake-Away, where you can get predator urine. We did not want mountain lions as they do not go after mice. So instead, we got bobcat urine. Unfortunately, there was a large colony of mice in the next lot from us. So we put out the Shake-Away product around the rig.

The mice were running scared, mainly when a bobcat was investigated. It could smell the new urine and think, "WHO IS THIS Stranger?" And then saw the mouse community. DINNER!

The bobcat left a huge hole where the mice had their colony. It sprayed its urine in a few places and left its scat around too. As if to say, "My Turf!"

July was the month of monsoons, the rainy season, which means no camping to escape the heat. It got hot at 7500 feet. But heat is relative here. Unlike the Canyonlands heat surrounded by red rocks, we saw 80 degrees and touched 90 once during the season. The piñon and juniper forests mean more moisture, but not as much as places like the east coast.

We took trips outside Grand Canyon to see other smaller parks and monuments. We went to Wupatki National Monument to see more extensive ruins and drove through Sunset Crater to Flagstaff.

We stayed at a Best Western in Flagstaff. They had the high-speed internet we craved. But, unfortunately, we got spoiled by the DSL in Canyonlands.

We also did more hiking in The Village area, including Hermit Rest Road. We were fortunate to walk and hike during the full moon; seeing it was a beautiful way.

Sometimes, Sasha hiked alone. I was not a fan of that. We never got the SPOT-like system, a GPS with two-way radio. When he hiked, he did not have a radio. He was checking out Cedar Mountain, thinking he could ride his motorcycle there, but there was no way.

We would go into Flagstaff almost every other week, eating at fun restaurants. Sasha would go grocery shopping while I applied for winter jobs.

While I never got a paying winter job, I did get into the Astronomy From the Ground Up NASA training class in Acadia National Park. It was a four-day program, all expenses paid, except for the flight and last night's stay. It would happen in September. Sasha would not go with me, but he worked instead.

I gave one of my best programs yet, a Tour Through Time, while Sasha and a co-worker of mine, Lauren, watched. The sunset was spectacular, and I finished at the perfect time.

June expenses: $3,973.62

July expenses: $2,206.71

Chapter 62
Another Health Scare

We visited the North Rim of the Grand Canyon (NPS), Glen Canyon National Recreation Area (NPS), Kaibab National Forest (FS), Grand Staircase - Escalante National Monument (BLM), and Bureau of Reclamation in one very long weekend of two nights and three days. It was a mishmash of the different agencies with their different rules.

We drove for most of the trip until we saw a visitor center. Then we would get out, walk around, read the signs, take pictures, ask questions, and fill our water bottles. Then go to the next place. I knew of dinosaur discoveries in southern Utah and wanted to see them.

We camped under the stars in Kaibab National Forest on our first night out. We had a little campfire, saw a coyote, and watched the shooting stars.

We were going to stay another night in Page, Arizona, but the prices were outrageous, from $150 to $250 a night. And if you went out a way, a ranch stay was $95. So I asked about the internet, and they said, "Cowboys don't need it!"

And I said, "Well, this cowgirl needs internet and ought to be blazing fast for $95 a night!" So we cut our trip a little short.

The following week, all of the female coworkers and I went to eat at El Tovar for dinner and drinks. We had a fabulous time with excellent food and great conversations. However, the next day I felt awful, as though my stomach had aliens trying to break free. So I skipped work and stayed by the bathroom for the day with a heating pad on my stomach.

My digestive problems were in disarray for almost a year. Some call it IBS: Irritable Bowel Syndrome, which most doctors say is caused by stress. Hrmph. What kind of stress did I have? Yes, I want my programs to go well. I did not want to look like a fool. I wanted to be healthy and did not want to run to the bathroom every time I ate. I did not stress about money, my relationship with Sasha, or my family. Why was I sick?

When I went to regular doctors, they told me to take antacids like Tums, Imodium, or Pepto-Bismol. I would go through this constant movement of eating crackers to calm my stomach to apples and peppers to things moved along. I was sick and tired of being sick and tired. So I made an appointment with a Naturopathic Doctor instead. They look at your whole body and figure out a solution that way.

I went to Root Natural Health Clinic. I spent an hour and a half with them, explaining my medical history, what I ate, and how I felt. Ultimately, the doctor suggested I go six weeks without eating wheat and see how I do. Of course, my first thought was a relief, a possible solution to my problems.

Of course, the second thought was, all those provisions, what would I eat?

I spent $135 on the doctor for almost two hours. The other part was medicines and an expensive test of $491.96 left us with no more doubts. I had gluten intolerance. I did not have Celiac disease. A prognosis would be the death of this New Jersey Italian woman. Spaghetti is a staple for us. Whatever would I do? A second doctor visit only confirmed what I knew, and another $75.

But at least we knew, and the RV toilet was back to its former pure white self.

September would be the last month working at Grand Canyon as a Park Ranger. I would go to Acadia for a week. Then came back and worked with Sasha as a Grand Canyon Association worker for a month.

Sasha seemed rushed, trying to push as many hiking or motorcycling days in as possible before we left. He came back from one trip as muddy as possible. He had gone on a dirt road that became a mud road with a quick shower. I said it was still monsoon season here, from July until mid-September, but he was determined to go. Along with him getting wet, his phone did too. It never fully recovered, so we had to get him a new one.

We also had an awesome end-of-the-season party with a campfire, great food, and dancing around a fire. It was a great end to the season. Sometimes, a group of people clicks and work well together. That was us by the end of the season.

Sasha was taking longer hikes to get back in shape for Lake Mead. We would be leading hikes again. He went on the famed Taner Trail and only went a little way down. However, it was a more technical trail, and he was tired when he finished. I had tried the path and did not like it, no matter how good the views were.

When I flew out of Phoenix, Arizona, it was a balmy 108 degrees F. I would take three flights, first to Atlanta, second to LaGuardia, and third on a puddle jumper to Maine. I got snacks before I went and only had an overnight bag. I met some fabulous people, including Kevin P., a Park Ranger and Dark Sky Ranger, and physicists and photographers. Plus, scientists from NASA taught us about telescopes and how to conduct star parties. This training would help as I planned to teach other rangers about telescopes and star parties in 2012.

August expenses: $3,386.10

September expenses: $3,160.44

Chapter 63
Do You Want To Change Jobs?

In 2011, we had some fantastic opportunities that fell into our laps with hardly any work. Yes, I did the work, like applying for a job I thought was a long shot (Grand Canyon National Park). Or I was requesting to be a Dark Sky Ranger with the AFGU program. We did not know until Grand Canyon that Sasha would do well as a salesperson. I got along with his co-workers. They offered me a job stay at the Grand Canyon for a month as a Sales Associate.

On October 4, my first day as a sales associate, I already knew how to use the cash register and about the museum. My boss told me that the selling goal at the museum was $300 a day. One of my co-workers had a great day and brought in $471.

Therefore, my mindset was to be friendly and nice and say, "Hello! Welcome to Tusuyan Museum and Ruin" to everyone who entered the museum. Maybe, I could do better than my co-worker. By lunchtime, I was up a little over $300. I had done the goal in half a day, and the donations were up. And by the time the museum closed, I had sold almost DOUBLE the goal at $579. There was much cheering and congratulations from my boss.

Some folks thought the first day was a fluke. I resolved to do better. I was nervous on the first day, but by the second day, I was ready. Again, at lunchtime, I went past the $300 mark. This time I resolved to do even better as I felt more comfortable, and I did it, over double the goal at $618.

While the weekend was harder to sell, I read all the books we sold at the museum. We had a great month of visitors. My parents came to Sedona. The day before we left for Sedona, it snowed at Desert View. We were happy to go down 3000 feet to the warmth of Sedona's red rocks.

We did some hiking with my parents, with a full moon hike, and checked out some lesser-known areas of Sedona. We went to the Chapel of the Holy Cross and saw an absurdly huge home from the church.

I was so happy that my parents liked to hike; we saw some exciting things. And they treated us to the Verde Canyon Railroad Wilderness Route train ride. Extremely fun to do, especially if you like historic trains. You went to a place where you can only go via train; you cannot see these places by car.

More fun was to be had back at Grand Canyon with our friends Leo and Karyn. They would visit us at the end of the month. We had a great dinner when Leo and Karyn were there, and they stayed at El Tovar. The dinner was fabulous, although we almost got kicked out as we talked and laughed so hard we were a bit loud. But when the laughter and talk flow as freely as water, you cannot stop the flow.

On October 27, we went hiking with them and saw a condor. It was close enough that we were able to see its tag number. They were excited, and I told them they were lucky to see one so close. Then, I got the statistics on the bird: when it was born, whether it was a male or female, and who its parents were, and they were amazed.

They asked, "How do you know all of this?"

"Training and website information," I replied.

They left after two days of fun, and we were also getting ready to go. I had three more days of work and knocked the ball out of the park each day. My boss told me I had made the most money during my one month at GCA than anyone working at the same store. I was their top seller.

October expenses: $1,089.62.

Chapter 64
Back to Lake Mead and Lost Power

I returned my keys at The Village and got a few specials at the grocery store. November was pretty quiet as it started to get cold. We were looking forward to getting down in elevation.

As we turned to Kingman, Arizona, we lost power. The truck would not go any faster than five miles per hour. It could not breathe, and the turbo was gone. However, a campground was nearby, and they had a space for us. Sasha got an appointment with the "Colorado River Ford Lincoln of Kingman" repair shop to diagnose and fix whatever was wrong with the truck.

It was the exhaust brake. It had failed and sealed shut, leaving no air to work through the brake. Michael stated, "Simple, Stupid Brake! Your engine couldn't breathe and couldn't build Turbo pressure, which equals no power. Your engine was constipated!" He did that on Facebook, and we laughed.

For those that do not know, an exhaust brake helps you slow down on a steep or long downhill. **As Sasha tells it**:

"Exhaust brakes are supplemental, often on medium-duty diesel trucks like our F450 that heavy tow loads. Unlike gasoline engines, diesel engines do not slow down simply by taking your foot off the accelerator; they rely on both service (disk) and supplemental brakes."

"Exhaust brakes use a vacuum or compressed air and a heavy-duty actuator valve to cut the normal exhaust flow. This function "retards" engine performance and slows the truck automatically."

We knew a different exhaust brake was in our future. But not this month.

Once we got to Lake Mead, we parked at a different site. Unfortunately, the lady in charge of the sites had not done anything to prepare our site. As a result, the trees planted hit the solar panels. It was a point of contention between us, but what could you do?

We visited Vegas to see if things had changed and attended a Volunteers' End of Season breakfast awards ceremony. Considering it was the start of our season, not the end, we felt pretty good. After that, we went along The Strip and found a new place, "The Grand Canyon Experience! Drink your beer while you hike up the stairs to see the mural of the Grand Canyon. Smoke, buy tee-shirts and shot glasses and act like a drunken fool!" Fortunately, this place is no longer in existence.

We did notice the prices were starting to tick up. Our favorite buffet at the Fiesta went up a dollar for any meal. Some other "freebies" were not so free anymore, but most Las Vegas seemed the same.

By November 6, we had met with our boss, Michelle, gone over dates for full moon hikes, and figured out our schedule. I would do night sky talks and full moon hikes. We also got our driving records to get a government vehicle. A vehicle we used most of the time to go to St. Thomas, Willow Bay, Bonelli Bay, and hiking.

We had no hikers show up for our first full moon hike, only a coyote. A sure sign that something is wrong is when you got a coyote this close to the road. Either that or they smell food.

We became social the next month. How social could those expenses get?

November expenses: $2,878.05

Chapter 65

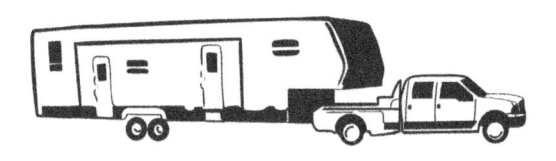

Social Expansion of Legs and Brains

I find it amazing, looking back on December 2011. We were out almost every day, going to the administration building, where Sasha and I could do some work or hiking. Or we would take the car and travel to another part of Lake Mead. The NPS site had the largest created reservoir in the US and the sixth largest (by landmass) in the continental US. It touches Grand Canyon to the east, Overton, Nevada to the north, Mojave Reservoir to the south, and Lake Las Vegas to the west.

We were in the Boulder City Parade with the NPS, and that year's focus was Explore The Dark Sky with Dark Sky Ranger Laura Jevtich! We walked the entire parade. One of the coworkers brought their dog, who was our Canis Major. The constellations were on our float, the ones you saw in the winter night sky. From there, we went down to the Boulder Marina to see the Boat Parade and the lights on the boats. That day and night had so much camaraderie, being with everyone and being the "Dark Sky Ranger."

The next day was fun, too, as we set up a table at Lakeview Overlook and had a stuffed tortoise, a tarantula, a tarantula hawk (insect), brochures, and a light pollution picture. These props are great ways to talk to people who might never visit the visitor center.

Leo and Karyn came into town the next day, and we went to the Las Vegas Sign and had dinner with them.

While we only had to work 16 hours a week each for our site, we took more time at the beginning of the month to work on projects. For example, I was asked to teach a class to park rangers within NPS, BLM, FS, and state parks in the surrounding Las Vegas area about the Night Sky. I helped Michelle figure out what telescopes to get and gave recommendations to rangers and students I worked with. It was an exciting, brain-draining month filled with beautiful scenery and long hikes over fantastic terrain.

We hiked and hiked some more, and Sasha found a motorcycle group to go riding. We went to their Christmas party too. After that, some would go on my full moon hikes in the winter months with their families.

Being social meant spending more, whether at the rig or away from it. However, we found that we enjoyed the work, and being social simultaneously was worth it.

December expenses: $3,895.65.

We spent a total of $35,024.63 for the 2011 year. We saved a little over 21 percent of our income.

Chapter 66
Changes and Added Stress

The winter of 2012 started a little differently for me. I was putting in more time than my "16" hours a week because I created a class for interpretation park rangers. I had a month to gather everything I had learned and make one eight-hour class. It was called "Astronomy for Interpreters." I became known in the Lake Mead area for creating a course while working on other programs to give to the public and hiking tours.

I conducted my first Evening with The Stars program, partly inside and partly outside. We had nine people for the program. Then, I created books for my class, which took forever, and I was worried I would run out of time.

On January 25, Astronomy for Interpreters class happened. It turned out well—a fabulous accomplishment for someone who was a volunteer. I instructed six park rangers; the first four hours were classroom time, and the next four were learning how to do a star party. I taught them how to set up the telescopes, check out the objects in the sky, watch the moon go down, look for Venus and Jupiter, and the Winter Hexagon. I gave them a constellation tour that evening. One of the budding Dark Sky Rangers gave another 18 folks from the Nevada Conservation Corps another tour.

I had been so focused, nervous, and scared that day. I was teaching Lead park rangers, higher pay grade people than myself, about interpretation and astronomy. Yet, once I started the program, my training skills kicked in, and I taught at better levels than before.

February, I was ready for hiking and my second class of Astronomy for Interpreters. Our hiking days in February 2012 were 3, 4, 5, 11, 18, 26, 28, and Leap Year Day, 29! I would go down to Phoenix to learn about the Maya Calendar from actual Mayan people. Sasha and I would take an oral history training class to prepare for an event in March—loads of learning for fun later.

I was so happy that I could take a governmental vehicle to Phoenix and use their credit card for gas. When I think about it now, Michelle gave me some unique opportunities I could not have gotten anywhere else. Yes, I had applied for a two-day workshop, but Lake Mead Interpretation paid for the car and gas. The workshop was one of the best I attended; I learned about the Maya culture, calendars, astronomy, and math. The presentations were excellent, and I met some fantastic people. These people helped me in the future.

We went to Death Valley and put our motorcycles on the back of the F450 truck, along with the ramps and tie-downs. We had an excellent adventure of riding. We stayed at a campground in the park. There would be no internet, but when you have a good book or three, you do not need it. Sasha checked out Titus Canyon, and we went on a full moon hike with my friend Naomi, whom I had met in Cape Hatteras. She worked at Death Valley during the winter and had gotten a full-time job there.

The full moon hike was great; she had an iPad to show what creatures might be around even if we could not see them. We heard the creatures of the night, the coyotes, and the foxes in the dunes. It was amazing to see the dunes at night. We even saw a kit fox!

We would spend almost a week camping in Death Valley, riding our motorcycles everywhere. While my seat is less comfortable than Sasha's, I guess I had more padding. Each ride made me more comfortable about being on the scooter.

Sasha and I went on motorcycles to Old Stovepipe Wells, Dante's View, K Point, West End Road to Devil's Golf Course and Speedway, and Artist's Road. Before we left, we went to Badwater, and I could taste the dry and salty air—nothing like it, being 200-plus feet below sea level.

After that ride, I was whipped. Yet, I managed to get my 125cc up a 15 percent grade hill to Dante's View. How my motorscooter did it, I do not know. But she did, and I was happy to see the views.

January expenses: $5,556.00.

February expenses: $3,581.91.

Chapter 67

Heritage and Family Visits

March was our last month at Lake Mead. We had to push to get the excitement into the first three weeks. We left for Grand Canyon early. It seemed, at the time, to be even earlier than before, and I needed winter uniforms to stay warm.

We received training in February for oral history and how to delicately ask questions to bring forth answers. The training was because we attended a special event: the St. Thomas Reunion. When Lake Mead's waters started to recede, the Town of St. Thomas was visible again.

The town was built by Mormons, who thought they were in Utah. The Hoover Dam, created during the Great Depression, drowned Lake Mead reservoir and St. Thomas. The people got out before that happened. With the waters dropping at an alarming rate, something happy was happening. St. Thomas became visible, and you could see the foundations again. Park Rangers came and talked about the town and those foundations.

Back then, there would be a reunion of the descendants. We had an extremely long day with the Chief of Interpretation, and the Superintendent came out. Tons of people came to this event. Many were the descendants, but others wanted to know what was happening. We were there to have a presence as part of the NPS. Plus, we got names and information from those who remembered or knew something about the town.

We had so much fun, getting to experience something that few Gentiles ever experience. This shindig happened at the beginning of the month.

We were excited to see Sasha's parents in the middle of the month. While they do not hike, there is much to see, and we showed them where we lived. They had never seen our second RV, so it was fun to show them our home. They also got a car rental, making driving around town easier. That rental was handy as we could put the new exhaust brakes on our truck while they were in town.

We showed them Lake Mead's surroundings. They, in turn, decided on a boat cruise to see the side of the dam you can only see from the water. It was a fun boat ride and something we had never done before. Next, they saw Sasha give a program about Wildflowers at the library, and they were very proud of his talk and photography of wild plants and flowers. Finally, we stayed at the Hoover Dam Hotel and Casino, ate delicious steak dinners, and saw the carp in the lake.

We also took them to the iconic "Welcome to Lake Mead" sign, where Dad J wore a shirt the same color as the rocks. One of the last places we took them was Valley of Fire State Park. I drove through the park at a slow pace. It went fine for the most part, but even with me driving, Dad was turning green. Valley of Fire is like that for those with motion sickness, with many hilly dips and highs. We had to go through the park to get to the highway.

As soon as it was a straight and even road, we put down the windows and let the fresh air flow. He felt better immediately. We then headed to Fremont Street to show them the lights of Downtown. They were fascinated by the neon lights. Fremont has more neon per square foot than the Strip.

We went with them to The Strip at MGM to see a show. Mom J picked it, thinking of a play with beautiful costumes and feathery hats. Instead, it was a nude review; with barely-there wear. I think they were shocked by it. We got front-row seats and more makeup and lighting than costumes, but that is Vegas, baby!

We would get to Grand Canyon by March 24 and be in the same spot. I would start working on March 26, and Sasha would start working again in April.

We had learned from the Mormons this month and prepared ourselves for a long remote season.

March expenses: $9,499.50, ouch.

Chapter 68
Tax Tribulations

April 2012 looked like a great start to my NPS year as we hiked some steep trails nearby our site. First, we took hikes to Cedar Mountain, long hiking trails with significant elevation changes. These trails go down to see beauty, but when you are the most tired, you hike up to get home.

In 2011, I worked in Utah and Arizona for a couple of extra months, which dinged us on our taxes. Unfortunately, I did not take enough out. I was also buying Municipal Bonds, a great way to learn a new income stream, as you only pay state taxes, not federal ones. Since we are domiciled in Texas, there is no state income tax. But we still had income.

Our rent went down for everyone in Desert View because they no longer had a fire truck in Desert View. It costs too much to keep one. If there were a fire, like an RV or housing apartment, it would take about an hour to come from the Village. At that point, why worry? Everything would be gone in an RV. That meant significant backups of everything we had and sending off hard drives to my parents.

There were upgrades and monthly charges for peace of mind for a satellite system called InReach by Delorme. This is for Sasha in case he has a problem with his motorcycle on his rides. He was adventuring without me, going off on solo trips, and I wanted not to worry as much about him.

I started worrying more this year than last, as he was hiking alone and riding alone. While doing the right things, like having good hiking boots and carrying plenty of water, my mind started to create these nerve-wracking scenarios I could not turn off.

We found out that April was cold at 7500 feet. Supposedly spring, but with no snow, it was bitterly cold for desert people. So we would head to Flagstaff and then further south to Scottsdale, home of palm trees and pools, for a few days of warmth.

At least in Scottsdale, you hike UP the mountains. I was also intrigued by the geology, plants, and lizards we saw on Camelback Mountain, and I took pictures whenever I got tired of hiking upwards.

We also found a few vacant lots with orange trees and picked as many as possible. We ate during happy hours and got tasty small plates. Amazingly, our food costs were low because we had spent so much on provisions during March.

We paid our taxes using H&R Block. And when we could not hike anymore because of the heat, we could go to the Recreation Center in the Village for $100 for the season. There was plenty to do there.

April expenses: $2,995.40.

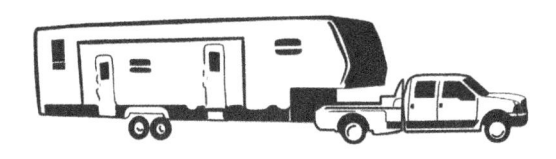

Chapter 69
Astronomy Dreams and Nightmares

This month was the start of the last NPS season, even though, at the time, I did not know it. I had a hard time reading my boss, Lisa. I was so excited to create night sky programming that I lost sight of what she wanted from me as a Park Ranger. Desert View is more about the archeology of the people, the Ancestral Puebloans, rather than the geology or astronomy.

I was happy to be asked back to Grand Canyon and join the 2012 Star Party. I created a talk and was the Keynote Speaker in June. I also asked her to pay for a SunSpotter telescope that showed the sunspots of the sun for the Solar Eclipse that would happen in May. In addition, I trained Desert View and The Village rangers about the sun, the coming eclipse, and the night sky.

May would be an astronomer's dream with a Super Moon and the Annular Solar Eclipse Party on May 20, 2012. I was coordinating with my contacts from NASA and AFGU people to get astronomers to Desert View and the overlook where we did our evening programs.

The number of stressors this month, of extreme highs and scary lows, cannot be overstated. I did not explain to Sasha what was happening to me during those times. Instead, I focused on doing so many programs, even though we only needed to do four. I lost sight of what I was at the Grand Canyon for and became full of myself because I knew things that other rangers did not.

Some of the male rangers questioned my knowledge, which made me angry and annoyed. It made me doubt myself. I did not let Sasha know of the turmoil that had started. I instead pushed those feelings down and piled more work upon myself.

I am not sure if Lisa saw this or what, but while the programs I had done last year were good, she wanted me to do a new evening program. It was a disaster for me. I wanted to do something about air pollution, but how it related to the Grand Canyon was never entirely revealed. I was speaking down to people rather than letting them enjoy the beautiful sunsets. And I would get annoyed when they did not stay for the talk but wandered off to take pictures.

Then Sasha would go off on a ride, a two-day trip after a long hike on Waldon to Hermit's Rest Trail. Sasha decided to go on the two-day camping trip but got a flat, and I had to get him in the truck. I was supposed to work on my programs that weekend but spent the time driving and bringing him home. We stayed at Cliff Dwellers Lodge and went into Page for grocery shopping and to view Horseshoe Bend. I was nervous about being close to the edge. However, it turned out to be a false ledge. Still, it was windy and a bit of a tiring day. I needed to get back to the work I had yet to accomplish. To say I was stressed was an understatement.

The Annular Solar Eclipse was a massive event for the Park. We had posters from Tyler Nordgen, whom I met at Acadia. We sold them at Desert View and in The Village. I asked for free solar glasses from AFGU, and they sent me over two hundred. NASA would be at our spot where we do the sunset programs and at the Watchtower. I coordinated with other rangers to explain what was happening so people did not look at the sun.

The biggest worry was that people would try to take pictures of the sun with their cameras. The sun's rays are magnified into a camera, which could lead to blindness. Just what I needed, a bunch of people blinded by my program!

While some idiots tried to use solar glasses over their camera lenses, I realized I could not police them. So instead, I went for the experience and excitement. Two folks from NASA came with their scopes to watch the eclipse and with the proper equipment. Our SunSpotter showed the entire eclipse as it was happening.

The weather cooperated with the clearest skies I have seen in a long time. The absolute bluest of skies before the eclipse only made an eclipse with the sun more amazing, excellent, and awe-inspiring than anything I could have done.

We had over 150 people come out just to our benches and the surrounding area. They looked at the three scopes, watched the eclipse with the sun scope, and listened to me as I said, "Two minutes to touchdown," and other cheers. There was a "ring of fire" around the sun and much joy throughout the crowd to have this shared experience.

Some astronomers came out from Tucson, Arizona, and brought their telescopes. Some with immense scopes and even a birder scope with a filter. It was one of the best experiences I have ever had. Everyone went away from it, happy and awe-struck. My co-worker and friend, Mandy, watched it with Sasha and me.

It was the best evening program ever.

The rest of May stayed strong, with more people coming into the park, more sales, and more hiking boots that had lost their soles.

I got new Vasque hiking boots that worked as a park ranger and for fun hiking, and I had spent my $150 allowance on a Gortex jacket for the winter weather. So I had to pay for the boots out of pocket.

May expenses: $1,796.52.

Chapter 70
Sky Adventures Before Family Visits

June was another month of stress and activities—the most exciting time since we started our journey and adventure. I led the way by staying as busy as possible, and Sasha decided to take even more trips alone. He spent the first weekend off on a motorcycle ride to the North Rim while I stayed up late and watched the lunar eclipse. He returned to watch the Transit of Venus on June 5, 2012. This year was full of sky events.

While I did not work on June 5, I went into The Village and "helped/volunteered" with Lead Park Ranger Marker. We used a reverse projection on a screen to show Venus going across the sun. It would ultimately take six hours, with some fabulous pictures taken, but I was not paid to help.

The following weekend, we had off and went to Las Vegas as our exhaust brake was acting up again. It stopped working this time. As we returned, my boss called and told me they had closed Desert View and Village road. There was a fire in the park! We had to turn around, return to Flagstaff, and go through the Navajo Nation to get home. At least we got enough notice.

At this time, Mandy had to go East to help care for her family. She would be gone the rest of the month. She would come back but left in early September. I was sad to see her go.

The smell of smoke was in the air as I did my sunset programs, but the start of the star party was clear skies for eight nights. I would work or "volunteer" every evening at the Star Party.

I gave the Keynote opening presentation on June 16, 2012. It was called "We Are All Made of Star Dust" to 250 to 300 people. Everyone got a little slip of paper. I said at the beginning it was essential to hold onto this paper for the game at the end.

The presentation was a little over 45 minutes long. Everyone had fun, holding up their slips of paper when I called out an element. We discovered that our bodies were made of materials that only happen when the stars (suns) explode, called a supernova. And if those stars did not explode? Well, there would not be planet Earth, nor us! That got the gasps I hoped for.

After my presentation, I went outside and gave constellation tours. I spoke of the Native American stories rather than the Greek stories. And we had great night skies with a 7.5 magnitude. We could see the Milky Way. I told stories of antelopes jumping across the sky, of shooting stars every time someone gets married, and of the creation of the earth by two opposite brothers.

In the end, I was exhausted in body and mind. But the evening and my program went well, and I enjoyed the rest of the Star Party. We would go back there on June 17 and 18 to work, June 19 to volunteer, and work again on June 21, 22, and 23, the last day and night of the star party.

The next day we would get up early for vacation for a week—our first vacation get-together for the Capuano family out west in Sedona and the Grand Canyon.

Chapter 71

Family Visits and Misunderstandings

While the vacation went well, there were misunderstandings and different vacation mindsets with family members. As full-time travelers and RVers, Sasha and I took our time to stay in a place to get to know it better.

However, Karen and James had only a certain amount of time each year to spend on vacations. As I said before, time is what separates tourists from full-time travelers. I think neither of us understood the other's vacation styles and what the Grand Canyon meant to us. Mom tried her best to mesh two different types.

Even though I never explained my feelings to my brother-in-law, I was hurt when he stated, "The Grand Canyon was just a big hole in the ground. So what is the point? You see it and then go do something else." He said it jokingly, of course. But I did not get the joke.

Looking back at it now, I realize our vacation styles differed. Again, it goes back to rushing to do everything within the time you have or taking it slow and coming back later. Sasha and I have different traveling mindsets and tend not to run to fit everything in. We have a taste here and there, and if we like it, we go back, as we had with Sedona and Las Vegas.

There is a phrase that park rangers use to separate tourists from visitors to national parks. The "tag it and bag it" crowd. The ones who drive five hours to a beautiful place. They then jump out of their car, get the stamp, snap pictures, and leave. We noticed it at almost every park, from Cape Hatteras to Lake Mead National Recreation Area. There is a sign as you drive towards the Lake where people stop and take pictures, never going into the park!

My parents, Sasha, and I had been to Sedona several times. While we had never been there in the summer, we enjoyed going to the pool and hot tub. In addition, we noticed more people around the town at this time, and the restaurants stayed open later.

The first day with the family was pool time with red rocks. It was amazing to see the blue sky, red rocks, and green trees everywhere. It was also quite warm. We went to a Mexican restaurant that evening, which worked well for me, as I could get primarily gluten-free items. They had good corn chips and great food.

However, there were disagreements between our families. The fact that we were eating out every night was different for us. We were used to going for a cheaper meal rather than dinner. My parents were used to eating later but having three meals a day. And my sister's family wanted dinner experiences.

Karen had set up to do an adventure kayak tour on the Verde River. The kids would go on tandem kayaks with their parents, and we all played with water guns. We also had a guide to help us figure out where to go. The water was low in some parts. The water guns became one of the better parts of the paddling adventure. We all had fun in the water. It was like we were back riding the ocean with our kayaks.

The ride down the river was close to Jerome, a town we went hiking with my parents in the past. Asylum Restaurant was a perfect way to end the day on the river. The city itself is filled with history and spooky stories.

The next day, we suggested Schnebly Hill after we found out Slide Rock State Park was closed. Slide Rock State Park's waters were too low to slide. We had done this park on another trip, where Mom amazed me by sliding down the rocks in her bathing suit. But this summer, the river waters had a rough time. With the water at low levels, the algae took over.

Instead, we went to Schnebly Hill. We would go up the hill to the viewpoints of the Forest Service and then down the rough road of Schnebly. My parents, Sasha, and I have taken this trip several times. The route can be scary for those not used to driving in remote areas, on rocks, and without pavement.

After that, I thought they were ready for anything. We would head to Desert View, where we work, and Grand Canyon Village.

We left Sedona first to drop off our stuff and gave the family directions to where our site was so we could have lunch together. Unfortunately, they were late and had only a quick lunch at our site. However, this was when Dad saw the sandwiches Sasha made for the family and said, "This is a $10 sandwich!"

High praise for a yummy sandwich. After lunch, we went to the Visitor Center where Sasha works.

We spent some time at the Watchtower, with its iconic paintings and Mary Colter's architectural design. However, we did not spend much time at my place of work, the Tusayan Museum, or any of the viewpoints.

We stopped at the museum and my workplace, where I tried to introduce my family to the park rangers on site, but the family was rushing to get to the Village. I felt deflated. I worked here most of the time. They only saw the rocks, not the ruins and the story. I tried to do my interpretive program to show them around the ruins, but it was a constant rush, rush, rush.

Mom planned a dinner at El Tovar for the early evening. It was a spectacular, elegant dinner for the eight of us. Knowing the prices for a dinner like that, Sasha and I thanked them and Dad profusely. Mom had gotten rooms for us at Bright Angel Lodge, less time traveling back and forth.

The next day was fun outdoor hiking, including the Trail of Time. We got pictures of us hiking and enjoying the rocks. While the kids got a little tired, they found a tree to climb. It got their energy up, and many pictures were taken. Then they were able to finish the trail. They did exactly what I always stated, "Take pictures of interesting stuff on the trail to catch your breath."

But it was bittersweet as they were leaving; they caught a flight the next day out of Phoenix.

My parents started a three-week tour. They took in the sunset at Hopi Point with us. We took fabulous photographs of my parents as the sun went down and the moon rose; I said, "Happiness is a good sunset and an extra special moonrise!"

We said goodbye to my parents on June 30, our last vacation day. They went to Yellowstone, Glacier, Grand Tetons, and Breckenridge, Colorado.

We went back to work.

June expenses: $3,249.49

Chapter 72
Of Hiking, Hotness and Sadness

We took it easy in July to spend less than in June. We took hikes, just at night instead of during the day. We took our first full moon hike down South Kaibab Trail for our gratification. We wanted to see how far we could go and still be able to get back up without problems.

One of the best features of these hiking trails happens at the top. There are water spigots to fill your canteens. We found a few elks hanging around for the water. The mom elk taught the baby elks to use their tongues to turn the faucet to get the water out.

"Ick," said we, "So glad we filled up at the RV!"

We went down and used the moon as our light.

A week later, we went down again, this time on Bright Angel Trail. Since there would not be a full moon, we wore headlamps. There was significant elevation steepness, and we often stopped for pictures. We had hoped to see the moon. Instead, we saw large clouds moving in.

As we watched the moon for a bit, we felt a drop of rain. Unfortunately, the clouds moved faster than we thought, and at the 1.5-mile rest house, we would have to book it back.

We stopped for nothing, moving as quickly as we could. We did a half mile in around 15 minutes, which was great for us, as there was a significant elevation change. We managed 1.5 miles in less than an hour and dogged raindrops before getting wet.

The Monsoon season had started. Our next hike was not into the canyon, but on top, with the Red Line. Every day it rained, and when we looked at the Colorado river, it looked brown.

By Sasha's birthday, July 22, 2012, we were ready to leave the park and see something new. So we went to Glen Canyon National Recreation Area and camped along the shores of Lake Powell at Lone Rock Campground. This was a great deal for $10 a night (now $14). And considering our truck was not a four-wheel drive, we managed to get a site closer to the water. Again, it was beautiful, seeing the water a blue-green with red rocks.

We saw a storm in the distance, but the rain did not come. Instead, it was a lightning storm. As it passed us, we greeted the Milky Way stars. I read in the tent while Sasha took pictures of the stars. We had thought of staying another night, but it was too hot.

When we came home, we worked the rest of the month, thinking of going back out at the very end. Instead, it rained so hard that we could not see the mountains or the trees. Lightning and thunder immediately following meant the storm was directly overhead. We lost power twice, and it came back later.

August seemed like we were working and riding between raindrops. Every middle of the day, it would storm with lightning and thunder. Of course, there was lightning when it was not raining, and we let visitors know how to protect themselves: go up on tippy-toes, put your heels together, and duck your head.

But not everyone paid attention to the ranger's warnings. A woman was hit by lightning in the Village. She hid under a tree. The tree's roots surged electricity, and she was thrown 10 feet from the power.

She was one of the twenty-two (22) deaths that year. Most of the deaths were not that powerful, but there were a few idiots who went down the trails and did not come back up. Or the young man who had survived two tours in Afghanistan and was celebrating with friends. He decided to jump the rocks. He jumped and slipped, landing about 25 feet down the ledge. His friends screamed at him, "DON'T MOVE!!!!"

"We'll get a ranger!"

He was dazed, we think, and moved. Unfortunately, he fell another 100 feet to his death.

August had many of these incidents. And because it was in a popular area, the park rangers specializing in search and rescue had to go down with ropes and retrieve the body.

One of the saddest incidents is when people come to National Parks to commit suicide. They either walk off the ledge or do a Thelma and Louise. However, the movie was not filmed at Grand Canyon. But because people THINK it happened at the Grand Canyon, they go there.

A young man did just that. He went through the barriers near El Tovar in the early morning hours with his car and drove to his death. What stunk to high heaven was that people were up and saw what he did. Kids saw him take out the fence and dive to his death.

And then, highly specialized rangers had to risk their lives to take his body and car out of the canyon. The amount of pain he put people through boggles the mind.

Sometimes it makes sense to leave the park so we do not see the madness. For example, we went to Kingman, Arizona, to look for storage places for our rig. After that, we would head east with only the truck.

When we returned, we found elk that had discovered my potted vegetable garden. I had everything in pots and on a table, so I did not have to worry about rabbits. There were tomatoes, jalapeño peppers, flowers, and other vegetables. The jalapeños surrounded everything to discourage the deer, but it did not work. A small herd of male elk came by, eating everything. They removed the few tomatoes, ate the leaves, and tried the jalapeños. The peppers were on the ground, partly chewed.

At least they were spanked by the spiciness. I figured that was it for my gardening.

We went out with the work gang in mid-August to El Tovar for our last get-together. Some rangers would leave soon, and we wanted to get together for a celebratory dinner.

By the end of August, Sasha suggested we get a 4x4 vehicle to take camping with us rather than the truck. But that little vehicle would end up costing us more than we knew.

July expenses: $1,117.

August expenses: $2,012.28.

Chapter 73

The End of My NPS Career

I wrote in my journal on September 1:

Dear Mom,

I need to talk to you about something I did...Something bad. I have made a mess of my career at the Grand Canyon. And I have messed up my marriage.

After the Star Party and the visit with everyone, I started having problems. I don't know if it was because of the excitement of those two events that the rest of the season would be a letdown. Or that parts of my season were not enjoyable. Or what? But I started letting incidents bother me more—stupid Stuff.

A co-worker who assessed my work upset me, yet I did not let Sasha know. Visitors parking in the lots and leaving their engines running. There is no law against it, but it was polluting the air. Junior Rangers were not getting badges because I felt they did not do the work. And I was annoyed they had not....and then finally, the straw that broke my mind's back.

Jill was a Grand Canyon Association person and a co-worker of Sasha. We have not worked well together. I have been short with her. Little incidents bothered me: allowing people to come into the museum past closing time, not being behind the desk, and putting too many displays on the desk. This last one, though, got me into deep trouble.

On Saturday, Jill and I worked together, and I was irked by everything. First, it seemed she had a book on the desk, and I, the great and mighty park ranger, told her to put it away. She ultimately did, but two hours later, she had two books out, and I...I lost it.

There were visitors there who saw me lose control.

I told my co-worker and boss for the day, Maci, what happened, and she talked to Jill. But the damage had been done. Yet, I did not even look back. I did not speak to Jill again or tell Sasha what I had done.

Sasha and I left for three days looking at Jeeps and returned to a mess. Jill was so upset by the altercation that I had a meeting with Lisa, and Sharon, Jill's boss. They told me that Jill had been crying for the past three days! About this incident!

I was floored. Part of me thought she stuck it to me to make me look bad. How could I believe that? But, on the other hand, part of me realized I hurt my reputation with bosses and co-workers. So there is no way we can return now, nor will I have Lisa as a reference.

I did talk to Jill on Wednesday night, and I apologized. But Sasha said there was something wrong with my brain. When I do this type of outburst repeatedly, he will not stay with me this time unless I get my brain fixed. He will divorce me if I cannot resolve my brain workings.

I hope you can help me figure out what to do,
Laura

Chapter 74

Snapped with Feelings of Guilt

I snapped. I do not remember what I said to her. I can barely remember the incident. I visualized myself getting angry and putting things back on the shelves. But my mind clouded over what I said to her. Why had she gotten under my skin so badly? I remember telling her I had done her job last year and nailed it. How hard could it be? I had sold more than any GCA person had done in one month at that store. She said I was bragging and not helping her do her job.

Either way, it was a death blow. In the space of three minutes, I had blown my reputation. Plus, my chance to come back for another season. This went on my record. I lost another person to recommend me.

For the next two weekends before we left, I found a psychologist who would take me on short notice. But, unfortunately, I could only get two sessions for free as a government employee. So after that, I got counseling in Fairfax, Virginia, using EAP Consultants.

I started journaling in a notebook immediately after I saw the therapist. She suggested journaling and listening to tapes or CDs to calm me. I bought two books on anger management, which we thought was my problem. The books were Overcoming Anger and The Anger Workbook for Women.

While I did have similar experiences with my Dad when I was younger, I realized it was more an anxiety issue than anything else. In a sense, I thought too much.

I thought people were out to get me. I feared that Sasha would go hiking and get attacked by a mountain lion. And I was constantly fearful of not saying the right thing.

My brain was constantly on. When I went to bed, my brain kept going, and I had horrific, vivid, multicolored nightmares that I could not remember in the morning. They would leave me in a cold sweat.

I would retreat to my games online or off. I knew these words could not go onto the website. The stigma of having a mental illness was too great. I had pushed it off. Hindsight was 20/20. I should have taken the pills back in 2001.

Sasha had been right too. First, he said I played too many games instead of doing what was needed. Then I would get frustrated and angry with him for "interrupting" my game. I was a Dr. Jekyll and Mr. Hyde but as a woman. And one that was pleasant and seemingly happy most of the time.

As I went through this process, I read other books to reduce stress and calm myself, including using a Franklin Covey planning system. Finally, I needed to find a way to settle down, think about my feelings, and talk to someone who could help.

While I journaled my thoughts, I still did not share everything with Sasha. I felt so upset about what had happened, yet I did nothing to stop buying the Jeep. I knew I could never drive it, as it was a stick shift, yet we got the vehicle anyway. I wished I had said no to Sasha about this vehicle. It added rather than subtracted stress.

I had tried to learn stick shift with Dad, and instead, I blew the muffler off. I tried learning with the little red motorcycle in

2006, but we sold it so I could get an ATV. So my adventures with stick-shift vehicles ended badly. And I feared this Jeep would also take the same run.

I tried calming myself, using books, tapes, and therapy. But as we would be traveling. There had to be more sessions and something else, which I did not realize then.

I received excellent advice from Mandy about getting help. She would not return to Grand Canyon as she took time off to help her family. Instead, she would go to Cape Hatteras National Seashore, Ocracoke, with its beautiful beaches. She worked at the lighthouse at the end of the Seashore.

"You got to go where you are appreciated and do what you love," she said.

First, I had to get my mind healthy.

September expenses: $10,776.24.

Chapter 75

Therapy and Travel

We headed into Seligman, Arizona, and went on Route 66. We took pictures of the signs while people took pictures of us. Then, into Kingman, where we dropped off the rig to store it for three months. We would stay in the Virginia area and go up and down the east coast visiting with family and friends. From Kingman, we went into Utah to buy the Jeep and hitch and see Bo.

Then we headed east to Dinosaur National Park, where I longed to be a park ranger. Instead, we had fun checking out the dinosaurs and exhibits. They had recently re-opened the Visitor Center, and I was happy. It brought back good memories of my first job as a geologist, "Dig for Dinosaurs," with the Milwaukee Public Museum.

We got to Virginia by October 3 and put the truck on a farm. Our dually truck seemed wider than my parents' driveway.

Once done, we headed down to the Outer Banks with my parents. My Aunt Tina and Uncle Joe came down and stayed with my parents and us for several days. After that, they went south to Hilton Head and their timeshare.

In October, we split our time with my parents for two weeks, then to Fairfax with Sasha's parents for two weeks. After that, we would travel around Virginia and New Jersey to see friends.

I was under significant stress during this time and wrote out my feelings.

While living with both sets of parents was hard on everyone, we were trying to be frugal. We did not want to spend money on hotels, nor did we want guilty feelings about not staying with the parents.

Sasha and I also added more stress to ourselves living with his parents at this time. I needed to apply for jobs, knowing I would not get a reference from Lisa or Sharon. Instead, I would get references from Marker, the lead of the Star Party, and Lesley, my Interpretation coach I had since Cape Hatteras days. I would spend hours upstairs working on these applications only to be told I was distant.

While Sasha and I created shakes for ourselves for breakfast, I had difficulty eating with his family. His parents eat bread, meat, and potatoes in that order. They have no reason to change, but it was hard for me. During this year, Sasha realized he had trouble swallowing denser meats like beef and pork, so we ate less meat. So strike two on the foods.

Therefore, stress, hunger, and jobs. How many arguments could we have? Plus, we took the Jeep to his parents. I did not have an escape route unless I borrowed a car.

However, I found an understanding therapist in Fairfax. I received twelve sessions, the maximum amount I could have with my healthcare plan. These sessions were paid for by the federal government, as I had worked for the NPS. Otherwise, each session was $60.

The therapist and I worked through my main hooks and stresses. She suggested I get up earlier than Sasha to do yoga, breathing, and exercises and then plan or list my day. She told work with the books I had and to journal my thoughts. She said it would be nice to bring my Dad too, but if that was not possible, to get Sasha to a session.

I realized that my Dad and I had similar communication skills during the sessions. I believed that I let too much worry me and that I overthought. What goes on in my mind does not get adequately communicated to others. I struggled with words to explain how I felt. What came out instead seemed to add fuel to the fire.

My therapist helped me tremendously with the words I needed to say or not say. She stated, "Sometimes it is best to say, "I *am not going to discuss "this"* with you (whatever "this" is)."

She also suggested walking away, either mentally or physically, or both. That was some of the best advice I got, but it took a while for me to implement it. Along the way, I was Hangry (hungry and angry), stressed, upset, fearful of the actions of others, and still applying for jobs.

Some of the stressors were ones we created. For example, Sasha spent hours digitalizing Mom's Fashion Notes, a cable show she put on about creative artists. She wanted those shows on YouTube, but they needed digitalizing. So Sasha got a machine to help him, and I put them onto YouTube.

Dad J had retired from the FDA at 85, and our family thought he should move from a PC to a Mac. So he had to learn how to do everything with a Mac. Unfortunately, most of that fell onto me, as Sasha could not help him. In addition, his office was disorganized, so I needed it fixed before we worked together.

There were cables and wires everywhere. And most did not plug into anything. And then there was the cable box. Dad did not like the flashing green lights on the cable box, which was high on the TV console. He felt like it was hurting his head. So he told us to turn off our electronic devices each night.

Oh, we did not take that well, Sasha especially.

Chapter 76
Arguments With Family

Before we traveled to New Jersey to visit my friends, we had a stressful couple of days with our families. We got into more arguments with Sasha's parents than ever before.

We watched the news about Hurricane Sandy possibly coming up the coast. Sasha said, "Maybe we should not go to New Jersey this Sunday."

I went into a tizzy, and we started to argue in front of his parents. Immediately, I thought he did not want to see my friends. I did not realize he did all the driving, as I had yet to learn how to drive a stick shift. We would be in THE most traffic-laden area, with some of the US's fastest-driving, lane-changing people.

It took a while for both of us to calm down. Then, finally, I went to my anger management books and saw I had done exactly what I was trying not to do! Sasha was looking out for me, trying to protect us from a possibly hazardous situation.

It probably did not help that we had a stressful previous evening with his parents. Dad J drove us to a restaurant and almost hit a woman. He had been having problems driving at night, which was part of the reason he retired. But if anyone else drove, he would get car sick. It made for an uncomfortable evening, with more arguing between Sasha and Dad.

Ultimately, I got them to apologize to each other, and the brandy and seltzer came out.

Sasha and I discussed going to New Jersey; we would go for dinner but drive back that night. We would not stay over.

We visited my girlfriends as I had not seen them in a few years. My childhood friends lasted through high school, college, marriages, deaths, and divorces. Five women manage to stay friends most of the time. Yet we had a great time together like time had not passed. We might be older but still friends.

We hung out with them as long as possible. Then, as much as I wanted to be there, in New Jersey, we had to go back. Hurricane Sandy was coming up the coast. There was no traffic coming back so late that night. It was as though everyone had hunkered down already.

We returned from New Jersey early on October 28, 2012. The governor of New Jersey issued a state of emergency and started mandatory evacuations in several parts of the state.

On October 29, during high tide, Hurricane Sandy hit New Jersey with sustained winds of 80 mph in Atlantic County. The hurricane moved up the coast, causing major havoc. My poor New Jersey!

Aunt Tina and Uncle Joe's basement and garages got hit with water as their sump pump failed. The Avon-by-the-Sea boardwalk was destroyed, and the sandy beach was swept away. North, south, and west New Jersey got hit. Mary Beth's beach home, where she married, moved off its foundations. There was a fire, and no way to know if they still had a beach home.

Denise had a home on the river, near the ocean, and her first floor flooded, mud reaching up at least six feet. She and her wife moved into Aunt Tina and Uncle Joe's home. Darlene lost hundreds of dollars in food supplies as the electricity was off for weeks.

Natyna's house flooded at her first level, and she lost thousands of materials for her business and home.

Ultimately, the electricity came back on. Darlene restocked her refrigerators, my aunt and uncle removed their stuff, and Natyna had to move. Denise got a FEMA loan to clean her home. But Mary Beth's home was destroyed.

What I learned, though, was that I could not control everything. I could not go up and help because I would need gas, which was in short supply. Food, which is no longer stored with electricity. And a place to stay, like the thousands who were displaced. Instead, I gave money to Red Cross and apologized again to Sasha for becoming hysterical.

Spending time with my therapist was good, especially during those terrible moments. She helped me.

While Sasha and I still had problems, confrontations, and disagreements, we had a session with her. It helped us both.

In the last session with her, she said, "You know, you might have a little less something in your brain that may make it harder to function. If you had a medication to help, do you think you could take it?"

In a sense, she said my brain lacked this critical ingredient that helps me function. By accepting that I lacked this integral part, I could become the fun-loving Laura I was beforehand.

It would mean a lifetime of taking a pill. And a lifetime of better, stronger, and more lasting relationships. I stated, "Yes, what is this elixir I need?"

She said, "Celexa is the brand, but the ingredient or generic is Citalopram."

"Will this do what I need?"

"Yes, it is not only for depression, which I do not believe you have but for anxiety. It would be the little help you need."

We went into December with the understanding that I would transfer her suggestions to a psychologist who could prescribe me medications.

October expenses: $1,991.43

November expenses: $1,137.17

December expenses: $3,585.71

We spent $47,324.68 and went into savings in 2012.

Chapter 77

New Year With High Hopes

Sometimes it is best to give up.

I went into 2013 knowing I needed a pill to help me be better. Or at least put me back to an even keel. So I scheduled an appointment to see a psychiatrist who can prescribe the medication on Thursday, January 3.

I got the message wrong. I had to pay $250 upfront on Thursday at Harmony Healthcare not to get a prescription. But to pay for the 15 minutes with the psychiatrist. They would only prescribe after the medical therapist decided I should get a prescription.

Those twelve sessions in Fairfax and the two in Flagstaff did not count. Another $100 to the medical therapist for the fifty minutes of me pleading my case. It still hurts my frugal soul all these years later. A $350 bill for a prescription that costs $4 for 30 pills! It is safe to say you would be mad too.

I had a hard time waiting for things. I received a three-month prescription, and they said to take a half dose, which meant cutting the pill in half with a sharp knife. The drugs have an indent in the middle. The half dose was for a week, then take the total amount. I was to call in a month and then in two months. I needed to get a prescription for longer than a three-month supply.

After taking the medication for four days, I found a dry mouth. This dry-mouth feel would continue for me. It would just be a part of me now. The health insurance did not pay for therapy visits. Is that messed up, or what?

We met my parents on Saturday, January 5. They were coming out for a meeting.

Saturday would be a crazy day. First, we hiked Liberty Bell Arch in Arizona, returned to the rig in Lake Mead, Nevada, and packed. Then, we went to Harmony Healthcare in Las Vegas, got the prescription, filled it out, and headed to the Marriott to be with Mom and Dad for the week.

We took Mom and Dad to the Fremont Experience to see the neon and then to the nature of Red Rock Canyon. We took great sunset pictures. The Marriott was perfect for when Dad had meetings in Las Vegas. He consulted and attended these meetings to discuss regulations and building codes.

Once the meetings were over, we took them to Valley of Fire for some hiking. We went on several different trails and saw some petroglyphs, the famed Mouse Tank (a natural basin in the rock called a tank). Mouse was the name of a lousy man hiding in the area and coming to this tank to get water. But fortunately, his family, who captured him, brought him to justice.

Before my parents left, we went for a strenuous hike at Red Rock Canyon National Conservation Area. We might have worn my parents out hiking on this trip, but they were great sports!

I still used games as an outlet when I got worried or stressed. Towards the end of January, I resolved to play less. I was on the computer so much that I saw wavy, weird lines in my eyesight. We spent money learning to deal with life.

January expenses: $2,277.19

Chapter 78
The Long Walk Out of The Desert

Whenever we were not hiking, I was applying for jobs. When I returned to Lake Mead, Michelle was surprised that we still wanted to volunteer. Someone had talked to her about my blow-up, and when she told me she knew, Sasha got upset again. I told her I had gone to therapy, was on medication, and that an incident like that would not happen again. But it caused strife in our marriage.

Instead of telling Sasha my fears about driving the Jeep, he tried getting me to drive it. So we went out on a supposed road more like a rocky path. Sasha had the Jeep in 4-wheel high when the Jeep started jumping and bouncing, and I hyperventilated and had a panic attack.

I screamed, "WHAT ARE YOU DOING?" My breathing was erratic and frantic.

Sasha slapped my leg and told me, "STOP!"

It was the catalyst I needed to take a deep breath.

He stopped the Jeep and explained, "The Jeep has a carburetor and was going through those options because there might not be enough gas. Sorry, I should have put it into four low and gone slower, but I thought we were having fun."

"NO, I am not having fun. I AM SCARED. I thought we were going to roll off the cliff." I said this to him as I started to calm down.

We went back to the campsite, slower. This irrational fear of the Jeep and my incapable ideal vision between Sasha and me continued into February. I did not drive the Jeep, even when we went on hikes. We continued to do longer and longer hikes; to lead people into gorgeous sceneries, such as Pinto Valley, of fantastic geology and historical signatures, a 9.12-mile through a wash—another of Tent Canyon, and six miles overland.

And then came **The Hike-Out, a Jeep MisAdventure**.

I do not know if this road was rated. It was called Bitter Springs Backcountry Byway, a 28-mile two-hour journey through the Muddy Mountains of Nevada. After two hours, my bleeping butt was red from the bumping, rocky road. There was no mud, only rocks left behind.

The road was near Valley of First State Park. But, the way Sasha read it, it was a way to bypass the state park and go from Lake Mead to the highway.

But NO.

Our Jeep started great, with a full tank of gas. We had our hiking sticks, hats, jackets, plenty of water, food, a first aid kit in our packs, and headlamps with batteries. But we wore sneakers. We both carried our wallets, even though I did not intend to drive.

We had turned off the pavement onto this four-wheel drive road, and for a while, it was fine, just slow. There was no mud, of course, as there rarely is in the desert, and instead, there were twists and turns and rocks! Nothing huge; it was rocky and jarring. We got a workout trying to stay still.

We went through an extremely rough patch of the road when the alternator had problems. First, the battery went low, and then the starter stopped working. As a result, we could not get up a hill. Instead, we stalled out. I do not know how these things go bad all at once. It looked as though we were almost out of gas!

Considering we had started around 3 pm, and it was 6:30 pm when this happened, I knew this would be a long day. We were on the road. But I was upset and primarily angry at the Jeep, which I thought was evil for doing this to us. Of course, I was mad at Sasha as well.

Sasha saw lights on the paved road, two sets. We were still on the dirt road, so we pushed onto the pavement. I stuck out my thumb.

And they drove past us.

Sasha said, "Well, if we had been them, would we have driven past too?" I guess, but I did not know.

I was discouraged. I figured it was another two to three miles, and I was tired. It was snowing, with a pebble or two in my worn-out sneakers with a hole. And then...

We saw headlights coming towards us. A truck slowed down. A guy asked if we needed a ride. And he was the same guy who blew past us 15 minutes before!

He said, "I was having problems with my truck, and I got my friend from St. George, Utah, to come out and help me." So he played the favor forward and got us to the travel center.

Sasha asked around. No one could help us on a Sunday night, but the manager would return in the morning. We got something to eat and drink, and they said we could stay in the traveler's lounge. So we put our hats over our eyes and went to sleep after seeing the Grammys.

It was hard to sleep. I had an interview the next afternoon and a project due by the end of business Sunday. So it was going to be late. I woke up before sunrise, found a book, and started reading. Sasha woke up around 7 am. He tried calling towing companies, who said it would cost more because it was a 4x4 road. Around 8 am, we were eating breakfast when the manager came over. He said he would check around.

He found Eric, a great man who would take his non-4x4 truck to our Jeep and connect his battery to ours. It gave enough charge but still would not start.

We pushed it up the hill. Sasha hopped into the Jeep, popped the clutch, and Eric and I pushed it down. It started!

Sasha had to turn the Jeep around and back up the hill to drive it out. Eric and I followed him. There were still a few tricky places, but Sasha kept the engine going the entire time.

When we got to the travel center, Sasha kept the engine running while I gave Eric money for getting us out. We filled the Jeep with gas, aired the tires, and returned to the rig at noon.

I set up to do the interview, sent out the project and returned dead tired. Do you know the weary, the twitchy kind that does not allow you to sleep?

We put the Jeep up on Craigslist the next day. We were able to sell the Jeep in a week.

February expenses: $2,784.05 and bye, bye Jeep.

Chapter 79

Traveling Across New Lands

The past year I bought some great corporate and municipal bonds at a loss but with great returns. So I went on a buying spree with them, using the same money repeatedly for higher returns. You buy, hold, get the money back and do it again. I did this through Zions Direct; they had at a time when you did not need a broker to transact the deals. Instead, you bid on a bond; if you were lucky or foolish, you won and paid. So by using the same $1000 or $5000 repeatedly that year, I received great returns. But I did not think of the tax implications.

We had H&R Block go over our taxes for 2012. We worried about paying taxes, either the federal or the two-state income taxes of Arizona and Utah, but it turned out not. She did an excellent job. We would only have to pay a little to the federal, nothing like before.

Our last hike at Lake Mead was on March 31, 2013. I consistently tried to find a job throughout the winter months but not even a nibble. I had a few interviews, but when they asked to see my exit interview from Lisa, they would not return my calls.

We were both disappointed that I had not secured a federal job, and we searched for another workamping job instead. I found one very quickly, and Sasha and I would be heading to Wisconsin to do gardening and landscaping in Jelly Bear Park.

It looked like Sequestration would happen. The budget cuts of 2013 were hitting the national parks, and having experience was not enough. Most of the parks I applied to were given two lists: those with veterans or spouses of veterans and everyone else.

If you did not have a full-time NPS job or a job where you went on leave for a couple of months, your job was up for grabs. Hiring officials would first ask every veteran on their list if they wanted the job. Then, they had to wait until they got an answer. If no veterans nor the spouses of veterans wanted it, then the most qualified previous park rangers got called. This pushed the job hiring process further into the season. If you were offered a job, you had better be nearby. Plus, you could not be in a remote area if you got a call or an email.

We left Lake Mead and went to Arizona, boondocking near National Parks. Sasha finally got to see Petrified Forest National Park in Arizona, and we took a hike. We saw Painted Desert. From there, we went into Albuquerque, New Mexico, and stopped at our favorite BBQ place, Rudy's.

On April 10, 2013, I got a call from Kristie of the US Forest Service, Mount St. Helens National Volcanic Monument, offering me a job. She had hired a veteran and wanted a ranger with a geology degree. I asked about living spaces, and she stated that Sasha could volunteer or work, whichever would allow us to be together. That was the clincher because she said we would be in shared housing. We were ok with it. How hard could it be?

We were in New Mexico and had to find a place to FAX the paperwork to them. We found a Choice Inn and used their printer and fax machines to get the paperwork out immediately. I would start working on April 23 for two weeks of training; April 21 was the move-in day!

March expenses: $3,561.44.

Chapter 80

Becoming a Forest Ranger

We rushed from New Mexico to Mount St. Helens at Johnston Ridge in Washington. We saw friends and hiked and boondocked along the way near Canyonlands National Park. A great dinner and caught up with Alice (my co-worker from Canyonlands) and her wife. She said she now worked at Arches National Park, doing Night Sky Programs! WOW! I told her congratulations and to let me know if she ever needed help.

Then we moved north to Green River and up in elevation to Midway, Utah. We had a late dinner with our friends Todd and Kimmy. It was great to catch up with them.

From there, we got to Jerome, Idaho, on April 16. We only had five more days to get to Kelso, Washington. We were starting to see more water, lakes, and reservoirs. We hoped to see Hagerman Fossil Beds National Monument, but the visitor center was closed on Tuesdays and Wednesdays. They did not have enough people to work throughout the week.

By April 20, we were 300 miles from our destination. We knew that as we entered the monument, we would lose internet and cell phone service. The only place with services was at work.

This job site was a new, different, remote work experience.

We lost internet and cell phone service as we went toward Johnston's Observatory. We did not know when service loss would occur on the mountain. Our shared housing had a phone, but we could only get calls in and needed a calling card to get calls out. It was as though we stepped back in time.

We went to the Science and Learning Center at Coldwater to see if anyone was there. We were supposed to meet Erik. We backed the RV in front of the house we would be staying at. We would not live in it but get everything out. There was a large living room, kitchen, deck, and dining room, with two bedrooms and one bathroom. Lovely. I would share this bathroom with three men. Two I did not know. Great.

We met the two men, Grady and Doug. Doug was the veteran Kristie had mentioned during my interview. We figured out where everything would go, as we had two refrigerators.

On the first day of work, April 23, we had training, and Sasha also went. So we had two weeks of training together. The training was on the geology and ecology of the monument, and we went on hikes. Sasha and I were gasping; they went up in elevations of thousand feet an hour, a fast pace for us. It was also very soggy, and we were not used to it.

By April 28, we had a day off and slept in. Then, we went to Vancouver for our weekend, found a place to stay, surfed the bandwidth, and let everyone know we were alive. By April 30, we returned and discovered that Sasha could work at Discover Your Northwest, the Association. He got a higher pay rate than expected, and we hoped to save more.

On May 1, we were still in training, learning about driving on the roads. We would go up to the observatory each day with the group, using the governmental Suburbans to go up, and we had to be by the vehicles at 8 am. We learned first aid, CPR, and wilderness first aid, as it would take over two hours to get to civilization.

Plus, we got to see Ape Cave, lava tubes, and more. However, I am not a fan of caves. Even though we had lanterns and lights, caves are creepy to me. While there is no way of getting lost, I am afraid of hitting my head.

Working for the Forest Service is different than the Park Service. In the Park Service, you buy your uniform; in the Forest Service, you borrow your clothes. Park has flat hats; Forest has ball caps. The Park Association sells items, but there is more cooperation between the Forest Service and their Association.

Plus, the Institute collects the fees for people coming into the Observatory, along with one of the Forest Service rangers. We had large numbers of school groups coming to the monument, more than I ever had at any park. So I created one program for school groups about the Building of a Volcano.

We would head into the season hoping to spend less while making more.

April expenses: $3,445.22

May expenses: $1,328.09.

Chapter 81

Internet Land and PTSD

We went to Portland, Oregon, during my first four-day weekend, again, something I never had with the NPS. Kristie had the entire season figured out, which amazed me. We knew precisely what days I had off, even months in advance. I thought this was perfect. When we talked to both Moms on Mother's Day, I figured out when my parents could visit. We decided on August with my two 4-day weekends almost back to back.

My first school program was on May 21, but before that, I learned about going down to the buses with other rangers and talking about the rules of the observatory. The kids liked the program, moved clay around the mountain, and asked questions. I even had a few come up, and thank me afterward!

We were getting close to the Memorial Weekend with a rainy season. Then on May 22, we had snow that was washed away soon afterward. So Sasha and I explored for two days before the holiday weekend. It was nice to go down to "Internet Land," as we called it, and eat out.

We were back on Memorial weekend. Sasha and I worked together and were thrilled by the people at the Monument. We were busy at the fees and information desk. I was at the fees booth most of the time, except for my two programs. Each one had between 50 to 60 people, way more than in National Park programs.

It was a great experience as we were unhappy in our home life. Living with a veteran who was divorced and a misogynist does not make living fun. He was chasing after some SCA students who were half his age. Or he was taking over an hour in the bathroom, which left little time for the rest of us. Grady was an SCA, Sasha an Association worker, but Doug and I were rangers who had to be at the vehicles at 8 am. He would watch TV until late, which is why we got earplugs, and then spend the early morning in the bathroom. And when he left the bathroom, it was a mess.

Finally, Sasha talked to him. I could not. He made my first month a living hell. I did yoga and meditation whenever possible, as my therapist had told me. He felt he deserved this job because he had tours in Afghanistan and could hike and walk faster than almost anyone except for Grady.

He said he had PTSD, but I think he was an entitled hater of women. While Sasha was right there, he told me that I should not have this job or should I be living in this house. He did not think it was appropriate for a woman to be a geologist, a ranger, or anything else work-related.

In the end, we found out on Memorial Day he got a full-time, higher-grade position in the Forest Service as a wilderness ranger. Perfect for him, as he hardly needed to talk to people about interpretation, but it would stink, too, as we would lose a ranger on the schedule. They might get an emergency hire. We were already down one person because of Sequestration. I hoped it would not mess up my plans as my parents had bought their plane tickets.

Because of that meanie, we would go away every weekend we could, leaving on our Saturday and coming back late on Sunday, to get away from him. I was so happy to escape the living conditions my frugality went out the window.

We took to Portland and stayed at a hotel within walking distance of everything. It is a great town, getting better with age. There are places to eat, with happy hour foods and crazy, fun things to see. I love the art that is everywhere, and Sasha loves the funkiness. We saw a person wearing a toga, and he said a parade was happening later that night. No real reason to have a parade. They just have them.

Even though Doug had left, he bad-mouthed Sasha to some of the younger women he pursued, and they formed a cliche against Sasha. So we went searching for something different. It would cost us, though.

June expenses: $2,314.01.

Chapter 82
We Work to Play

On July 1, we moved our rig down to Brookhollow RV Park, but we called it Internet Land. We paid monthly and got the internet for free. It is a quiet park with 150 spots. We met some folks down there, but we mostly kept to ourselves. When you talk to hundreds of people daily, you must retreat and play on your days off. On my days off, I was happiest listening to the birds, playing online games, listening to music, and being with Sasha.

We would Work To Play, a phrase I learned in Oregon. You worked to enjoy your weekends and activities. Since we worked and hiked, we stayed put on our days off, except when we went berry picking. We would get two large buckets of blueberries in July, 15 pounds worth. After we got back up the mountain, we would freeze the berries.

We also went to county fairs, and these were quite large. Some 4-H kids take care of pigs, sheep, and goats. I had to get my fill of goats, petting them as much as possible. They were fun to watch.

Before my parents came out, Sasha and I had been hiking for work. I did an interpretive hike, and he volunteered to hike. As a volunteer, he tries to meet folks and offer advice or directions on the trail.

With my hikes, I did not take pictures of people but took pictures of flowers. I loved zooming in as much as possible to see the intricacies of the flower parts. The visitor center is visually appealing and has so much to offer. This is why there are fees, to help pay for the cost of the building and to pay for our salaries.

My parents came to visit from August 24 through September 3. I loved how they tried to go everywhere I worked, even in the odd years. We picked them up at Portland, Oregon airport and brought them to Homewood Suites, which had a great breakfast and lovely bedrooms.

The first night we went down to the docks. People had homes on the canals and river, and they had it looking like Miami or South Beach, with neon and bright colors of their painted homes. After yummy food and the steep gangplank back up, we went back full and tired. My parents got a modified SUV to come up to the monument while we were working.

I led a guided hike with my parents and 20 people. I had my hiking poles and my backpack, which matched my green and light gray uniform. For borrowed clothes, they looked good on me.

Another talk with my parents was the Crater Talk, where I dub everyone geologists for 20 minutes. I talk about how Mount St. Helens was doomed from the beginning because of lousy construction. We played a game with clay, learned about rocks, and then blew up the mountain.

My parents left after the second program to get down before dark. The road is a long way down. While they were visiting, we had to work for four days.

The next day they would participate in two more programs: The 1980 Eruption and Life Returns. The 1980 Eruption was my best program; it is accurate, raw, and emotional. One of the goals or objectives of the program is to make a person cry or wipe their eyes. Every time I talk, I get emotional. I wanted my audience to feel the terror, excitement, fear, and loss of life felt in the community. I gave my audience speaking roles and short and powerful words. When my parents came to the program, I had Dad read one speaking part, and Mom took pictures. I managed to get Dad to shed a tear or two.

They would go to the second program about life returning, a fun program I did with string. I showed how animals and plants interconnect in the web of life. I asked Mom and Dad to wait until we finished work to come to housing with us so they could see it. Sasha made dinner for us then my parents drove back down.

Their last hike on the mountain was with Sasha, where they would go five miles downhill. Again, they saw incredible sights, including a rare herd of elks running in the distance. After that, they went back to housing together; he made lunch, and they took naps.

We showed Mom and Dad Windy Ridge and the Smokey Bear statue, the Forest Service's mascot. We saw falls and flowers, lakes and reservoirs. The many steps as we climbed Windy Ridge. With these spots, whether hiking or driving, are many beautiful vistas to stop and get your fill of colors. It was a long day full of adventure, sights, and smells.

When we had enough of nature, we headed to Portland.

All of us revisited Portland. We saw but did not try the bicycling bar. There was art galore, and every corner had a coffee shop. Plus, the iconic Powell Books, we had to go in there. Go to this bookstore and get lost in the stacks. We got happy hour food at a tavern with beers and ciders and returned to the hotel comfortably.

On September 1, we went to Frank Lloyd Wright's building. It was neat to see, with built-in bookcases and sliding doors similar to what you see in an RV—each day seemed like a hurry up to adventure because we would not see each other for a year. It was bittersweet when it ended, on September 4, after a relaxing day. A sad sort of goodbye, we decided to make plans for 2014. We would go back in the fall of 2014 to ease the goodbye. Finally, we had something to look forward to next year.

In 2013, I applied to over 150 jobs, and the Forest Service was the only one that offered me a job. So after four and a half seasons of paid employment, five seasons of volunteering, and a BS degree in geology, it was a no-go with the NPS. Life was uncertain.

July expenses: $2,420.73

August expenses: $2,176.77.

Chapter 83

Government Shut Down

At the end of September, around the equinox, we started to see the frogs. They were tiny frogs but an essential part of the ecosystem. Like other frogs, they keep the insect population down and tell you of seasonal change.

Even though October 2013 was my birthday and our anniversary month, it was a sad month for me. It was just another nail in the coffin for an NPS or a Forest Service job for next year. We were put on furlough for sixteen days.

Before we were furloughed, I knew it would happen before my peers saw it. Or they said it would only last a day or two. Not a week, surely not! We were somewhat prepared.

But. Still. NOT.

My emotions were running high, even with good medicine, meditation, and yoga. People gave NPS rangers, the seasonals especially, a hard time. People had rallied outside National Parks, stepping over fences, taking down signs, and yelling at Park Rangers who were just there doing what Congress could not do, trying to work together. No NPS Park Ranger wanted a furlough. They wanted to protect the resources. At least the Forest Service, which is the Department of Agriculture, did not get as many disgusting comments or attitudes.

Most Forest Service Rangers were off fighting forest fires, and they were considered essential. The Law Enforcement rangers were necessary workers. Those in interpretation were not.

Some said that the federal government should go into default. For those that depend on national government services like social security, veteran's aid, Medicare, Medicaid, and Treasury Bonds, this sounded insane. Everything was already bought but not paid for. The federal government's expenses were not things they could bring back to a store for a refund. It does not work that way.

The expenses at the end of each chapter are bills we paid. If we did not pay them, collection agencies would come, and our credit rating would spiral downwards.

My emotions ran high enough that I said, screw it, no more being on social media for a while. I would not watch the news; I would read books, play games, and only go back online for my birthday and anniversary. So finally, after a week of weirdness, we decided to do something productive.

We did over 20 different chores on the rig during the furlough. One of the biggest chores was cleaning the roof. After that, we planned for boondocking over the winter. I organized the closets, cabinets, and shelves and knew exactly how much stuff we had in the rig.

We found leaks, fixed them, designed a closet system in the garage, and backed up our electronics and website. I cleaned every little nook and cranny in the RV.

We went to housing to bring everything to the rig as we had heard of thefts in NPS sites. As we went, I started taking pictures. It had snowed on Mount St. Helens, and the mountain had her winter coat. Coldwater Lake was closed and had a gate across it. Thankfully, there was no trash or anything else there. There were hikers, and we saw cars, but no mess. Many were solemn about coming here like they knew it was not the same. I hoped that was the case.

After I saw the mountain, I felt better. I knew we would go off and have adventures, go apple picking and festival hopping, and go to Portland again. People respected the Monument, what it stood for, and by admission, for myself and what park rangers do. So we left and had fun. We came back to work on October 18 for one week. I had brought only uniform clothing with just one pair of jeans and street clothes for the return back. We left the Monument on October 24, having timed it perfectly for the amount of food and clothing. We cleaned up our housing area and work areas.

September expenses: $1,744.22

October expenses: $2,888.55

Note: we were both furloughed as Sasha cannot work if the rangers are not working. Something most do not realize when the federal government goes into furlough.

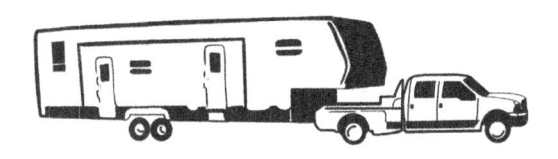

Chapter 84
Into The Desert to Renew

After the furlough, I still felt the effects of a government shutdown with the conference for the National Association of Interpreters. I should have known better but did not. Less than half of the one thousand people who signed up attended the networking event. Nevertheless, I buckled down and made the most of it.

I went to every seminar or workshop, got my name into every person's hands, and made the most of the dire situation. We also stayed in the same campground as what Amazon workers stay in at Fenley, Nevada—a campground 35 miles away from the facility. The new owners ripped out the trees and grass and made it into parking lots. I called the campground Slot Canyon as there was nothing to look at but another RV.

After that experience, we boondocked near a lake before heading to another campground experience. This time we would meet friends we had only known through Facebook, Stephen, Joanne, and their three children. We "met" in 2012 and face-to-face met in 2013.

Do you ever feel like this? You meet someone new for the first time, and you click? We felt that way with them. They have three kids that Joanne homeschools, and she did a great job.

Sasha and Stephen took an epic ride through Titus Canyon in Death Valley while I had fun with Joanne and the kids. We were so happy to finally meet them and spent as much time as we could.

From there, we headed south to meet with Sasha's family and stow the rig at the Clark County Shooting Range. When we went to the campground in November, it was empty. The sites were huge, 100 feet long with 50 amp service, and you could stay as long as you like. So we thought this campground was the best place to stow it. We could plug it in, recharge the batteries, keep the food cold, and it was safe as the campground was a gated community.

This year we decided to be in Las Vegas rather than Lake Mead. We had given Lake Mead four winter seasons, and that was enough. So this year, besides the parents, Yvonne and Kristina joined us. We got a two-bedroom suite at Homewood Suites in Henderson, Nevada. It was perfect for the four of us and two more during the weekend. We saw the show: LOVE, a Cirque du Soleil and Beatles tribute, which worked very well for us. The parents stayed for a week, and we enjoyed being together, eating out, and having great conversations.

Afterward, we went to the rig and did our epic and most extended time-lapsed video of *Taking the Graphics Off the Rig*. It took us ten days to do it. By doing this video, our views and money from Google Adsense skyrocketed from 2013 to 2017. We took off the graphics that were peeling off. Then we cleaned, waxed, sealed, vacuumed, and organized the rig the first weeks of December.

By December 15, we headed to boondocking nirvana, Searchlight, Nevada, and beyond, to Quartzsite, Arizona.

We got our permit to be on BLM lands called Long Term Visitor Areas (LTVA) of Quartzsite (Q) and Imperial Dam. While Q is where the action is, Imperial Dam is where the water is. They have more dump stations and water facilities. And they are closer to a large city, Yuma, and Mexico.

On December 19, 2013, I found several ways to make money while we figured out what to do. First, I started writing for websites: HubPages, BlogMutt (now Verblio), Amazon Mechanical Turk, and Bubblews, a social media site for writers. You write short articles and get paid for every click, view, or like.

We found a great place to boondock and went for 17 days without having to dump the tanks. We rode to farmer's markets, date farms, and solar cooking dinners. We found a community both online and offline in the desert.

I would end this year by getting myself mentally healthy for my next job. We found a job that would last four summer seasons using our old standby, Workamper News. And become even closer to Sasha than ever before.

November expenses: $3,078.90

December expenses: $2,203.89

In 2013, we spent barely over $30,425 and saved money again by 22 percent.

Chapter 85

Living In the Desert

The Story of Bubblews and Blogmutt: both websites enticed me to write for them, but they did not make us much money. We did not live as cheaply as I had hoped. I started writing for Bubblews in December 2013 and continued throughout the winter into mid-spring 2014, when I stopped. I always got paid for my work, but it was a time drain.

Our website languished again. Bubblews was a social media site for writers who could write short stories, articles, and posts about anything they wanted. Writers made the most when discussing how to make money on Bubblews. The other aspect was the social end. I became friends with people I followed and followed back. We liked and commented on each others' posts.

The time there was spent on posts which I equated to more money. Sharing posts on other social media sites, such as Google+ and Facebook, was encouraged. The time drain was real, and I was on it most afternoons. I could immerse myself yet still be outside.

We were in the desert to enjoy ourselves. While I wrote about frugality, cooking with a solar oven, and exercising in the desert, we became part of a community.

One of the thrills of living in Imperial Dam LTVA was the independence and co-dependence of the community. For example, there was "Liberrty," a lending library where you could drop off a book and pick one up. It was in a travel trailer that someone stored during the summer and brought back in the winter.

The "season" in Imperial Dam was either September or October through February or March. Those that stayed until April were pushing their luck with hotter weather. The permits from the BLM were good for five months of the year for $180 a season. So you could come back year after year and go to roughly the same spot to see your friends.

We felt like interlopers, being younger than most yet having the motivation and drive to experience something different. We went 17 days without moving our rig to dump the black tank. How we did, it still eludes me to this day. But Sasha marked his area well.

I would get up early and exercise with an Army guy who held an aerobic class at 8 am daily. Another type followed, a yoga class at 9 am. The friendliness of the two classes helped me focus on the day ahead.

We became friends with a few people in the desert and one couple in particular. They took us under their wing and showed us how to cook using a solar oven. They had ten different gadgets used to create, cook, and wash their midday meal. One of the most ingenious was the turntable.

The turntable was set on a 12-hour timer and would move every hour the same way as the sun moved across the sky. This gadget would hold their main dish for the meal. They also had glass water jugs painted black and filled with water. They used them to mix with cold water and wash their dishes. I learned so much from them about frugality and cooking in the desert.

We got news from Washington that my old job was available but without housing. I needed to drive up with Kristie for every day I worked. I declined the position.

Instead, we returned to our trusty Workamper News to find a job. We quickly revamped our combined resume and found one with Yellowstone Nature Connection (YNC). It was an outdoor education center geared towards children learning about forest fires and the people who fought them.

We would still have one more month of fun before heading north to West Yellowstone, Montana, to work the day after Mother's Day. After that, we went to Nevada and Colorado to sell our motorcycles. And we would buy an adventure vehicle.

January expenses: $1,668.50
February expenses: $1,667.66
March expenses: $4,489.60

Chapter 86

Our Adventure Vehicle

We took some mountainous passes with full water tanks as we headed out of Imperial Dam in late March. We emptied the gray and black and refilled the water into every possible container. We knew we needed to take it slow on some inclines going up, usually at 35 miles per hour. So like the 18-wheeled trucks, we put on our blinkers and slowly descended the passes. But in Gila, Arizona, we experienced a hill pass that made us go even slower, down to five mph. In addition, the transmission on our truck was hurting on these hills.

We managed, slowly, to make it to Las Vegas and Clark County Shooting Range. We immediately booked a campground stay and called Diesel Underground. They were able to get to us to rebuild our transmission.

I had sold my scooter at the end of March in preparation for our adventure vehicle, a Ural Sidecar Motorcycle. So we went to San Diego, California, to test drive one. We saw the beach, rode the bike, and Sasha got them to let him test drive it with me in the sidecar.

My first time flying the chair, I was petrified when the sidecar went up in the air when making a right turn. However, I soon got used to this feeling of riding low. The bike was unique, with only 2,500 sold yearly in the US.

In early April, Sasha sold his dual sport motorcycle, and then we sold the motorcycle ramps we used for the truck. The Ural would go further than my scooter ever could. And it came with an external gas tank in case we ran out of gas.

Three weeks into April, the tranny was fixed, and we were good to go. We headed to Fort Collins, Colorado, as our Ural Sidecar Motorcycle was shipped from Russia (now Kazakhstan) through the US on two large crates. The dealer in Fort Collins would take those crates and start building the Ural Sidecar. We wanted to be there to watch the process.

Sasha was especially interested in watching the build. It was a very different bike. Certain parts would be easy to find. Any car shop had the filters for oil changes and other pieces.

The dealer and his wife allowed us to stay on their property while the build was ongoing. Along the way, we met friends in Fort Collins. We swam for several days at his old college; there was a pool with a climbing gym, showers, and a great lounge. Finally, we felt refreshed to head to Montana. This was good as the temperatures in West Yellowstone went below freezing.

When we arrived at our spot for the season, we were worried. Mark, our landlord, did not realize how large our rig was nor how much room we needed to get into the spot. Having a fifth wheel with the truck meant our length was 56 feet long. As a result, we required 112 feet to maneuver, yet piles of snow, some higher than our 13-and-a-half-foot tall rig, were on either side of our spot.

In front of the spot was a mound of snow and ice. Mark had a bobcat and dug, pushed, and gave us enough room. Sasha straightened the rig. He gunned the engine. The rear-wheel drive rig moved over the icy patch and shoehorned into the spot without hitting me or either fence on the first try!

By June, my Bubblews articles were no more, as a glitch in the system only allowed one picture, and the rest were wiped away. However, I saved the essays in Word documents for future use. And we had other work to do, including learning a new program and promoting YNC.

April expenses: $21,260.96

May expenses: $2,272.44

June expenses: $1,683.98

Chapter 87

Who Is YNC?

We went to the Chamber of Commerce (the Chamber) and Visitor Center when we went into West Yellowstone. There was a National Park Service portion and the Chamber portion of the building. I still remember going over to the park ranger on duty and asking them where Yellowstone Nature Connection was located. And they, in turn, gave us blank looks. They had no clue!

We went over to the Chamber and asked them. The first person we met was a huge proponent of forming the nonprofit Mary Sue. She showed us the building across the parking lot and said, "Welcome to West Yellowstone!" Her warm welcome made us feel good, especially after the response from the ranger.

We started the season in May, with a cold beginning as spring had not come close to Montana. School groups visited at the end of May and June, and Sasha and I would meet Amy, our boss, and Joel, our intern. Sasha and I would work Sunday through Thursday, eight-hour days, and each got paid $10 an hour.

While I got a decrease in the hourly rate, Sasha got an increase. They would pay for our RV spot. But after talking with the Board of Directors (Barry, Sandy, Mark P, and Rick), we asked to pay for our camp spot as there was less paperwork and taxes. We were paid $13 an hour; Amy, our boss, would make $14. As the season continued, Amy, Sasha, and I worked very hard at the promotion and marketing of the organization. We put up signage that was sure to stand out and be noticed. We became a great team, working together.

Amy was a kindergarten teacher. She worked hard to get those children prepared for the first grade. She had the patience to work with the children, and they loved her in return.

She would spend part of her time reading to the kids at the library and then come over to YNC on Thursdays to figure out the week with us. One of the ways we could promote YNC was through the Fourth of July parade. She picked one of the best students she had, a girl who could fit in the sidecar of our motorcycle, put on the smokejumper outfit, and ride in the parade. Sasha would drive while Amy, Joel, and I threw Fire Balls and cinnamon candy.

We were the hit of the town and won third place. The townsfolk were so used to the name National Smokejumper Center, the name YNC was before, that seeing us in orange, yellow, and green was utterly different.

We would continue to do events that summer, including contacting the marketing department of Disney for coloring pages for the *Planes: Fire & Rescue* movie. That allowed us to bring out a few real smokejumpers who jump out of planes to fight wildfires. The Junior Smokejumper program started with retired smokejumpers coming together to teach children about the outdoors, exercise, and nature in a fun and safe environment.

Each child would get a goodie bag, and we would get their email address to send pictures. In addition, they got an activity book, crayons or pens, and coloring pages. I brought educational books, puppets, Fire and Rescue figures, and other items. That way, children could buy small tokens to remember their adventures.

Because the building had a look of olden times, our sidecar motorcycle fit right in. Whenever we would go to the store or for a ride, I would wear my NPS jacket (without the patches) of the same army green as the matte color of the bike. Of course, with my helmet overwhelmed by pink, glittery butterflies, and an unusual motorcycle, we stood out.

We told our parents we would be back in 2014, and we bought airline tickets in August to fly east in the fall. But first, we had another adventure waiting after Yellowstone.

July expenses: $1,924.04

August expenses: $2,629.17

September expenses: $1,433.76

Chapter 88
Dipping Our Toes in Real Estate

When we sold the house and everything in it in May 2007, I put over $100,000 into seven-year CDs. They earned over 5 percent then and accrued interest that compounded (rolled over and snowballed) into more savings. We were compounding and saving money for our retirement at a later date. However, most of those CDs came due in 2014, and the interest rates were horrible at the banks and credit unions. Even our old standby, ING/CapitalOne, had dismal savings and interest rates. I was trying to figure out what to do when an opportunity hit us squarely in the face.

We left YNC on a high note at the end of September. We celebrated Smokey Bear's birthday on the campus, with smokejumpers coming out, fire trucks, and pictures with Smokey Bear.

After that season, we went south to Moab, Utah, our old stomping grounds. Typically, we boondock somewhere, but we hoped to get with a group of people doing a Ural rally. Unfortunately, we missed the rally but stayed in a campground called Portal RV Resort.

This campground had two parts: one regular side with gravel spots and one side for large rigs or small casitas with a pool. The beautiful RV lot with 200 amps service, 240 feet long, and twenty feet wide pink concrete slab was on sale for around $100,000. We did not take too long to think about it.

We could rent out the spot, and as long as it earned us four percent net, I was happy. The campground owners would take care of everything, and their service meant a 40-60 split. It still seems high even now.

We had been looking for other rental spaces. We checked out Yuma and other southern Arizona places, but their season might be six months. There are very few places in the US where it is temperate AND where RVers want to go. Texas was not warm enough, and Florida was prone to hurricanes and other natural disasters. Utah is an outdoor haven, and Moab has three seasons. We had liquid cash, which would be the best way to use it.

Once we decided, we went through the paperwork and became owners of an RV lot. From there, we drove back to Las Vegas and stored our RV. Then, we flew to the East Coast. Mom and Dad J were going up to Atlantic City, New Jersey, for the Ms. Senior America Pageant. Mom had won the Ms. Senior Virginia pageant in 2003, and she regularly went with Dad to Atlantic City to celebrate and socialize. So this time we would go with them.

I never went to Atlantic City. The beaches were large and deep, as well as the boardwalk, but it was off-season. It did not matter as we had a great time with them.

When we headed home, I suggested we go to a diner. You typically can get anything at a New Jersey diner, and I wanted the parents to experience it.

I remember Dad's order with perfection. He wanted a salad but "hold the lettuce." Just tomatoes and onions, please. And then, he'd have the lobster tails! These were the most expensive items on the menu. After that, there was so much fawning over him. I doubt they ever sold an order like that. So my plan of showing an NJ diner was either a success or something else. But Sasha and Mom still recall that event even now.

We also visited Williamsburg to see my parents and took a trip to Corolla, North Carolina. We spent time with both families and even had a small Capuano reunion in Florida. We would stay until Orthodox Christmas, January 7, 2015, and then fly back. I would change my spreadsheets for the new year, as buying that lot now needed a new line item. I could hardly wait.

October expenses (excluding the lot): $3,744.74

November expenses: $2,218.11

December expenses: $838.08

Expenses of 2014: $45,832.12. We went into savings to buy the Ural.

Chapter 89

Winter Work First Time Ever

Yellowstone Nature Connection asked me to work on grants in the winter. So during the fall and winter, I worked and volunteered my time. However, I did not want to charge them while I learned. So I waited to bill them for the fall and winter in January. Otherwise, our income would put us into another tax bracket.

I paid for the ability to see grants through a Foundation Center database. I could do searches for Montana or outdoor education programs. Going small was best, and I received two grants that year: A Reading in the Garden of $1000 and $500 from Miracle Grow. Our push this year for YNC would be to get local and visiting children to listen to stories read outdoors and give them books to keep.

January 2015, I worked like never before, trying to find larger grants to get our other project and program, The Fire Naturalist, off the ground. If we created a native plant garden and got a few objects like plastic scat and footprints, we could show what creatures lived in Yellowstone. Amy and I developed this program in 2014. We incorporated fire ecology and looked at the natural world through young adult eyes.

But Sasha was restless and wanted to go back down to Arizona. I could hardly blame him. We now had the perfect rig for boondocking: a white RV with a white truck, and a get-around vehicle, our Ural sidecar motorcycle. It fit into the garage, with only minor worries of hitting me when driven up the ramp.

We would place the wheel chock on the floor. Then, he had to align the motorcycle perfectly, speed up the ramp, and fit the front wheel into the chock. Easy peasy, right? No, not really. Sometimes the bike was cold and easing the motorcycle, which had reverse, back down the ramp.

Ultimately, it got easier. We headed to Hi Jolly, Quartzsite (Q), Arizona, in February. We checked out some of the Q shows and tried our hand at boondocking for two weeks.

We wanted to go to Mexico for my prescription and medication this time. It was not covered through health insurance. I needed a yearly supply, not a ridiculous one of 30 days. Not only that, the medications would go to Texas and then to me.

Instead, we went to Mexico with another couple to go to the dentist. You park your car in a secure area, on a Native American parking lot, pay the $10 or so for the day, and then walk in. Hundreds of other people from the US and Canada do the same thing every day. People are hawking their businesses, the American-trained dentists, the pharmacies, and eyeglass businesses.

What I liked most was that there was no upselling at the dentist. Usually, going to a dentist means you have to pay more than quoted. They wanted to extract more money. In Mexico, that was not the case. They cleaned your teeth, you paid, and you left. You did not get a new toothbrush or an appointment to come back. You paid cash, and that was it.

The same was true for my prescription. I found the perfect pharmacy that had the best price for 200 pills. I cut those pills in half, and each bottle lasted a year or more. The pills cost $50, giving me peace of mind. I knew 2015 became more manageable with the medications.

In March, we went to Joshua Tree National Park and boondocked to the south of the park. We were on BLM land and had great views of the Joshua trees. It was perfect for us, with cool nights and sunny days to ride into the park or explore.

During the spring, I worked for YNC, figuring out how to do drawings. I researched more about children's books and nature studies.

We were going back earlier. YNC wanted us to be there in early May rather than waiting until May 13 for Bear Creek Days. This event happened for the children in grammar and middle schools in Gallatin County. They experience shortened programs by different organizations. We needed to get our stuff ready. The first school group was in May, and we needed to hit the ground running.

Once we returned, I became the Program Manager, while Sasha was the Senior Presenter, Amy the Director of Education, and Belle was our intern. The Board created my job title while the rest made up their names.

I tried to bring money in from other sources. I created The Fire Naturalist program to make a Native Plant Garden. I designed and maintained the social media, the website, and the enewsletter, and getting students and school groups to come to our Junior Smokejumper program. We would also start offering The Fire Naturalist program every day starting in June.

It was a pleasure driving to and from work with our Ural. We would get on our gear, navigate to the campus, and go about our day. Sasha made yummy lunches in the volunteer housing kitchen while I was in the store. Sasha used Adobe software to make the flyers and brochures, called rack cards, which you see in most visitor centers. I read or ordered products and created something for social media, the newsletter, or photographs to send to the schools.

We geared up for a larger school group who came to West Yellowstone. They would stay several days and participate in our programs: Junior Smokejumper, The Fire Naturalist, and my night sky program. They would be on campus on June 2, 2015.

After they came, we started to get even more schools visiting, and my parents said they would like to see us. They would be doing the Grand Tour of many national parks and wanted to visit. It would be a perfect time, September, and they would stay in the volunteer house.

And an organization called InterGenerational (Intergen) would come throughout the summer. So we changed the program with them. Before we worked there, the grandparents had their talk separately from the grandkids. So we decided to put them together and see how the interactions went. In a word, fabulous!

Learning about nature and science together helped make the class better than just learning with peers. Plus, everyone loved taking pictures of the kids, jumping out of the mock plane, and playing the parachute game. Some adults even mentioned doing that when they were in school.

By the time June 30 came around, we would be ready.

January expenses: $2,650.32

February expenses: $1,601.38

March expenses: $2,103.41

April expenses: $3,101.67

May expenses: $2,587.59

June expenses: $1,956.48

Chapter 90

Book Seller with Grants

July turned into an excellent adventure for us. Again, we started the month with a bang, the Fourth of July Parade, this time with a teddy bear the size of a large child in the sidecar seat, with a Yellowstone Nature Connection tee shirt on. We had large YNC signs with our logo on the front and back of the motorcycle and Sasha driving with a Smokejumper helmet. Amy, Belle, and I threw red hot cinnamon candies to the kids in the crowd, and everyone was happy. We won second place this time.

July is among the best times to visit West Yellowstone and Yellowstone National Park. The weather is perfect nearly every day, the lines are long to get into the park, and the town hustles to make money. Our grocery bills were ever-increasing because, like every resort town we lived in, they also had to make money.

I participated in a local woman's group called the United Women. They had lunch and learns every month, where you brought your lunch and learned about something about the area. It was a great networking event. I went each month to be a part of the community. At the same time, they welcomed me even if Sasha and I were seasonal. We cared about the organization and wanted it to be successful for the community.

In August, the weather turned. It was still summer, but the fires of the West had started. Most smokejumpers worked in Montana, Oregon, Washington, northern California, and a few in Alaska. Few people entered the store, and the schools were back in session. Intergen's last visit was the first week of August. I pleaded to the West Yellowstone public schools, where I held a book fair to sell books to grammar and middle school children.

September, the days flew by with some groups coming in each week. Sasha and I had the West Yellowstone book fair during the first week in September. We got a volunteer to help take pictures while Sasha did the programs. Both Belle and Amy returned to school. I saw between 25 to fifty children each day at the book fair and was able to sell many of the books. They remembered me from Reading in Nature over the summer and the events we held for them.

After that week, we had enough money to create the Native Plant Garden. Ten volunteers came to push soil, installed the brick wall, planted bushes, trees, and flowers, and gave their time. The entire Garden Club came out to lend a hand!

The following week my parents came out and helped as volunteers. The volunteer house still needed work, and the basement had three bedrooms and two baths which needed painting. Mom and Dad took to it enthusiastically. Dad loved using the wood tools, and Mom, with intense concentration, painted.

They stayed in the volunteer house, saw the programs we put on, and toured the area, which made us happy. They were on tour checking out this part of the West. They saw our excitement about working for the nonprofit and were thrilled when we told them we would be back east in 2016. They helped us with ideas for saving money in the fall and about our RV lot in Moab.

I found book shows in Utah and Arizona when given the OK to sell books during the winter season. There were three in rapid succession: Big Water, Utah, for a dinosaur festival. Page, Arizona, for their fall festival, and Moab, Utah, for their folk festival.

Sasha and I boondocked in most places between the festivals and fairs, except for the Moab folk festival, where we stayed in our RV spot. For the past six months, we received between $500 to $900 a month for our split of the rental fee. We felt fortunate to get rental income from a concrete pad.

We saw Bo in Utah. Then, we had fun in Huntington and Antelope Island. We toured the island, did some hiking, and got great photos of the artwork. In Huntington, Sasha and Bo took an all-day ride around the area with Bo in the sidecar.

We stayed two weeks in Moab, with only part of it at the folk festival. The rest of the time, we hiked in Arches National Park. We were excited when we could ride the motorcycle and go to Arches and hike. October is the best time to be there, and we took full advantage of our RV site to come and go.

We headed further south to Pahrump, Nevada. We had researched the area over the summer and found it a perfect place for full-time RVers. While we had mail service through Escapees in Livingston, Texas, we found our Affordable Care Act health insurance in Texas was going up in price.

We were not going to get more services. We were getting less as we did not go to Texas. If we got sick, we went to the emergency room and paid as though we were uninsured. Most often, we were in mountain or pacific time zones, nowhere near Texas. As we saw it, we paid $60 each month or $120 for both of us. If we stayed with Texas health insurance, it would be $600 for one of us or $1300 for the family plan. They did not have a couples plan.

We went with Nevada health plans. Their health insurance payments were much cheaper and went DOWN in price. We got the couple rate of $105 per month. However, we had to pay more to register a new motorcycle and an older model truck. We went through being domiciled in Nevada with new license plates, driver's licenses, and a new mail service. Nevada does not have a state income tax; they have a lower cost of living and no sales tax on food.

We stayed at Wine Ridge RV Resort and Cottages for two months because we liked the people and had fun. Most were older than us, and most were retired and traveling. They had card games, lunch get-togethers, and *Walked Away the Pounds* low-impact aerobics. Sasha and I ultimately got into this idea to work out. He was the only man there, but I loved that he exercised with me.

We headed south as the others did but waited until after the holidays, New Year, and Orthodox Christmas to connect with friends and family that year. We looked forward to more boondocking and checking out southern Arizona and California to see where the Ural could go.

July expenses: $1,499.02

August expenses: $1,700.31

September expenses: $1,008.22

October expenses: $2,348.05

November expenses: $5,954.24

December expenses: $1,851.04. Total Expenses for 2015: $25,099.26 with 21% savings.

Chapter 91

Following the Sun

We stayed in Pahrump a little longer in January 2016 to get the full benefit of a monthly stay. We headed to Salton Sea Beach at a casino before reaching our first destination, Borrego Springs, a dry lakebed. Borrego Springs was a great town, a feast for your eyes place. The city was arty, and the area surrounding it was perfect.

We saw perfect temperatures for sleeping with open windows and snuggling under down duvets. We spent days riding our Ural motorcycle and hiking to the springs or the metal art. The Galleta Meadows, LLC is a privately-owned desert estate allowing people to come onto their land to see this artwork. We saw dinosaurs, mythical beasts, shamans, desert tortoises, javelinas, and tigers in different spots, all rust-colored patina brown. Most were on concrete pads that must have weighed a ton.

We parked close to a road but not close to anyone this time. Most people did not know of the place. We went riding and saw an orange stand. They had it on an honor system, and we gladly dropped a few bucks to get sacks of oranges. The air smelled sweet, with oranges and grapefruit picked right from the trees.

I put my hummingbird feeder against the dinette window and opened the window. I never expected hummingbirds, but they came. Their wings moved so fast that I patiently waited for them to stop to drink or look around and then snap a picture or two.

We checked out the State Park, a swath of land with cuts in the dry lake bed that looked like a dinosaur swiped at the hills with claws. Inspired by rock art, we took pictures of ourselves as shadows during sunset, looking like shamans of old.

And then, we headed to the deepest of deserts, Desert Hot Springs, Palm Springs RVing cousin. This area has so many RV parks and resorts. But, unfortunately, we realized they run a bit of a racket.

How it worked was this. We pulled into a park without a reservation. We would only spend a night, charge our batteries, dump, and take on fresh water. They suggested we purchase Passport America and get the two-week discounted rate. Then you go out of the park for another week to a different resort (possibly discounted) and then come to this one for another two weeks with the discount.

We found out they had a heated pool fed by thermal springs. Plus, three hot tubs heated by springs of various temperatures. Oh boy, we were in heaven.

They had different classes and fun events every day. Burgers by the pool, chili cook-offs with prizes, ice cream socials, oh my! They did not rent by the month.

We decided we did not want to move from our spot, so we paid for two weeks at the discounted rate, one week at the non-discount rate, and another two weeks at the discounted rate. Yowza, but we had fun. It was the perfect time from February to mid-March. We got tan and met many Canadians and seniors who played water volleyball and aerobics. And we *Walked Away the Pounds*, too.

We went north again to Las Vegas and Clark County Shooting Range campground. We went from a quiet park of hummingbirds' wings to the constant bang, bang, bang of the shooting range. The shooting range was the perfect place to prepare for another season at YNC, where school groups came en masse.

I had broken down and bought a monthly Mead planner and FriXion erasable pens for the changes I knew would happen. I had gone from digital planning to paper because there was so much to put down. Also, it was easier to see the week in a paper planner. Little did I realize that this would spark my creativity and writing.

April was full of adventure for us, spending the entire month in Utah. We rode our Ural motorcycle into Zion, Capital Reef National Parks, and Goblin State Park. And this would be the year of the parks for sure. Not only were we going back to West Yellowstone and YNC for our third season, but we were also going back the earliest yet, May 1! Of course, we bought as much food and provisions as possible.

The Ural was perfect for the back roads. We visited Bo and went to hot springs near him. They had pools, waterfalls, and even a few slides to the pool below. I was most content to swim in warm water, only getting out when it was time.

You see, the work I did during the winter had paid off. Mark P, the treasurer, and I managed to get the entire Belgrade middle school to YNC for the Junior Smokejumper program. It was a huge accomplishment. The Fire Naturalist program was hitting its stride. And more schools signed up for all classes. So we were going to be busy this May.

Amy and I also worked on having the Summer Recreation program come to our campus during June, July, and August. Besides the Junior SmokeJumper program, we would do different parts of the Naturalist program with them. We taught how to draw, listen, and observe wildlife.

May was extremely busy, and Sasha and I were doing the work. We did have volunteers come in, from Board members to the occasional volunteer wanting to get more teaching experience on their resume. Each volunteer like that had to have a background check, which cost YNC $20 a pop.

They asked Amy if she would like to be a board member this year. Then, another person was asked to be a board member, someone we had never heard of, nor read about, in any of the paperwork or history of the organization. The person was Jim.

He had been a smokejumper before and an integral part of the Forest Service in the area. Another board member was brought in, Phil, who lived in Washington state. They would be given different amounts of years, Amy for one, Phil for two, and Jim for three.

By June, we had started to get into a rhythm. We had Intergen on Mondays and Summer Rec on Wednesdays. I worked on ten sponsorships of $100 each for the Children's Outdoor Bill of Rights scavenger hunt program. We gave a sheet to the kids to do fun things within West Yellowstone. Each business would get a stamp, so they would stamp that part of the page when the kids came in. When they completed a row, they would get a sticker, a patch, or a pin, depending on how many different places they went. By completing the sheet, they received a $5 prize. It was a way to get the kids to know about the town.

My Mead monthly calendar was so filled with daily activities. So when I went to the Chamber of Commerce for a meeting with Katrina, I drooled over her beautiful planner.

"What is this beauty?" I queried Katrina.

"Ah, this is an Erin Condren Life Planner I ordered online," she answered.

My love affair with decorative planners had begun. So I ordered the same type of planner, with a different cover, in June, with several other appurtenances for the office.

January expenses: $2,650.23

February expenses: $1,601.38

March expenses: $2,103.32

April expenses: $2,393.24

May expenses: $2,087.00

June expenses: $1,542.80

Chapter 92
Florida Living

I had the planner shipped to the Chamber as they did not accept PO Boxes or the address at YNC. It would come in July, the day before the parade. This time YNC was in the parade with Sasha and me riding the Ural motorcycle in smokejumper helmets with yellow long-sleeve shirts and flying the chair. I would throw the fireball candies, and summer was looking sweet. We won first place!

When I bought the EC planner in June, I was able to get it started for July 2016. It was nice to have a place to list my weekly to-do's. And be able to see when each reservation had which program. I could also see just by looking at the week what the weather was and whether we would need to set up indoors or out.

August was looking pretty grim for us, though. This year, kids seemed to head back to school earlier, and there were fires throughout the west. As a result, we had summer camps come twice in August. They were cute kids, wearing the same colorful tee shirts, and were happy to visit YNC.

It was good timing that they came in early August because, by the time Jim and his family came to YNC in mid-August, the campus got smoky, and we had hacking coughs. In addition, there were several large fires around West Yellowstone, and the biggest one was in Yellowstone National Park.

August went into September with continued smoky conditions. By the middle of September, when we had tons of work to shut down the season, we got sick. It was from the continuous smoke in the area, but we continued as the end of September was nearing, and we looked excitedly toward fall. We would be heading east for our yearly trip.

We had another couple of school programs in the last two weeks in September and the first day of October. So on October 1, we drove our rig to the campus, as the snow was coming, and we did not want to be stuck.

The class went great; we hiked in the forest, looking at burned trees and their surroundings. This was with a high school class. Seeing how a children's program could be expanded to teach young adults about the environment was exciting. My days as an environmental geologist and naturalist helped create this program.

This year we did not go to Portal. We would head east instead. And we were making money this year as more people came to Moab in their larger rigs. Our spot was perfect for them, with 200 feet of pink concrete for their toys and rigs. We were looking forward to the best time of the year for traveling.

I used the Erin Condren Life Planner (ECLP) not just for figuring out my day, week, or month but also for color, journal, and memory keeping. Our rig had browns and tans; I love purples, pinks, and blues. So my planner became my coloring, journaling, and memory keeping, a way to get off the screens and play with color. I am not an artist, but the colors meant something when my black-and-white life turned topsy-turvy.

We headed into Utah and checked out Mars Station. With red rocks around, very little water, and hot, the site could be the perfect place to experience Mars. Or they could go up the road and get groceries. The buildings looked like white biospheres, with two long arms covering up the plants grown on either side. They had signs saying private property, but it looked empty.

We had tried to get storage reservations before we left. But a hurricane had gone through North Carolina, and the open campgrounds were booked solid.

We looked around Surf City, North Carolina, on Google Maps and found an open space with the words Loyal Order of Moose. We had no idea there were any moose around North Carolina, and we looked up what it meant. Moose was a fraternal organization that they had all over the country. WOW, who knew that? Certainly not us, as we never grew up with it, and pictures from *The Flintstones* as our only clue.

Sasha went in first, asking how we could park our rig there. They said they needed more women members than men, and for a woman, it was cheaper to join. So I became a Moose, got a card, paid my dues, and then paid only a little more for monthly storage. In return, they gave me free drinks and seemed very welcoming.

November was in North Carolina and Virginia. We would stay with Mom and Dad J in Surf City, NC, at Yvonne and John's beach house for several weeks, and to Wilmington, NC, the weekend after election day, November 8. I wrote in my planner: delete news sites, delete polls sites, find beauty, take walks, drink more water, and do yoga to release my mind of negativity. My cousin's wedding in Wilmington was beautiful, with an outside/inside plantation property. We got to see family we had not seen in years.

Thanksgiving was at Yvonne's house, and my parents came up to Fairfax. There were some tense moments and others filled with silliness. We took pictures of the silly and tried to forget the rest.

After Thanksgiving, we pulled our rig out of storage at the Moose, had dinner with them, and headed south. We went to an RV campground that we never saw, only through Google maps, to try our luck with camping in Florida. We would revisit my parents in Florida for a few weeks, staying at their timeshare in Bonita Springs. It was beautiful and warm, and I got a new bathing suit at a thrift store as my old one was worn out. Winter in Florida, how lucky were we?

July expenses: $2,159.59

August expenses: $1,574.61

September expenses: $3,395.01

October expenses: $3,791.68

November expenses: $2,628.57

December expenses: $2,402.29

For 2016, we spent $28,700.09 and saved 11 percent.

Chapter 93

Trying to Find My Groove

This year, 2017, for the first year ever, we were in Florida on New Year's Eve and for the winter months. Also, Sasha and I felt healthier with aerobics inside and outside a pool. I started a water aerobics class and created it with movements similar to *Walk Away the Pounds*, yoga, and tai chi classes. Sasha would join me and get other men to join in. We had fun and got great tans, enjoying every day outside if we could.

There were a few downsides to living on the Gulf Coast of Florida. We were directly under the Coast Guard's flight path to the ocean. Oil particles from the jets would come down on the rig and the motorcycle. We had barely shoehorned our rig into a spot, the only site that could fit our large rig. The truck took up most of our patio. We could put the Ural under the nose of the rig, and it did not get as dirty.

But we are desert people. We were used to going to a pool, drying off, and being dry! Hanging our towels outside the rig was not an option, so we left them in the garage. But it would take at least two days for a towel to dry. The humidity was still very high for us. When we exercised, we had more sweat running down our backs than we thought possible.

We were spending more money. I always envisioned Florida with citrus farms like what we experienced in Borrego Springs. The air would smell sweet, and the oranges and grapefruits sold for cheap. But no, this was not the case. Instead of farmer's markets, there were fruit and vegetable stands. Instead of picking-your-own farms, there were Italian and Mexican grocery stores.

The campground had so many events that we did not need to go out as much. So instead, we paid extra for the parties and pool time. But at least we were having fun.

I was learning about economics and financial freedom too. When I saw an interview with Vicki Robin, the author of *Your Money or Your Life*, she stated she had a new version of the book. Mr. Money Mustache (MMM) had written the forward of her book. His blog and a few podcasts kept me entertained rather than watching the news. I immersed myself in this new economics as more of our money was no longer earning anything. I wanted to become confident again about putting money in the stock market without us losing money in the process.

You see, Zions Direct (ZD), the company I bought municipal bonds at auction prices, was changing how it did business. Before, you paid a difference in price to ZD but no broker fees. Now, ZD would charge for every buy that happened and how much money you had in the account as a user fee. So I had to get the money out, and pulling the plug took me a while.

Based on MMM recommendations, I bought Vanguard Index Funds. We went back into the stock market. I moved the municipal bonds I bought over to Vanguard without selling them. Ultimately, I changed the account from being in my name to our name as a joint account. I was thankful that I had not messed up our savings.

February was when my content writing hit its stride. I created posts on Instagram, Facebook, Pinterest, and YouTube while learning to be an ultimate social media person and writer. While trying to figure it out, I encountered a social media guru called Alexis, *Miss Trenchcoat.*

I tried to create more content on the website and made the title pages mean something more regarding search engine optimization. After twelve years of blog posts, I knew that meant re-inventing the wheel. I was never consistent, and I wanted the site to make money as it had before. So I signed up for Empire Building, a $300 purchase for an online course. I hoped it would work for me.

We were excited to return to the desert when we decided to head west.

We left on March 1 to travel west. We would take the I-10 across the country. We were east of Tallahassee, Florida, when we lost power and surged. It was pretty scary. We had no clue as to what was going on.

Nevertheless, we managed to limp to an abandoned truck stop. We were prepared, and Sasha had his tuner reader, which scanned the truck's error bank. He did an oil change that evening.

We took off again the next day thinking everything was good, but NO! We had gone 30 miles more and had problems. This time, we limped to a Flying J, and our trusty CoachNet roadside assistance came in handy. Since our engine was International, we went there. Because CoachNet is for RVers, they knew to get us a tow truck to handle our vehicle and RV. We were transported by a monster International Medium Duty tow truck. They towed us to Ward International.

Ward figured out the problem by dropping the engine, replacing a feed line, and installing a new fuel pump. We had the most fantastic crew help us figure out the problem.

We headed back to Flying J, figuring we would spend the night and head out in the morning. We got over there without a problem, no surges or sputtering. Saturday morning, as we drove out, we got about 100 yards from the Flying J, and the surging started again! On a Saturday. On the side of the road of a busy interstate. Our engine died as we were idling, thinking about what to do. AHHH!

Since Ward International was not open on the weekends, and CoachNet was concerned about our safety, the monster tow truck came out. While he brought us back to Ward International, Sasha looked back at the rig and saw a bubble on the roof. *"Truck Conked and Roof Snafu!"* What else could go wrong?

We had the supplies we needed to temporarily fix the roof, with Sasha going up there. So we would batten down the hatches for now.

On Monday, March 6, International returned and found the second problem. It had nothing to do with the engine but our external fuel station. The problem was the additional tank filter that was plugged up. The tech said the filter was not a good quality one, and this was the cause of the tank blockage.

International installed a full-flow auxiliary filter and water separator with a cut-off ball valve. As a result, when Sasha changes the filters, he will not get the diesel all over himself.

The moral of the story? Make sure you have backups and extras and make sure you have the money when you are traveling. By Tuesday, we were back on the road to reach Pahrump, Nevada, by March 19. We would stay there for a month, getting other work done, fixing the roof, and gearing up to head back for our fourth season in West Yellowstone.

We started with YNC on May 1 as school groups were coming in. This time, Mark P. and I got eleven school groups, plus Pacific Heritage Academy would come in May.

However, the vibe this year seemed off. It might have been the Board going in two different directions. First, there was worry that we might not keep going after this year if we did not get federal grants from the Forest Service and BLM.

The Board suggested we need more people on the committees to get more money coming in and told us they were "auctioning" a week in West Yellowstone at our volunteer house. People still had to volunteer, but it wasn't evident. We did not know who was in charge of the volunteers. I did not know what my position would be. So I went into May with trepidation and hoped for a good year.

This year my parents planned to visit during the Solar Eclipse. So there were activities to plan and events to look forward to. But the vibe was different, and everything was different too.

The next couple of chapters is as hard to write as they are to relive them. I decided to take some stuff out as it was giving me heartache and anxiety. I am glad I can provide you with this shortened version of what happened and leave it at that.

The information and recollections came from my notes, documents, Excel spreadsheets, and planners. I was under significant stress to find ways to create more money. I am thankful for Sasha as we tried to understand the organization. They kept rehashing their mission statement, name, organizational charts, or how they wanted volunteers to work.

Every one of our long-term volunteers had fizzled. If they were working on the house, I had nothing to do with what they did. A board member directed them instead of me. When working on the programs and being around children and money, we had to do background checks on them. We had tried to do longer-term volunteer last year, and our expectations did not mesh. If they were short-term volunteers, they gave two hours at the nonprofit for a week. If anything longer, we expected more time.

Sasha and I dealt with the fact that his Dad was failing health. May was becoming a nightmare for us, and it was only the second week. We worked in the evenings to accommodate the schools' schedules.

I created a book for The Naturalist program called the Naturalist Fire Notebook. It was much larger than our Children's Outdoor

Bill of Rights. There would be sponsors for the inside and outside covers, and it had the animals and plants of the Yellowstone area, the fire ecology, maps, how to draw animals, landscapes, and more.

It was a way to make money with the sponsors and create something completely different. You could add pages to it, like the Happy Planner. And use it as a naturalist would with graph and dot grid paper. I managed to get the West Yellowstone Chamber of Commerce on the front cover with us.

On May 19, 2017, the Board meeting changed almost everything. First, they gave Sasha and me a lifetime membership and pay raises. The second was that Bob would be the volunteer executive director (he was the Vice President) even though he did not live in West Yellowstone. He believed he could run the outreach and the fundraising from Washington state. Third, Jim would be the President of the Board; Rick would be the past president. Mark P., Treasurer, and Bob, VP/Executive Director. Finally, Bob started a relationship with The Land Council from Washington state and brought in a new board member, Chris.

Bob had never won a grant while we worked there. I wanted the position as a natural move as Program Manager. In addition, I brought in more money because of the outreach from the Town of West Yellowstone.

And in June, I got the Belgrade School to attend our programs. Ian, Stephen and Joanne's son, volunteered on Thursdays and Fridays. He did not stay in the volunteer house, but he helped.

June was super busy with the school groups. In addition, I was working with an International group who found me when they were looking for Night Sky Rangers. They were very interested in what we could offer them.

January expenses: $2,432.01
February expenses: $2,514.03
March expenses: $4,652.00

April expenses: $2,974.86
May expenses: $3,199.99
June expenses: $2,433.72

Chapter 94

We Start to Drink

An excruciating experience for us. It led to some hard feelings with YNC. Yet, the experience solidified our relationship as we celebrated our 20th wedding anniversary in October.

This is the chapter I dreaded writing: July 2017. We were productive and brought in thousands of dollars in May, June, and the beginning of July. The early season was one of our best, four years running. We did not participate in the parade as we had too much to do. Instead, we worked every day. Bob, his family, Jim, and his friends volunteered at the house.

We had a smokejumper volunteer come in and stay in the house for three days. He helped me put together the Naturalist Fire Notebook with the sponsors for the summer. Sasha and I created the front and back covers and laminated them. They were cut, punched, and put together, along with the inside notebook. Creating and publishing in-house took time but was still cheaper than offsite.

Gayle came to visit on Friday, July 14, 2017. She wanted to be a long-term volunteer. And she had a teacher's resume.

Gayle had another name, but we did not know it. We did a background check on the name she gave, and she checked out. I offered her a two-week probation period to stay at the house and volunteer to see how she did with my direction and work. Sasha and I did not work weekends, as we needed time off. I ask her to water the trees and the Native Plant Garden during the weekend.

On the same day, Bob, Mark, Rick, and I reviewed the Memorandum of Understanding between The Land Council (TLC) and YNC that our newest board member Chris wrote. It had glaring problems and was very one-sided, not for our benefit. They wanted our connections but would not give us the money to have those connections. That was the start of the day.

I got Gayle's timesheet on Monday, and she put down eight hours "working" on Friday and half hours on Saturday and Sunday. There was no way she worked on Friday for eight hours; it was the day she applied. I asked her to help with The Naturalist Notebook, but she ruined more books than she made. She turned sneaky; I started to distrust her.

Bob came the following week. There were too many people in the volunteer house: Bob, Gayle, Rick, friends of Jim's family (four), and Jim's family (three). The house was for eight volunteers, with five bedrooms and three baths. And we used the kitchen for our lunches as well.

We had many disagreements with Gayle from that point forward. First, she did not sign the volunteer agreement, stating she wanted to do other things. Then, she got Chris and Jim to believe her rather than Sasha and me.

But still, I tried. On July 21, 2017, I asked her to do Teacher packets like the ones we used in Mount St. Helens. These packets would explain the program and suggest what the class could do to prepare for the program. I asked Gayle to do a package a week. She could do it in eight hours or shorter. I stated she worked 24 hours a week to help with her resume. Then she said she could not do it.

I said, "Well then, we do not need you here."

She stated she was on vacation. She did not want to volunteer at all. After a week of trying to pin her down to do some volunteering, she caused significant headaches for Sasha and me. There were massive disagreements and stomachaches for us.

We always said that we changed our working mindset to do enjoyable jobs. We did them to make ourselves feel good. But, unfortunately, this volunteer turned our excellent job into a nightmare we could not awaken.

Gayle tried to get out of doing any work. She lied, stating that Jim asked her to stay through the rest of the season. She said she would only work with Chris on TLC programs, not for YNC.

Sasha lost his temper at our meeting with Gayle. It was very unusual, and I had not seen that happen in a long time. This woman had caused his lack of sleep, stomach upset, and severe stress. We drank more each night, trying to dull the pain of a passive-aggressive woman.

Gayle was about to leave, but I asked her to stay. I got Sasha out of the building and talked to him. I got him to calm down. He went back in and apologized to Gayle for losing his temper. We went back to discussions about the volunteer agreement. She asked for an hour to look over it.

I called Jim immediately after our almost two-hour meeting with Gayle. I told him I was stressed and mentally exhausted from dealing with Gayle and wanted her out. She was draining our life energy. He said I had the authority to fire Gayle but to call him that evening.

Since she did not return to the office, I searched for her. She and Chris were in the volunteer house and started questioning me. She was not going to sign the agreement. They acted like my boss and superiors. Sasha came looking for me. The arguments ensued, and

Sasha lost his temper again. While he apologized for his outburst, the meeting was over.

I had already discussed the Gayle problem with Chris. He stated he was not volunteering for YNC even though he lived in the Volunteer house.

We got ready for a Junior Smokejumper program, and I told Gayle I did not need her there. Instead, I would take pictures. The program went well, even with Gayle looming in and out of Sasha's vision. He ignored her and gave them a great program.

Ultimately, I called Jim, stating that Gayle had to go. But this time, Jim said that he was sick of this drama and to do nothing with Gayle or Chris. So I told him we would take a personal day the next day and return on Monday, July 25, 2017.

So what did happen to Gayle?

Chapter 95

Relationships

In August, Gayle left after two weeks. She did not stay in the house as much, and we had nothing to do with her. In August, we worked on firming up a contract with a Chinese High School that had found me through the night sky network. I created the Solar Fest activities for the same week my parents visited. Solar Fest would happen on August 21, my parents would come on August 18, and Gayle would leave on August 18.

She and Jim did "West Yellowstone Ambassadors" for two weeks, bringing in no money, sales, or donations.

The Chinese school came to YNC on August 15 for an extended Fire Naturalist program. While I had hoped for more money from them, I got the full attention of 35 students and ten adults for whom English was their second language. They came willing to learn and enjoyed every single moment of the program. We took some of the best pictures and had great camaraderie. They stated more Chinese student groups would come next year.

We used the entire campus to help them understand nature in Yellowstone. They came back for a fun Junior Smokejumper program. They would go off and see the night sky in another part of the park.

When the Solar Fest happened on August 21, 2017, we saw an almost perfect solar eclipse with over 100 people on our campus. We sold solar glasses beforehand and during the event, created solar beaded bracelets, and made solar ovens for creating s'mores and solar tea. We had cookies and did not spend much.

The money made that day was considered "donations" as we had closed the store. At least 25 children were there doing the different activities. Considering how many people saw the eclipse in the park, I thought our event went well.

Our relationship was more vital than ever before. We came together, leaned on each other, and helped get through this stress of a woman and a Board that pushed and pulled us this way. My brain was spinning even with my parents there, and the board was gone. Sasha helped me slow the spin. My parents and I might have done activities, gone out to eat, or eaten at the volunteer cabin, but I do not remember.

I knew that this would be the end of working for YNC. They still had Chris on the board, Gayle had stayed until my parents came, and Jim's children acted out.

We had no school groups in September, not a single one. So, instead, Jim started doing these "free short programs" that brought no money or people to the store.

I did one program for adults, bringing in Project Learning Tree and Project Wild for Environmental Education for formal and informal educators. Eleven adults, including Mark P, came to our class, and we enjoyed learning.

In the end, as September reached its forgone conclusion, The Board decided there was not enough money to have us return. So we cleaned up the volunteer house, put away or sold the books, deposited money, and handed over our keys.

I found out later that I had won a $5,000 grant to fund the summer camps for 2018.

July expenses: $3,162.21

August expenses: $1,794.78

September expenses: $3,258.64

Chapter 96

Beginning of the End

Before entering Utah, we bought food at Winco in Idaho, yet we broke the trailer suspension. We could not do anything or go anywhere with the rig, so we traveled with the Ural. So many places to see, and we celebrated our 20th Anniversary in Hanksville, Utah.

After the repair of the rig, we headed south to Avi Casino in Laughlin, NV. We had never been that way for an extended stay. We boondocked in their parking lot and paid for the beautiful pool passes. We stayed there for almost three weeks, with only one night in the hotel because of the high temperatures in October. Who thought Laughlin could be 100 degrees at the end of October?

We met Danny and Lisa, friends of Stephen and Joanne, at the KOA. The KOA was across the street from the Avi Casino and did not have a pool. So we did our laundry there and got the shower codes. That way, we conserved our water tanks.

But something was happening with Sasha's big toe. It looked gnarly and inflamed. So he used a web app with the doctors in NV who told him, "Go to the emergency room immediately. The toe might have to be amputated!"

We went, and they said, "No, that toe is OK. You must bandage it correctly and go to a podiatrist when you return home." Hahaha, we are home (Home Is Where You Park It). We had to go to a regular doctor in Las Vegas and get a specialist to look at Sasha's toe.

We headed back in November to the Clark County Shooting Range and were surprised by the number of volunteers and people staying there full-time. Then, we went to Pahrump to the doctor and got a referral for a podiatrist in Las Vegas.

We put those worries behind us and headed to Big Bear, California, to see our friend, Richard, during Thanksgiving weekend. I would drive up the mountain, and Sasha would drive down it, giving his toe time to heal. It was great to see Richard and be in a cool temperature.

We had fun during the fall, but we were paying a bit. So we decided to stay at the Clark County Shooting Range until the first part of 2018 and then head south to warmer weather.

Changes were happening at the county park. Something about not having people stay longer than two weeks: as we made plans for 2018 and met new people, we had to decide what to do.

I found my passion again for writing long-form blog posts. I wrote about frugality and finances. I wrote over 20 articles in two months, including articles and a boondocking series. Plus, Sasha and I signed up for a new club of the Escapees called Xscapers. Xscapers were people who were younger than 65 and who still worked while living in their RVs.

We still had ways to figure out what we wanted to do. Would I be able to make money by writing? Can we deal with the fees of the Rental property? We were tired of the continual problems with the truck, motorcycle, and keeping the rig up to speed. 2018 was coming, and we were still not sure of what was going to happen.

October expenses: $4,051.70

November expenses: $4,631.37

December expenses: $5,598.18

Expenses of 2017: $40,694.04. We managed to save 12 percent over the year.

Chapter 97
Decisions Made

We met with like-minded people called Xscapers, and I created a seminar: *Frugality In An RV*. My writing period was in full swing, and we used my knowledge to figure out what to do next. However, life was still uncertain for Mom and Dad J, who visited in February.

Looking back and remembering, I used my planners rather than my computers. I poured my life and ideas into those planners to figure out what to do. Did I want to try and work at another job? I had many questions, although not the worry like last year.

Sasha and I started to look at finances and see what we could accomplish this year. Unfortunately, we noticed some sad events, such as the social media and affiliate marking conference.

I went in January 2018, and they stated that:

1. Cookie language had to be clearly stated on a website, or you would get into legal trouble.

2. If links on a website or social media went to an affiliate link, you had to state it on the opening post or along the way at the beginning of the post.

3. You had to put the words affiliate links and what that means on everything that makes you money or the possibility of money. This meant YouTube, Facebook, Instagram, Pinterest, or other social media.

4. Your websites and blogs had to have disclaimers, legalese, and explanations.

Gone were the days of linking everything people bought, and you got some money from it. Amazon decreased its cookie length. By cookie, I mean the digital data that connects a buyer to your link. My percentages were going down, and I wanted to understand why. Instead, I got this doom and gloom at the conference.

As soon as it was over, I got sick and got Sasha sick. We got the flu in early January; we were nowhere near a store. As I stockpiled provisions that meant over-the-counter medications, we used what we had. We went into Quartzsite (Q), Arizona, to the Xscapers Bash and Rally as soon as we were well to move again. There were two parts, one in Q and one in American Girl Mine in California.

The second part was the one I was most excited to see. I would teach fellow RVers how to live frugally and still have fun in an RV. My seminar was 45 minutes and had 15 minutes of Q&A, which went longer as people had questions. More than fifty people were there, and we met some who became life-long friends.

We stayed after the rally for another week, solidifying friendships and enjoying ourselves with lunar eclipses and superb photography. Then, we returned to Las Vegas to stay with Mom and Dad J for four weeks at an Airbnb in Lake Las Vegas. We had found something larger and hoped to help Mom care for Dad.

The month of Dad was sad, happy, frustrating, confusing, heartbreaking, joyous, and painful. But ultimately, we were glad to live and care for him in February 2018. Yvonne told us he had fallen out of bed, and the fire department had to come to pick him up. Every night or morning.

When the parents came, they were in wheelchairs to be picked up by us. Mom looked tired. Dad was a mess, with long, wild hair and significant facial hair. He did not know where he was and why he was there.

The second social media event happened while we were with the parents. YouTube turned off monetizing for those publishers who had less than 1,000 subscribers. I started a YouTube channel in 2005 and had never had more than 200 subscribers, but I had the views and watch time. Now we were not going to earn money on YouTube. It was as though another earning avenue closed.

But we had little time to worry about it. Every day we washed sheets or tried to ensure Dad did not slither out of bed. First, we put bars on the bed so he did not slide out. Then, on one of the first days with him, we took a shower to get him clean. Yes, I showered with him, in my bathing suit, and with Sasha. The main bathroom did not have handrails, so we got him a bench to sit on, and Sasha had the front and I the back. We would wash his hair and body and ensure he did not slip off the chair.

Sasha made cocktails each evening and put Rose's lime juice into Dad's non-alcoholic drink. Dad would say, "This is a million-dollar drink!"

His moments of clarity were phenomenal and made you think he did not have Alzheimer's. But I knew he did, even if the rest of the family denied it.

Las Vegas has a large senior population, and they have geriatric-centered doctors. So I told Mom and Yvonne he should get tested for Alzheimer's. This allowed them to understand what he had and what was wrong with him, how he was not the same as he was five years ago. They finally agreed, and on the second to last day of the visit, I drove all of them to the appointment. He got tested, and Yvonne, Sasha, and Mom watched him take the tests.

To say they were shocked when they came out would be an understatement. He would get support by receiving this diagnosis, whether they stayed in Virginia or came to Nevada. Hospital beds, hospice care, and other items are easier to get with the diagnosis. Yvonne suggested they stay in Nevada, but Mom did not want that.

It was hard to make any decision about your spouse. They were together for over sixty years of marriage. How tough it must have been for her to ask for help, and now, she knew he was in stage four of the disease and would not get better.

For us, it was hard to know the future. We might have helped by storing the RV and moving in with his parents. But we tried it before and could not foresee doing it again.

Instead, we just waited.

January expenses: $3,210.69

February expenses: $809.57

Chapter 98

Desert Decisions

I had fallen while taking care of Dad J. I was rushing. I kept pushing myself, and by doing so, I could not write for almost a month. So instead, I waited until the parents left and finally went to a doctor. I needed a splint for my hand and wrist. We searched for a rental home we could live in with the parents. There would be swaying back and forth for a few more weeks on whether or not they would come. Then, boom! Mom decided it was too much, and she could not do it.

We pivoted and said OK, and decided to go into the desert. Being in the desert helps us understand ourselves. You are part of the environment when you are out there. You learn to go without as much water or showers. You listen more to the wind and the animals. A calmness makes me feel good when I go into the desert.

We decided to sell our RV lot in Moab, Utah. The fees were getting too high. The maintenance fees and property taxes went up yearly, yet the split between management and its clients stayed the same. In addition, we noticed that not as many people were coming out in their bigger rigs and staying on the more expensive sites.

We realized four percent net each year of renting for three and a half years. It was an annual return of over 13.5 percent for each year when we sold the lot for over $40,000 what we paid. We were happy about the sale. We could figure out life with the extra money, even with an uncertain future.

Once Mom said they were not moving, we went to The Pads, a boondocking paradise. It was an old mining town. The town and the mine went bust, and the company took the buildings but left the concrete pads. The Pads were perfect for RVers who needed to go into the desert. At the time, there was no internet, and our friends were nervous.

However, we headed over there and had a blast. We each got a "Pad" to put our RV on and tried to group ourselves. What was perfect about it was the proximity to Death Valley National Park and The Oasis, a resort located just inside the boundary. They had a pool, showers, cabanas, and semi-decent WiFi.

When we needed internet, we went there. When we wanted community, we were at the rig getting to know our new friends. I was writing a series that gave me focus on my writing. I was reading constantly and looking at the stars at night. The weather seemed perfect for it.

When we had been at The Pads for almost 20 days, our friends decided they had had enough of No Internet. So we decided to be "available just in case" we were needed by Sasha's parents and went to Pahrump, Nevada.

This decision was not made lightly. We felt we needed to put down some roots. Dad J could live longer, or he could get worse. We did not know.

We also wanted to see if we could live in the desert for the summer. We had heard of 120-degree days and frying eggs on cars and other wild stories; would that be true for us in Pahrump? Can I make friends and live frugally in a town of snowbirds and outdoor enthusiasts? Would we become part of a community? We felt we had the summer to try and BE part of something.

March expenses: $3,991.74

April expenses: $2,307.44

Chapter 99

Finding Fun Communities

We moved to long-term RVing, paid month by month, at Wine Ridge RV Resort and Cottages. It was beautiful, but summer came early, by mid-May, with temperatures in the 90s. However, the price for the RV spot was never higher than $300, as it was off-season. So we decided to stay and get acquainted with our RV neighbors.

A woman I met in a Michaels Craft Store told me about this Facebook group that did regular meetups. They would get together, swap stickers, and talk about life. They would show off their different planners, things used to stay organized, and I thought, "WOW! Women who like stickers - Sign me up! Ever since I was little, I loved all that color; this was me to a T!"

And by June, I had a new planner, an A5 six-ring binder with inserts. Plus, a few more friends and I enjoyed the beauty and color of the planners.

We had gone to the Moose Lodge in Pahrump as we did in North Carolina, thinking of joining there, but it was so smoky we did not enjoy the food. Instead, a friend I met at Wine Ridge told us about the Elks, a similar type of fraternal organization but with more social benefits, including RV sites. We decided I would join, and Sasha could be my spouse or plus one. It was easy to become a member. We went and met many people in the Pahrump community.

June came and went with swimming laps in the pool and whatever club we could find. We researched water rights, a big issue in the desert, especially in Pahrump. There is a large aquifer under the town and the valley. Pahrump Valley does not rely on the Colorado River for our water as Las Vegas does.

Dad J was getting worse. I kept hoping he would not die on Sasha's birthday, July 22; thankfully, he did not. Instead, it happened a week later, on July 31, 2018.

We made our final decision. We would buy property in Pahrump and build our dream home. We could take the heat if we built a sustainable home. But, as we moved towards making that happen, we had to do something else to close the past.

We sold the Ural Sidecar Motorcycle to a gentleman in East Texas. We did this as the vehicle was no longer suitable for our situation. You had to gear up to buy milk during 110-degree summers. Sasha put it on Craigslist and Facebook. While we were sad for a little while, we still had great memories and pictures.

The man bought it and paid for it without riding it first. Sasha's detailed records showed trustworthiness. He stayed in a cottage at the RV park. He took off the next day. He would travel the back roads to his home in east Texas. We wished him well and many happy adventures.

In August, we bought our Jeep, a 4x4 white Jeep with automatic transmission. This would be our fun, go-around town vehicle. We would be part of a Jeep club in the winter. We were excited for this new adventure to begin.

May expenses: $1,912.73

June expenses: $1,557.75

July expenses: $2,460.46
August expenses: $2,717.14

Chapter 100

We Come Full Circle

In August, we found a Realtor who knew the land in Pahrump, and her husband was a water well driller. Debra and Larry, her husband, and their daughter were part of the team. While water well drilling is not the same as environmental drilling, we had the basic concept down and what drilling a well would mean. We told them we wanted a lot on a quiet street, close enough to Home Depot, of two acres or more, not in a floodplain, and a square lot.

At the end of August, we found our piece of land and closed the day after Labor Day. We managed to get the ground for a lower price because of several factors. First, the seller was in Massachusetts and had never been to Pahrump. They wanted it off their books. The listing agent stated that the property did not have relinquished water rights. This meant that an owner needed to buy rights costing around $18,000.

But the listing agent was WRONG! Debra went to a website showing the entire valley's relinquished water rights. By "relinquished," the subdivision's developer gave each lot their water rights.

Based on Mom J's suggestion, the lot was going for $20,000, and we offered $18,000. It was as though we wanted it but did not.

The strategy worked, and we closed the deal on September 5. Now would come the hard part, the actual building of a home.

At the same time as we bought the property, Sasha asked for and was granted volunteer work at Wine Ridge RV Resorts. He would clean the pools and hot tub, and we would get our site and electricity for free.

We scheduled Larry to do our well, septic system, and electricity of 200 amps. First, I sketched out where we wanted everything located. Then, I used my geology knowledge to make a landscape map. But first, we needed a surveyor to know our property.

Once that happened, we decided to sketch out the land. We wanted the well away from any house nearby. There were horses to our east, so the well would go on the western side of the property. We also found that those horses were rubbing against the salt cedar plants. They are invasive plants that pull water from the ground and kill anything around it by dropping their salty leaves. Therefore, no house or well on that side.

At the end of September, Pahrump had a fall festival. We went and met more people. I met the Master Gardeners, who judged the fruits and vegetables. From there, I learned that they scheduled a Master Gardener's class. I stated that I wanted to take part. It had been a dream ever since I started gardening back in Virginia.

A unique opportunity came as we figured out what I would do as work. I would get my hands dirty and learn something new and different.

September expenses: $3,406.58

September would be the last month of calculations as we started to work on a spreadsheet for the house.

Chapter 101
Plans Become Actions As I Turn 50

We joined clubs to meet people, such as the Garden Club, the book club at the library, the 4-Wheelers club, and the Elks, and I learned about sustainable living in the desert. I bought books on positioning your property for passive solar heating and cooling. And I designed our home and the lot.

Turning fifty was not a big deal to me. It might have been different if I had worked at a nine-to-five job. But instead, I worked on my birthday, October 6, 2018, on a hemp farm. I came home from an exhaustive day of standing and clipping buds for only a few hours. I wanted to learn about hemp but was this the way to do it?

I stuck it out and got a back brace and leather gloves. Each day I came home smelling hemp, which smelt the same as marijuana. I met interesting people and wore my callouses with pride. When asked if people wanted longer shifts, I said, "Give my hours to others. I want to do less!"

I was not in it for the money, but it was a way to "work" on something interesting. Hemp and its products were delisted from the felony drugs in the Farm Bill in 2018, and Nevada actively pursued growing the CBD industry. Yet, I wanted the hemp industry to go towards building production.

Sasha and I went to Springs Preserve in October after our anniversary to see Desert Sol. University engineering students created this building to create a sustainable, energy-efficient home.

I called the educator onsite to find out how to get a personalized tour of the building. Aaron spent the day with us. He showed us Desert Sol and other structures that used passive cooling systems and other features. These became features we would use in our new home.

I learned about a company called Hempiture. They were touting hempcrete, a mixture of hemp, lime, and concrete, to create building walls. However, the walls were not load-bearing, and you still needed wood and chicken wire. When I first stated my desire to build with hempcrete at the building department, the inspector looked at me cross-eyed.

He wanted detailed specifications on how good the fireproofing was, what tests had been done, and how those tests were backed up.

We were also becoming frustrated with Larry and the family business. They stated that we were on their list for the fall, but problems existed. We paid in four installments, but that did not move them faster.

Finally, we spray-painted on the property each place where the septic tank, electricity box, and transformer would go. We took my landscaped drawing and drew lines on the property where all the water and septic lines should go. We made ourselves a bother to Larry and the team to find out when they would come out.

We did not watch the proceedings, unfortunately. Larry got sick. We were worried for him. So, instead, we waited and hoped for a well to go in before we left.

When Dad J died in July, Mom was too distraught to have a funeral or mass. Instead, Mom and Yvonne decided to do a cremation service. We had the Celebration of Life memorial service on December 21, 2018, Dad's birthday. That way, everyone could be there. Everyone from the west and north, the kids and family, would converge to come. We got plane tickets and flew into Norfolk, Virginia, to stay with my parents and Mom J.

We found this year was sad for the Jevtich extended family. Marcus, Sasha's first cousin, had died of a heart attack in May. John's mom, Sandy, passed away the day after Thanksgiving.

We left on December 2, 2018, with no well in place. I told them I needed videos when they did the work.

Chapter 102

Celebration of Life

I stopped counting every dollar, in or out of our bank accounts, as I had done for eleven years. Once September ended, there were huge numbers, and they screwed up most of the calculations. So instead, we made a shareable spreadsheet of the vendors, things bought, and people met who could help us build our property and home. It ended up being for the best.

Not only that, but I stopped trying to find work. I was the project manager for building our home; it meant calling and speaking to many people to get what we wanted. Sasha would still work at the pools in 2019, and we stayed there until December 2019. After that, we would be owner-builders, even though we had no real experience. We knew what we wanted and made sure we got it.

Around this time, I decided to let go of the website and our domain, Laura-n-Sasha dot com. I put my efforts into Facebook and other social media sites instead. Unfortunately, the YouTube money had dried up, and Amazon's payouts got lower as I focused on building the home.

I decided to let go of the website because, every time I went on, I said, "Sorry, Fans, I haven't been on here awhile."

We did not think anyone was interested in learning about our normal day-to-day operations. I had hoped our website would make money through passive income. Instead, what truly made us money was actively managing and saving money by being frugal. Being frugal allowed us to decide if a doodad would give us pleasure or was something we needed to dust.

The guilt trip I felt each time I went into the website to update it was another factor. Why should I feel unhappy about something that should give us joy?

Plus, in 2018, hackers and spammers found my website. We were consistently getting spammed with junk emails. The hosting company used a shared server; I can't guess who might have shared the server with us. Problems persisted.

I created my pros and cons list in my Big Happy Planner. Then, with Sasha's help and encouragement, I decided to jump with both feet into being the contact person for our property. First, I would call General Steel to build our metal building. Then, I would call the contractors and the building inspectors and talk to the geo-tech about the soil report, the grading, and other factors.

I had my pretty pictures. I wrote what we did on Facebook and Instagram. I did not worry about how many followers I had. Instead, we would create a livable, sustainable home for ourselves.

We went back east in December 2018. I showed Dad, a professional engineer, my drawing of our home and landscape. He had many questions, and I was able to answer them all. We had decided to stay in Virginia until mid-January 2019 to be there for Mom J's first Orthodox Christmas without Dad J, for Slava, and for the Celebration of Life memorial event.

When we think back to Dad J and his long life, we remember how he told us to pursue our dreams and what we wanted with gusto.

And so, with both Dads' blessings, we have.

Epilogue: Where Are LauraNSasha Now?

This memoir and story take place from 1995 to the end of 2018. In 2019, and throughout the COVID pandemic, we created our sustainable, solar-powered home. We took occupancy in September 2020, two years after we bought it.

We sold our F450 truck and fifth wheel toyhauler soon afterward. We sold the truck to a campground near us, and the fifth-wheel toyhauler went to a woman in California. She will never use it on the road. We sold the top of the Jeep to a guy in Oregon as it was an unusual white top. We figured the Jeep would always be in the garage.

I set up a nonprofit at the start of the pandemic in December 2019, only to close it a year later as COVID kicked its butt to the exit. It was about how planners, scrapbooks, and journaling helped bring mental happiness and wellness. When you cannot attend conferences and meetups, a nonprofit like that is hard to achieve.

Instead, we saw my family in 2020 when they visited us right before the lockdowns. We would travel east in 2022, four years after not being on the east coast. We hopped into the CamperVan experience and built ourselves a camper using an E350 van. Sasha has to take most of the credit as he made something extraordinary. I, at last, got my hemp, in the form of hemp wool, and put it into the insulation of the van.

I got back into videos and writing long articles on other websites and social media. I have Dad to thank for his insistence on writing this book. There might be another book about our self-sustainable home and how we built it once we finished the backyard.

We are in good health and are happy. We are not as busy as before the pandemic, but we are still in touch with our RVing, East Coast, and Pahrump friends and family. I have finally figured out the best thing I can do for work: write.

Please: if you liked this book, review it here: with the link: https://amzn.to/445S6Kv.

Stay tuned for my series coming in the Fall of 2023, Organizing Your Life.

About the Author

Laura C Jevtich works as a writer, author, and social media creator. She enjoys being part of a community, whether at home, online, or traveling. She is a Master Gardener without a garden, a Dark Sky ranger with beautiful stars and stories, and continually strives to read, write, and play well with others. You can find her in Pahrump, Nevada, with her husband, Sasha, and online: @LauraNSasha and @LauraJevtich.

Laura and Sasha as shadow art

Made in the USA
Las Vegas, NV
07 July 2023